Managing poverty

Since the second world war, the means test has played a role of growing importance in British social security provision. Beveridge's vision, fifty years ago, of a society protected by a national system of social insurance has never been realized and, instead, social assistance, designed as a residual and diminishing means of support, has gradually been expanded to make up for the inadequacies of a national insurance system which was at first neglected and then attacked by governments. This important shift in the founding principles of the British income maintenance programme occurred without any public or parliamentary debate and without public acknowledgement by government that it was happening. As a result, British social assistance provision has continually been stretched beyond reasonable limits.

Managing Poverty examines the reasons for the growing importance of social assistance in British social security policy, traces the many changes introduced by successive governments, and examines in detail why both Conservative and Labour governments have been unsuccessful in finding permanent solutions to the recurrent problems that have emerged. Most of the previous literature on this subject has concentrated on the policy-making process, but Carol Walker looks at the efficacy of these policies from the point of view of the service users, the claimants. She uses empirical evidence on the experiences and views of claimants to evaluate benefit provision.

This book will be an invaluable text to all undergraduates and postgraduates in the social sciences, particularly social policy, and to all welfare professionals.

Carol Walker is a Senior Lecturer in Sociology and Social Policy at Sheffield Hallam University.

The State of Welfare
Edited by Mary Langan

Nearly half a century after its post-war consolidation, the British welfare state is once again at the centre of political controversy. After a decade in which the role of the state in the provision of welfare was steadily reduced in favour of the private, voluntary and informal sectors, with relatively little public debate or resistance, the further extension of the new mixed economy of welfare in the spheres of health and education became a major political issue in the early 1990s. At the same time the impact of deepening recession has begun to expose some of the deficiencies of market forces in areas, such as housing and income maintenance, where their role had expanded dramatically during the 1980s. *The State of Welfare* provides a forum for continuing the debate about the services we need in the 1990s.

Titles of Related Interest
Also in *The State of Welfare Series*

The Dynamics of British Health Policy
Stephen Harrison, David Hunter, Christopher Pollitt

Radical Social Work Today
Edited by Mary Langan, Phil Lee

Taking Child Abuse Seriously
The Violence Against Children Study Group

Ideologies of Welfare: from Dreams to Disillusion
John Clarke, Ian Cochrane, Carol Smart

Women, Oppression and Social Work
Edited by Mary Langan and Lesley Day

Managing poverty
The limits of social assistance

Carol Walker

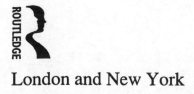

London and New York

First published 1993
by Routledge
11 New Fetter Lane, London EC4P 4EE

Typeset in Times New Roman by Michael Mepham, Frome, Somerset
Printed and bound in Great Britain by
T.J. Press (Padstow) Ltd, Padstow, Cornwall

British Library Cataloguing in Publication Data
A catalogue record for this book is available from the British Library.

Library of Congress Calaloging-in-Publication Data
A catalogue record for this book is available from the Library of Congress

ISBN 0–415–08454–7
      0–415–08455–5 (pbk)

To Alan

Contents

Tables

Acknowledgements

I am fortunate never to have had to live on social assistance. However, over the past twenty years, as a voluntary welfare rights worker and then as a social science researcher, I have worked closely with many people who have and for whom 'managing poverty' is a major focus and concern of their lives. That contact has left a lasting impression on me. Different people cope differently with claiming benefit and respond differently to being a claimant. However, no one finds it easy. No one is proud of being on social security. And if there is one lesson which I learnt from working with claimants, it is that they deserve better: better treatment and a better standard of living. I hope that this book goes some way to making the case for such improvements.

Writing a book is a very individual activity but not one which can take place in isolation. Many people have helped me over the years both in developing my ideas and in supporting me in the lengthy process of committing them to paper. Peter Townsend and Jean Corston provided a much needed boost to my flagging morale on more than one occasion. This book has gained much from the stimulating conversations and clarity of thought provided by Peter. Mary Langan proved a patient and supportive editor. I am grateful to her for that and for her many pertinent comments on earlier drafts.

Inevitably the main burden has fallen to my family. During my preoccupation with this project, often at their expense, Alison and Christopher provided a much needed and appreciated diversion. My final, but not least, thanks go to Alan Walker, who, in addition to commenting on most chapters, provided both intellectual and emotional support in equal measure. This book owes as much to his resilience as to mine. I could not have finished this project without him.

Series editor's preface

Nearly half a century after its post-war consolidation, the British welfare state is once again at the centre of political controversy. After a decade in which the role of the state in the provision of welfare was steadily reduced in favour of the private, voluntary and informal sectors, with relatively little public debate or resistance, the further extension of the new mixed economy of welfare in the spheres of health and education became a major political issue in the early 1990s. At the same time the impact of deepening recession has begun to expose some of the deficiencies of market forces in areas, such as housing and income maintenance, where their role had expanded dramatically during the 1980s.

The shift away from the post-war pattern of welfare services, in which the state played the central role, towards the new mixed economy of welfare began under James Callaghan's Labour government in the late 1970s, but received its real impetus from Margaret Thatcher's Conservative regime after 1979. The new framework was motivated above all by a concern to curb the burden of public expenditure on Britain's crisis-stricken economy. It received ideological legitimation from the anti-welfare and pro-market outlook adumbrated by the New Right theorists and incorporated into the Conservative programme from the mid-1970s onwards. The restructuring of welfare was also profoundly influenced by the gradual subordination of local government – the key agency in the provision of education, housing and personal social services – to central financial control and, ultimately, political direction, in the course of the 1980s.

The central features of the new mixed economy of welfare are the greater role of the private and voluntary sectors, a greater reliance on informal care in the community (that is, in general, by women in the family) and a reduced role for formal public services. The expansion of private provision is most striking in housing, with the success of the 'right to buy' schemes in transferring council properties into the ownership of their former tenants and the wider growth of owner-occupation, encouraged by tax relief on mortgages. Similar trends are also apparent in the spread of private pension and sickness benefit schemes, in the boom in private nursing homes and in the growth of the private health and education sectors – all assisted by various direct and indirect state subsidies.

The voluntary sector has assumed much wider responsibilities in the social services field, as organizations like Age Concern, Mind and others now tender to supply council services. The promotion of community care policies has meant placing greater reliance on informal carers, to compensate for the decline in public and institutional provision. The shift away from universal and insurance benefits towards selective and means-tested benefits in the sphere of income maintenance has led to the revival of two traditional forms of informal social security provision – begging and charity.

However, under the new welfare regime, the role of the state has not merely been cut back, but transformed. Market forces, which in the past acted as an external constraint setting ultimate budget limits on public services, have now become an internal organizing principle within the state sector itself. Public services have been subjected to reorganization according to the managerial principles of private enterprise. Throughout the new welfare state the rhetoric of delegated financial responsibility, decentralized budgetary targets, localized cost centres and putting the customer/consumer/user first, now prevails. The establishment of local management of schools and the 'internal market' in health care, with self-financing trust hospitals and budget-holding GPs, are some of the more radical developments of a policy that has been spreading through local government for a decade.

In surveying recent trends in welfare there are striking differences both in the government's approach and in the public response to changes in different spheres of welfare. Thus, for example, the reforms promoted by the Conservative governments of the 1980s in housing were the most popular and least controversial. They were introduced at an early stage, they proceeded rapidly and the opposition parties soon recognized the appeal of home ownership and the unpopularity of council housing and adjusted their policies accordingly. Similarly in income maintenance, the marginal position of claimants and the impact of propaganda against 'idlers' and 'scroungers' gave the government a powerful advantage over the poverty lobby.

On the other hand, when, after her third election victory, Mrs Thatcher turned to step up the pace of 'reform' in the spheres of health and education in an increasingly unfavourable economic and political climate, she – and her successor – faced much stiffer opposition. The NHS enjoyed relatively high public esteem and contained in the medical profession a well-organized and influential lobby. Though there was some public resonance for Conservative campaigns about declining education standards and the scapegoating of trendy teachers and liberal teaching methods, there was also widespread concern about the evident under-financing of the education system at every level from nurseries through schools to polytechnics and universities.

In the late 1980s and early 1990s the deepening economic slump throughout the advanced capitalist world has exposed the exhaustion of the New Right programme of free market policies, espoused with such apparent success by Reagan and Thatcher in the 1980s. In both the USA and in Britain there was an evident swing back from the extreme anti-state, pro-market policies of the recent past towards more the pragmatic, interventionist approach personified by George Bush and John Major, and the dominant opposition parties. In the sphere of welfare, the intensity of the recession in Britain has undermined some of the much-vaunted achievements of the new mixed economy of welfare established in the 1980s.

The collapse of the housing market has destabilized the building societies and banks whose easy credit policies had fuelled the home-ownership boom. It has led to a wave of repossessions of houses from owners unable to meet their mortgage repayments. The collapse of the Maxwell publishing empire at the end of 1991, after the owner's mysterious death and revelations about the use of his employees' pension fund to underwrite massive debts, revealed the vulnerability of private pension schemes in a period of wider financial instability. Pressures for the state to intervene to safeguard homes and pensions revived memories of the fact that it was the failures of private market forces in these and other areas of welfare that prompted state intervention in the first place.

Economic recession and political insecurity have thus combined to cast a shadow of uncertainty and insecurity over the welfare state in the 1990s. Whereas populist anti-welfare postures helped the Conservatives to power in 1979 and, to a lesser extent, in 1983 and 1987, by the 1992 election the crisis of welfare had become something of an electoral liability for the Conservatives. Yet a simple swing of the pendulum back towards the post-war welfare regime is unlikely. It is striking that, despite the evident difficulties of the New Right programme in confronting the economic and social problems of the 1990s, it has in its essentials been accepted by the major opposition parties as well as by the Conservative Party. Even though Conservative polices on health and education remain unpopular, the Labour Party has constantly shifted its position to endorse the key themes of the internal market and managerialism. Thus the ascendancy of market forces over the new mixed economy of welfare is likely to prevail for the foreseeable future.

1 Introduction
Managing poverty

This book examines the development and impact of social assistance policy in Britain. There are several perspectives on which such an exercise can be based but most of the previous literature on the subject has concentrated on the policy-making process (Hill 1990; Deacon and Bradshaw 1983). In contrast, this study looks at the efficacy of social assistance policy from the point of view of its service users: the claimants. In so doing it has to be acknowledged from the outset that the concerns and aspirations of users may be quite different from the other key actors: the policy-makers, including government ministers and officials who determine provision, and service providers who have an important role in influencing the quality, if not the nature, of the service given.

The British post-war welfare state has been slow to develop user-centred services. Universal services such as health and education have been criticized for putting the needs of bureau-professionals before those of users. Benefits and services that go predominantly to poor people, such as social security, have been even more reluctant to involve their users in their planning and delivery. Instead, since the second world war, social security policy has been managed, not with the needs of poor people to the fore, but within a framework of ideological, economic and political philosophies, which have often been anti-poor both in sentiment and application.

Opportunities for claimants to respond to such negative attitudes are limited. The nature of benefit administration and the circumstances which have brought people to dependence on state benefits often lead to isolation and alienation. Thus, attempts to form and sustain pressure groups comprised of claimants themselves have been fraught with difficulty and there are few successful examples which have been sustained over a prolonged period to argue for claimants' rights. The history of the claimants' union movement during the post-war period has been understandably erratic. The most well-known and effective pressure groups working in the field of social security, such as the Child Poverty Action Group and the Disability Alliance, campaign on behalf of claimants; few of their members are drawn from among claimants themselves (McCarthy 1986; Whiteley and Winyard 1983).

This book then examines the social assistance scheme from the users' perspective. It draws together evidence collected in a number of empirical studies of claimants of social security, to present their views and their experiences. One of the main sources of data used, especially for the quotations from claimants, is the interviews conducted with over 400 claimants in Leeds as part of a study to monitor the impact of changes made to social assistance policy in 1980 (Walker with Dant 1984). This, together with a national study of claimants by Richard Berthoud for the Policy Studies Institute (PSI) (Berthoud 1984), a study of the impact of earnings disregards on lone parents (Weale *et al.* 1984) and another on the appeals system, probably constituted the most thorough empirical exploration of the working of British social assistance policy at any one time during the post-war period. It would be a welcome criticism if the findings of these studies were seen to be out of date and the weaknesses of the social assistance system revealed had been overcome by subsequent developments. Unfortunately, more recent data on the circumstances of claimants and the operation of the scheme, which are also used in this book, show that this is not the case. There is a growing body of research evidence to show that social assistance claimants in the 1990s are experiencing the kinds of difficulties and hardships faced by claimants in the past. There is a dispiriting similarity to be found in the results of the numerous empirical studies which have been conducted into the living standards of claimants over the last three decades. The picture which emerges, from Townsend's national study of poverty in 1969 (Townsend 1979) to smaller studies in the late 1980s (Bradshaw and Holmes 1989; Noble *et al.* 1989; Ritchie 1990), is that a majority of families on benefit struggle to make ends meet and that debt and deprivation are the key to their managing their poverty. This is the pre-eminent message of this book. It is a message which successive post-war governments have chosen to ignore.

THE IMPORTANCE OF SOCIAL ASSISTANCE

'Social assistance' is sometimes used as the generic term to cover the whole means-tested sector of social security policy and in particular the three main means-tested benefits, which after the Social Security Act 1986 were called income support, family credit and housing benefit. Throughout this book the term 'social assistance' is used in the sense that Beveridge (1942) first used it. It refers only to the first of these benefits: that aspect of means-tested income maintenance provision which was created as a safety net for those out of work who were not provided for by social insurance, which was intended to be the bulwark of the state's social security provision. The subsequent introduction of help with some housing costs, most recently in the form of housing benefit, and of a benefit to enhance the incomes of low-paid working parents (at the time of writing in the form of family credit) reveals the growing acceptance by governments of the means test as the favoured strategy for helping poor people. The growth of these means-tested schemes, like that of social assistance, has illustrated the abandonment of policies to prevent poverty in favour of those which seek only to mitigate its worst effects. Britain is increasingly a means-tested society.

Many of the problems associated with social assistance discussed in the following pages apply equally well to other parts of means-tested provision. Since 1988, both housing benefit and family credit entitlement have been linked to the income support rates, so the level of income support affects the standard of living of people on these other benefits. The less claimants can receive from income support, the less people in similar circumstances can get from housing benefit or family credit.

Over the years, and to the chagrin of the Conservative governments in the 1980s, the social assistance rates came to be regarded, unofficially, as a national 'poverty line'. This was justified on the grounds that these rates were approved annually by Parliament. As the Supplementary Benefits Commission (SBC) said when it was responsible for the administration of social assistance, the social assistance rates bore 'the unique stamp of authority, having been approved by Parliament as a minimum standard of income applicable to large sections of the population' (SBC/DHSS 1977, p. 2). The social assistance rates became an unofficial poverty line because they provided a benchmark against which the standards of living and expectations of poor people could be measured. Thus, for example, this nationally determined minimum standard was adopted by many local authorities in devising eligibility criteria for local services or for charges on them. Sometimes the line was drawn at the level of the basic weekly rates but, more usually, researchers added a margin of 20 per cent or 40 per cent to reflect the additional help available to social assistance claimants in the form of both weekly and lump sum additions (e.g. Abel-Smith and Townsend 1966, who were the first to use this method).

In the 1980s, for reasons which are discussed in Chapter 2, the Conservative government did not accept that the supplementary benefit levels constituted a poverty line. Indeed, under the Thatcher governments it was not even accepted that poverty existed in Britain (Moore 1989). The word 'poverty' was abolished from the vocabulary of official reports; the 'poor' were replaced by people 'on low incomes' and 'those in greatest need'. However, it was implicitly acknowledged that those in receipt of supplementary benefit and later income support, together with those working families with children in receipt of family income supplement (later family credit), were among the least well-off. During the 1980s government financial support was increasingly confined to these two groups: recipients of income support and recipients of family credit. Financial support to other families with an income just above these levels was quickly reduced. The electricity discount scheme was abolished, free school meals were restricted to those on income support only, child benefit was frozen for three years, universal grants to help with funeral and maternity costs were replaced by means-tested benefits, and housing benefit to anyone with an income above supplementary benefit or income support level was cut severely.

HOLES IN THE SAFETY NET

Our primary focus is on the circumstances of people who receive social assistance and how they manage on this state-defined minimum. In so doing, it is recognized that there are many other people, in different circumstances, who have to survive on incomes which are as low or even lower than that provided by this state safety net. Figures produced by the Institute for Fiscal Studies (Johnson and Webb 1990) showed that, in 1987 (the latest year for which these particular figures are available), in addition to the 4.3 million families (7.3 million people) in receipt of supplementary benefit or housing benefit supplement,[1] 1.9 million families were living on incomes *below* supplementary benefit level, a further 0.7 million families were living on incomes up to 10 per cent above supplementary benefit level, and a further 2.1 million were living on incomes no more than 40 per cent above.[2] Altogether over 8 million people were living in families whose incomes were less than 40 per cent above supplementary benefit level. Of those whose incomes were *below* SB level, one-fifth were in full-time work or were self-employed, 16 per cent were young people living with their parents and 42 per cent were failing to take up housing benefit, housing benefit supplement or supplementary benefit.

Changes in the social assistance rules, particularly during the 1980s, meant that new groups of people were no longer protected by the safety net. They included most 16 and 17 year olds, full-time students and people with savings over the capital limit. In addition, there were growing numbers of people on social assistance who were 'struggling to survive below benefit level' (Rhodes 1991). Growing numbers of claimants found themselves falling foul of the increasingly punitive 'voluntary' unemployment rules, paying back social fund loans, including crisis loans taken out to tide them over the first two weeks of a claim, or having to meet a sizeable proportion of their housing costs because of increasing deductions for non-dependants. From 1992 onwards, lone parents who refuse to name the father of their children will also have their benefit reduced.

The social assistance recipients whose lives are described in this book are, therefore, not the only poor people in Britain, nor are they necessarily the poorest. However, benefit recipients are particularly vulnerable to poverty, as an analysis of government statistics has revealed.

In 1987, over 63 per cent of the poorest 10 per cent (of the population) received supplementary benefit or housing benefit in comparison with 24 per cent for the population as a whole... Benefits made a crucial contribution to the incomes of the poorest. In 1987, 70 per cent of the income of the poorest 10 per cent came from social security benefits, compared with 17 per cent for the population as a whole.

(Oppenheim 1990, p. 36)

The material presented here describes the sort of lifestyle that can be afforded by the level of income provided by the state safety net. In so doing it is intended to contribute to a key current debate on the efficacy of social assistance provision, on whether it can be said to constitute a state of poverty. Is social assistance the answer, or the cause of much poverty? The reader can easily extrapolate how far these experiences might be shared by other poor people.

While social assistance claimants share with many other people the experience of poverty, a condition which in itself is stigmatizing, the experience of claiming and being supported by this last-resort means-tested benefit is unique to them. For example, in 1977 the Supplementary Benefits Commission remarked in its evidence to the Royal Commission on the Distribution of Incomes and Wealth (DHSS/SBC 1977, p. 1) that the administration of benefit added to the stigma already experienced by poor people:

The social services, of which social security is a part, can to some extent counteract the stigmatizing effects of poverty and the factors with which it is associated. They can also have the opposite effect, by separating the poor from other users of the services, providing different and inferior services for them, or simply marking them out as poor. Means-testing is one way in which this can happen.

Despite the best efforts of the staff who administer it, the procedures and the practices of any system of means-tested assistance provided as last resort for the poor must inevitably be stigmatizing to some extent.

(DHSS/SBC 1977, p. 32)

Following their study of the treatment of social security in the media, Golding and Middleton (1982, p. 164) reached a similar conclusion:

The evidence suggests a sharp move away from the individual notion of stigma... to a broader view of the social obloquy surrounding institutions, the practices they employ and the people who use them.

DEVELOPMENT OF BRITISH SOCIAL SECURITY

The British post-war social security system was based on the recommendations of Sir William Beveridge fifty years ago. His proposals for a comprehensive scheme of social security were laid out in the best-selling report, *Social Insurance and Allied Services* (Beveridge 1942). Beveridge proposed that the bulwark of state-provided social security should be a system of social insurance. In return for contributions paid while in work, people would draw out benefits when they were unable to work. Benefits paid under this system were to be adequate in amount and duration. Whether benefits are paid for as long as the need lasts is easy to measure; judging whether they are adequate in amount is more contentious and is the question at the heart of the debate on the effectiveness of the benefits system. Chapter 2 considers some of the arguments surrounding this debate; Chapters 3, 4 and 5 explore the empirical evidence available on the lives of the people who live on social assistance.

Alongside state insurance provision, Beveridge recommended a national system of means-tested social assistance as a 'minor but integral part' of income maintenance provision (Beveridge 1942, para. 369). Beveridge anticipated that once the insurance proposals were fully implemented the 'permanent scope of assistance (would be) much less than that of public assistance and of the Assistance Board' which it replaced (1942, para. 371). Very few people would need to rely on social assistance and the numbers who were dependent on it would fall as the social insurance scheme became established. In fact, that model was never fully realized. National insurance has met neither of Beveridge's conditions of being adequate in amount and duration and increasing numbers of people have fallen outside its net (Lister 1978; Atkinson 1989). Thus the post-war period has seen a decline in the significance of national insurance benefits and a rise in reliance on means-tested benefits in general and social assistance in particular. This change in the balance of provision, which is discussed more fully in Chapter 2, had important implications for the success of social assistance in the post-war period.

There have been three social assistance schemes in operation in Britain since the war. While the structures of the three schemes differed, their function was the same: to provide benefits, on a means-tested basis, to those not in full-time work, whose incomes fell below a prescribed level. From 1948 to 1966 the scheme was known as national assistance, and it was administered by an independent body, the National Assistance Board (NAB).

From 1966 to 1986 it was called supplementary benefit, and was adminis-tered up to 1980 by the Supplementary Benefits Commission (SBC) and from 1980 to 1986 by the Department of Health and Social Security (DHSS). In 1988, income support replaced supplementary benefit. In addition to the two changes of name, one other major reform stands out above many other minor interim changes which occurred between 1966 and 1986. That is the reform introduced in the Social Security Act 1980, which came into effect in November 1980. This legislation ended most of the discretionary powers of the SBC and, before it, the NAB, and replaced them with claimants' rights which were laid down in regulations approved by Parliament.

Both the NAB and the SBC had held varying degrees of control on how the system was administered and the formulation of policy, for example on such issues as which needs could be met and in what circumstances weekly or lump-sum payments could be made. After the abolition of the SBC in 1980, responsibility for administration fell to the Department of Health and Social Security (DHSS) and policy was made only by ministers, via Parliament.[3] A Social Security Advisory Committee (SSAC) was created, as its name implies, to advise the government on all aspects of social security but not, as the SBC or the NAB had done, to make policy. Since its creation, the SSAC has been very critical of certain aspects of government policy, especially with respect to social assistance (for example Cmnd 9296 1984, Cmnd 9791 1985). However, the Conservative government often ignored the advice and recommendations of this advisory committee. In October 1990, responsib-ility for the administration of social security was passed from the Department of Social Security (DSS) to a new executive agency, the Social Security Benefits Agency. Officially, the new agency has no control over policy. Its first chief executive pointed out soon after taking office that it was respon-sible only for the operation of the system:

> It's no good saying we can change policy. We have a role in ensuring policy takes account of operational issues, but at the end of the day policy issues remain with ministers. We may not be able to improve the level of benefits our customers think they need, but we can improve the way they're delivered.
>
> (Lunn 1990)

However, the impartiality of the new agency was called into question when it was revealed that it had played a key role in effecting an important policy change in 1991. A letter from the chief executive, which was leaked to a Labour MP, suggested that the agency had actively campaigned for a change in policy. Facing a Social Security Commissioner's decision which would have led to some 35,000 people with learning difficulties claiming arrears of benefit going as far back as 1948, the Benefits Agency responded 'to the views of, and pressure on, local services faced with mounting requests for review following take-up campaigns' (letter from M. Bichard, quoted in the *Guardian*, 5 September 1991) by lobbying the policy group of the DSS to get the law changed. This was duly effected in August 1991. Thus, in a situation where the legitimate rights of claimants unduly pressurized benefits administration, the Benefits Agency sought to protect the latter.

The changes in structure of the various British social assistance schemes have been influenced most by the administrative and financial pressures which have confronted it in its various guises. The structure of the first national and comprehensive social assistance scheme, national assistance, was based on the assumption that it would only have to cope with a minority of claimants. Consequently there was considerable scope in the scheme for adjustment to individual need and circumstance. Under the national assistance scheme, two types of financial support were available. First, the basic weekly scale rates were intended to cover all day-to-day needs up to subsistence level. A second tier of support was added to meet the 'abnormal needs' of a minority of claimants (Beveridge 1942, para. 371). Extra help was provided in the form of weekly additions to benefit for regular expenses, like special diets, and lump sum payments to meet occasional large expenses, such as furniture. This system of subsidiary support assumed a growing significance, both for claimants, to whom it provided a welcome boost to their fixed weekly income, and to the benefits system, for which it was a source of complexity and increased administrative pressure.

This dual structure was seen to be untenable when it became clear that social assistance was not, as intended, a residual scheme, but a 'mass' scheme, dealing with millions of claims each year. From 1966 onwards, Labour and Conservative governments looked for ways of adjusting the structure of social assistance to make it fit the role it was actually having to perform, rather than the residual role that had been planned for it. However, it was not until 1976, in the report of a review of supplementary benefit set up by the Labour government, that this crucial development was publicly acknowledged and proposals put forward to tackle it. Previously, both Labour and Conservative governments had been publicly committed to reducing dependence on means tests, even if their actions had the opposite effect.

Since the second world war, social assistance has been subjected to numerous changes, both major and minor. All sought to find the most effective way of making a scheme, designed to meet the needs of a minority, operate effectively on a much wider scale. The frequency of attempts made to reform British social assistance proves the difficulty of finding a workable mass means-tested scheme. However, none of the numerous reforms of social assistance was accompanied by any serious public discussion of the role of social assistance or, most importantly, its relationship with the national insurance system. Furthermore, little heed was paid to the key problem faced by social assistance claimants: the low level of benefits. Without tackling these fundamental issues, and instead merely revamping administrative structures and procedures, the search for an administratively simple means-tested system was bound to fail. The income support scheme abandoned all flexibility to individual need and therefore has a relatively simple structure and rules of entitlement. It is too early to say how well the latest social assistance scheme is working. It would appear that, in restricted administrative terms, it stands a greater chance of success than its predecessors. The rigid structure offers less scope for pressure to build up. However, as the growing demand on income support's minor companion scheme, the social fund, shows (see Chapter 7), any simplification has been achieved only by ignoring the financial hardship of claimants. The next section considers how, despite the obvious failures of previous reforms, successive governments continued to look for changes *within* the social assistance scheme to tackle problems which were, in the main, caused by factors *external* to it (e.g. Lister 1978).

MAKING IT WORK: REFORMING SOCIAL ASSISTANCE

The first national, comprehensive scheme of social assistance was introduced in the National Assistance Act 1948. The scheme ran relatively unchanged until 1966 despite the fact that the National Assistance Board (NAB) found itself performing a much wider role than that envisaged in 1948. Demand for social assistance was greater than Beveridge had recommended and more than ministers had anticipated. This came about because, almost as an afterthought, provision was made in the original legislation for social assistance to be paid in supplementation of national insurance benefits (Deacon 1982). Furthermore, contrary to Beveridge's expressed recommendation, social assistance entitlement for many people was higher than their social insurance entitlement. As a result, between 1948 and 1965 the number of weekly payments grew from just over one million, supporting 1,750,000 people in December 1948 to two million, supporting 2,800,000 claimants and their dependants by December 1965 (Walker 1983, table 1). There were increases among lone mothers, widows under 60 and people with disabilities, but the largest growth was among beneficiaries over retirement age. During this period, no fewer than two-thirds of all national assistance payments were paid in supplementation of national insurance benefits.

Despite the growing numbers wholly or partially dependent on national assistance, data became available from the 1950s onwards which showed that many people were not taking up the benefits to which they were entitled. In their research into the economic circumstances of older people, Cole and Utting estimated in 1962 that up to half a million pensioners might be entitled to, but were not receiving, assistance. They attributed this to three factors: the complexity of the regulations which made it difficult for potential claimants to understand entitlement and eligibility; the inconsistent decision-making of the NAB's officers, particularly with regard to discretionary payments; and, finally, to the continued presence of stigma (Cole and Utting 1962).

Partly in response to the public outcry created by these findings, a second study, carried out by the Ministry of Pensions and National Insurance and the NAB, was set up by the Conservative government to explore the problem of take-up, particularly among older people (HMSO 1966). The survey, conducted in 1965, found that reluctance to claim was not confined to older people though it was among this group that the problem was most acute. In all, it was estimated that 700,000 pensioner households were entitled to, but not receiving, national assistance.

From the 1960s onwards, another significant problem emerged: that of the administrative burden caused by the enormous growth of the system of extra payments. Between 1948 and 1965, the proportion of claimants receiving a weekly addition to benefit doubled from 26.2 per cent (265,000 claimants) to 57.9 per cent (1,157,000). Similarly, the number of lump sum payments trebled from 100,000 in 1948 to 345,500 in 1965 (Walker 1983).

The growing body of evidence on poor take-up, the increasing complexity of the scheme caused by the growth of additional payments, and the more frequent criticism of the national assistance scheme in Parliament led both the Labour and Conservative parties to consider reforms. In opposition in the early 1960s, the Labour Party put forward proposals to lift people off means-tested assistance. These more adventurous plans were shelved in office in the face of a deteriorating economic situation (Hall, Land, Parker and Webb 1975). Instead the 1964–66 Labour government allocated more limited resources to reform the national assistance scheme. The aims of this change were, first, to make the system of means-tested support more acceptable to those it was intended to reach and, secondly, to reduce the number of discretionary additions which were 'not only administratively costly and inefficient but ... increasingly recognized to be inequitable' (SBC 1977, p. 209).

The changes were implemented in the Supplementary Benefits Act 1966. The new name, supplementary benefit, was thought to connote the notion of rights better than the term 'assistance'. The second objective of the reforms was to reduce the number of additional payments, especially the weekly additions to benefits. To achieve this, a long-term addition of nine shillings was introduced to be paid to all supplementary pensioners and to all those under pensionable age who did not have to sign on for work (ie those registered as unemployed), who had been on benefit or assistance for more than two years.

Apart from these changes, the detail of the new supplementary benefit scheme differed little from national assistance legislation or the policy of the NAB. It was, therefore, inevitable that the supplementary benefits scheme should continue to be beset with by then familiar problems. First of all, despite the new name, there was no new image. Take-up was still a problem, remaining at around 75 per cent. The new supplementary benefits scheme faced even tougher problems than its predecessor, as the number of claimants continued to grow and, even more importantly, the profile of claimants changed. While the number of people over retirement age stayed almost constant, the numbers of claimants below retirement age gradually formed a higher proportion of all claimants. By 1981, the number of claimants below pension age exceeded those above retirement age; in 1982, the number of unemployed claimants alone exceeded the number of supplementary pensioners (Walker 1983). The implications of this for the system were and remain extremely significant and help to explain the changing attitude of post-war governments towards means-tested provision.

The first impact that the increase in younger claimants made was to increase pressure on benefit administration. Claimants under retirement age undergo more changes in their circumstances which affect their entitlement, and they move on and off benefit more frequently. The younger claimant population, who were more likely to have children, also put pressure on the subsidiary system of extra weekly or occasional payments. The consequent increased demand provoked the SBC to launch a debate centred on the widespread use of discretionary powers to supplement the weekly benefit rates and the problems this posed for equity of treatment between claimants (SBC 1977, Chapter 6). What was not stated so explicitly were the expenditure implications of a discretionary decision-making process set within an Act which placed few limits on the circumstances in which an extra payment could be made (Donnison 1982). The Labour government was concerned because these payments, like the social security system generally and unlike almost any other area of public expenditure, were demand-led (Bradshaw 1982); neither ministers nor the SBC had any means of controlling the costs of these extra payments.

The second consequence of there being more claimants below retirement age was that younger claimants attracted criticism. During the 1970s, there was growing antagonism towards the social security system and its claimants. Considerable criticism was made in the tabloid press and by various Members of Parliament (see Golding and Middleton 1982), which was overwhelmingly directed at those groups who had been traditionally regarded as 'undeserving' – mainly unemployed claimants and, to a lesser but significant extent, lone parents. One of the most tawdry episodes of 'scroungerbashing' took place in the national press in the summer of 1976. The trigger for this adverse attention was an increase in benefit levels which, because of high inflation and a statutory incomes policy, exceeded some wage increases.

In the midst of the furore, the Labour government announced an internal review of supplementary benefit in 1976. The SBC regarded the creation of any enquiry at a time of public expenditure cuts as a victory (DHSS/SBC 1979). Most groups who represented claimants were more critical, because the enquiry failed to address the inadequacies elsewhere in the social security system from which the problems facing social assistance stemmed. They sought a more wide-ranging enquiry which would look at the adequacy of the whole system, and especially the interrelationship between social insurance and social assistance (Lister 1978; Lister 1979).

The review team's report *Social Assistance* (DHSS 1978) was published in 1978. The review team toured the country discussing their report at public meetings and received over 1,000 pieces of written evidence (for further discussion of this see Walker 1983). They even produced a report summarizing the comments which had been submitted in response to *Social Assistance* despite the fact that the majority were critical (DHSS 1979; Walker 1982). By the time the Labour government might have been expected to comment on the review, a general election had been announced. No reference was made to the reform of social assistance in any of the major political parties' manifestos.

Though no official pronouncements were made, it is clear that Labour ministers did have considerable sympathy with the main tenor of the review team's report and did see the recommendations as a way forward. The key concepts in the review – acceptance of the principle of social assistance as a 'mass system', simplification of the system, primarily for administrative and cost reasons, and the need for financial stringency within the social security budget – received the support of Labour ministers (see Walker 1983). However, it fell to the incoming Conservative government to implement the implied changes to supplementary benefit. This was done in the first of several Conservative Social Security Acts. The aims of the social assistance reforms in the Social Security Act 1980 were twofold: first, to simplify the scheme, and, second, to move from a highly discretionary system to one determined by legal entitlement. The conflict between these two goals was realized only after, but very shortly after, the reforms had taken effect. The conflict arose from the fact that means tests are by nature complex. Simplification can only be achieved if provision is made on a broader group basis. This in turn can only be achieved by putting more money into the system or by making some people worse off. The Conservative government was not prepared to commit extra resources and, although they were prepared to introduce changes which would make people worse off, they were not prepared to be as ruthless in 1980 as they became in future legislation. It soon became clear that the 1980 reforms had merely replaced one type of complexity with another.

> There is an essential conflict between trying to contain the availability of additional payments to the minority for whom they are intended and trying to keep the system simple. By catering for the exceptional cases, the regulations have to be extremely precise and over-definitive and can themselves give rise to new anomalies.
>
> (Walker 1983a, p. 194)

The switch from discretionary decision-making to a regulation-based system did not curb the demand for extra help. The number of weekly additions continued to rise, though their administration was considerably streamlined. After falling back by one-fifth in the first year, the demand for lump sum payments increased fourfold by 1986. This led the government to announce huge cutbacks in the regulations governing lump sum payments which took effect in October 1986 (see Chapter 6).

The reformed SB scheme had been in operation for less than three years when, in 1983, the Secretary of State for Social Services, Norman Fowler, announced a second review of the system. This was just one of four reviews which he set up to examine social security provision. The others were on housing benefit, benefits for children and young people, and pensions. Though packaged rather grandiosely, the scope of the second supplementary benefits review was little different from the first. It was concerned only with the internal structure and operation of the scheme, not with wider external factors which many regarded as being the real cause of supplementary benefits' problems. Like its predecessor, the Fowler review team was given a no-cost remit and therefore the scope for substantial reform leading to genuine improvements in the level of benefits for claimants was impossible. Both *Social Assistance* (DHSS 1978) and *Reform of Social Security*, the Green Paper in which the Fowler review's proposals were set out (Cmnd 9517 1985), contained numerous references to the need for financial stringency. Both analyses of the system's problems were cost-driven, and the solutions set within fixed financial targets.

The Fowler review of supplementary benefits had three major objectives, none of which was new: to tackle the complexity of the scheme, to reduce the number of extra additions which 'swamped' the scheme, and to target help more effectively 'to those who need help most' (Cmnd 9517 1985, p. 31). The proposals relating to social assistance which were published in the 1985 Green Paper survived virtually intact and were enacted in the Social

Security Act 1986. Most of the social assistance changes took effect in April 1988. Now under the name of income support, British social assistance provision became less flexible. Additional weekly payments were entirely abolished, replaced in part by a system of premiums. The system of lump sum payments was abolished and, in its place, the social fund was set up. The social fund was the most controversial aspect of the 1986 legislation. It was quite different from any previous type of British social security provision in that it was cash-limited not demand-led; it could make grants, but most payments were made in the form of loans; claimants became applicants to the social fund, as they had no rights to a social fund payment and all decisions were discretionary; finally, there was no independent right of appeal.

Building on the spirit of the 1980 legislation, the Social Security Act 1986 buried once and for all the notion that social assistance would ever be a scheme for the minority. The legislation firmly placed means-tested benefits at the heart of future benefit provision. Some changes, like the severe curtailment of the State Earnings Related Pensions Scheme, had the impact of increasing the number of people likely to need social assistance in the future. The only reduction in dependence on social assistance was among young people. This was achieved not by raising their income above social assistance level but by removing their right to benefit. Subsequently, most full-time students also lost their right to benefit.

The 1986 legislation paid even less attention to the impact of its policies on the lifestyles of claimants than previous reforms. The new income support scheme set up in 1988 owed more to the government's desire to restrict spending, and to devise a means-tested benefit which could be computerized, than to a commitment to providing better or more adequate benefits for claimants. Experience had shown that it was impossible to bring the subsidiary system of help under control and it was impossible to computerize this plethora of payments. The solution found was to abolish weekly additions and lump sum payments and to provide only token compensation for the latter through the social fund. While it is obviously in the interests of claimants to have an efficiently run system, the structure and administration of any service should reflect user needs rather than determining the extent and level to which need will be recognized.

THE REST OF THIS BOOK: OUTLINE

The next chapter looks at the development of the British social security system and, in particular, at the influence and legacy of the Beveridge Report (1942). It explores the changing balance between benefits provided by the national insurance scheme and those provided on a means-tested basis, and how that change has come about without any public discussion on the efficacy of such a shift. It looks at the 'ambiguities' (Atkinson 1989) in social security policy-making, whereby governments endeavour to maintain the appearance of providing adequate benefit levels while being equally, or more, concerned to contain expenditure and avoid the creation of work disincentives.

Chapter 3 looks at the arguments which have been waged on the adequacy of benefit rates and the different measurements that might be used. It looks at how post-war governments soon abandoned the subsistence principle but how the legacy of the concept of the national minimum continued to influence the definition of adequacy which governments adopted. Chapters 4 and 5 look at adequacy from the point of view of benefit recipients. Is social assistance enough to live on? What kind of living standards does it allow? The chapters draw on many empirical studies of claimants conducted over three decades. Chapter 6 deals with the system of supplementary support which was a central feature of social assistance provision until 1988. It examines the different ways in which this extra help has been provided, on a discretionary and a regulated basis, and how well the different schemes have met claimants' needs.

Chapter 7 looks at the reforms to social assistance set out in the Social Security Act 1986, most of which took effect in April 1988. It examines how the very radical changes which were introduced were a reaction to the failure of the many reforms which had gone before, and considers how far they solved the problems which had beset social assistance since the war. Chapter 8 examines the less tangible effects of being a claimant. It looks at claimants' status within society and how they perceive themselves and other claimants, and considers their relationship with those administering the scheme.

CONCLUSION

This book traces developments in the provision of means-tested social assistance in Britain, and the increasingly important role it has played in state social security provision. Over the post-war period it has been subject to a series of minor and major changes. However, the question which needs to be answered is what impact these changes have had on those who depend on this system for their income. Have the needs of claimants been adequately considered? My thesis is that they have not. Governments have various reasons for changing policy and, since the mid-1970s in particular, social assistance policy has been determined by factors other than the needs of claimants. Governments have sought to manage poverty by controlling the amount of resources available to alleviate its worst effects, not by preventing it. Later government concern concentrated on the definition of poverty, which first reduced the numbers officially defined as poor and then led to it being redefined out of existence. As a result claimants have lost out to wider economic objectives and to anti-welfare state ideologies. Social assistance recipients have to manage their own poverty in a hostile climate, on inadequate incomes. It is on them that the failures of state provision fall. As long as the debate on social security in general and social assistance in particular concentrates on financial and administrative concerns, the actual impact of policies on the poor is ignored. The danger then is that their needs are allowed to disappear, into poor and deprived homes or on to the streets.

NOTES

1 HBS was introduced in 1982 when the rent and general rates costs of SB claimants were transferred to the housing benefit scheme. HBS was introduced to make up the incomes of those claimants who would have been made worse off by the change.

2 Forty per cent above supplementary benefit level was the usual 'poverty line' used in many studies, from Abel-Smith and Townsend 1966 to the definition of 'on the margins of poverty' used by Townsend (1979) and later by CPAG (Oppenheim 1990).

3 The DHSS was split into the Department of Health and the Department of Social Security (DSS) in July 1988. This book uses the title which is appropriate to the time under discussion.

2 The shifting sands of British social security

When a national programme of income maintenance was introduced by the post-war Labour government, social assistance was expected to play a small and diminishing role. National insurance was intended to provide for the majority of people unable to support themselves. This chapter considers how British social security policy shifted away from the goal of a predominantly social insurance-based system to one increasingly dominated by means tests. It looks at how this happened despite the professed commitment of all governments up to the Thatcher governments of the 1980s to reduce dependence on means tests and without the public rejection by any government of the insurance principle. It considers how this growth in significance of means-tested social assistance inevitably led to the numerous attempts to reform the scheme described in the previous chapter and eventually led to the abandonment of key principles underlying the structure and provisions of post-war social assistance.

BACK TO BEVERIDGE: WHERE DID IT GO WRONG?

Publication of *Social Insurance and Allied Services* (the Beveridge Report) in 1942 was a landmark in the development of British social security policy. Beveridge's plan drew together and built on the existing pre-war income maintenance provisions rather than putting forward radical new ideas. However, half a century later, his vision and goals stand above any subsequent government analysis of the British social security system, despite attempts by various Secretaries of State, Labour and Conservative, to compare their work to that of Beveridge. The significance and uniqueness of *Social Insurance and Allied Services* was twofold: first, it was the result of a thorough rethink of the aims and goals of state income maintenance policy and, secondly, it set out to provide a comprehensive plan to both prevent and alleviate poverty. The plan for social security set out in the report took 'abolition of want after this war as its aim' (1942, para. 14). Subsequent reviews of the social security system have been set much more modest goals of an administrative or financial nature (see Walker, C. 1986) within the context of a system designed only to alleviate, not prevent, poverty.

The state social security programme proposed by Beveridge was designed to assist those not able to participate in the labour market. The problem of poverty of those in work was identified as being confined to the mismatch between earnings and family size. Universal children's allowances were proposed to tackle this. Other benefits to assist low-paid families were not introduced until over twenty years later. The plan for social security proposed by Beveridge was one based on social insurance for the majority backed up by means-tested social assistance for the residual few and topped up, as appropriate, by voluntary insurance (1942, para. 17). However, Beveridge recognized that even comprehensive social security provision could not solve the problem of poverty if implemented in isolation. Thus, half a century ago Beveridge saw that the prevention of poverty depended on the availability of decent housing, education, employment and appropriate health care as well as adequate income.

> Want is one only of five giants on the road of reconstruction and in some ways the easiest to attack. The others are Disease, Ignorance, Squalor and Idleness.
>
> (Beveridge 1942, para. 8)

Beveridge argued that, to be successful, his social security programme needed to be underpinned by three measures: the maintenance of full employment, the provision of an allowance for each child, and the provision of free health care. These three 'assumptions' were discussed at length in the report because Beveridge believed that the success of the social security provisions were particularly dependent on these wider aspects of 'a concerted social policy' (1942, para. 409).

The Beveridge Report has had a longstanding influence on generations of policy-makers in Britain and abroad. Even today, politicians and policy-makers refer back to Beveridge for support for their ideas in this field (see, for example, the Green Paper on the *Reform of Social Security*, Cmnd 9517 1985). And yet the British social security system has never worked as Beveridge envisaged. The question which then needs to be addressed is why Beveridge's vision did not become reality. The answer to this question begins to give some pointers to the continuing difficulties faced by the social security system and those dependent upon it.

The demise of Beveridge's vision has been caused by a number of factors. First, the goals which made up Beveridge's three underlying assumptions have not been achieved. Secondly, successive governments failed to implement some key aspects of Beveridge's proposals, at the heart of which was a national system of compulsory social insurance with just 'back-up' support from a means-tested system of national assistance and voluntary insurance. Thirdly, weaknesses in the original plan were not rectified as they became apparent over time.

The three assumptions

Beveridge's proposals assumed an unemployment rate of no more than 8.5 per cent. His arguments in favour of full employment revealed his concern to prevent the waste of human and economic resources *and* also to ensure that people could and would work when they were able. He argued that full employment was necessary for five reasons (1942, paras 440–443):

1 Unemployment is demoralizing: to combat this the report made payment of unemployment benefit conditional upon attendance at a worker training centre after a period of time – a condition, it was argued, which would be impracticable if applied to large numbers of people as has happened with the mass schemes implemented in the 1980s.
2 'The only satisfactory test of unemployment is an offer of work. Such a test cannot be effectively administered if there is no work' (para. 440).
3 To encourage ill or disabled people to become fit enough to re-enter the labour market, there needs to be work available for them.
4 'Income security which is all that can be given by social insurance is so inadequate a provision for human happiness that to put it forward by itself as a sole or principal measure of reconstruction hardly seems worth doing. It should be accompanied by an announced determination to use the powers of the State to whatever extent may prove necessary to ensure for all, not indeed absolute continuity of work, but a reasonable chance of productive employment' (para. 440).
5 Unemployment is wasteful both 'through increasing expenditure on benefit and through reducing the income to bear those costs' (para. 440). In particular he stressed that long-term unemployment (which he defined as 26 weeks, in contrast to the more recent British definition of 52 weeks) would be 'a rare thing in normal times'.

The post-war picture of employment and unemployment has been very different to that which Beveridge argued was necessary to allow his social security plan to work. The unemployment rate reported by the Department of Employment was just under 3 per cent in 1971; between 1979 and 1981 the number of unemployed claimants doubled, reaching its peak of 3.3 million in 1986. It then gradually fell back to 1.6 million in 1990, after which it began to increase once again. By August 1991, 2.4 million people were on the official unemployment count. Furthermore, far from long-term unemployment being the rare thing envisaged by Beveridge, in 1989 41.5 per cent of men on the unemployment register and 30 per cent of women – a total of 567,000 people – had been out of work for over a year. None of these would have had any entitlement to national insurance unemployment benefit as it is paid for 12 months only.

British official unemployment statistics should be treated with great caution. Between 1979 and 1991 there were more than thirty changes (Unemployment Unit and Youthaid October 1991) in the way they are calculated (see Atkinson 1989 for an account of the most important twenty-two changes). The most significant occurred in 1982 since when, instead of recording the number of people registered as looking for work at Job Centres and Careers Offices, the official statistics have included only those registered unemployed *and* claiming benefit. Thus large numbers of people who are out of work and looking for work are not included in the official count because they are not entitled to or not drawing state benefit. The rules of entitlement to national insurance benefits has become more restrictive in the 1980s and cuts in national insurance benefits have reduced payments below social assistance levels for many. However, many of the people so affected would not be entitled to means-tested benefits for other reasons.

The change to a 'benefit count' rather than an 'unemployment count' fell particularly harshly on certain groups of people. Married or cohabiting women are more likely to be excluded because the earnings of a partner disqualify them from social assistance. Since April 1983, claimants over the age of 60 have received a higher rate of social assistance if they cease to sign on as available for work (a requirement which is made of those under 60 who draw benefit), and since October 1988 the majority of 16 and 17 year olds have lost their right to income support, thus also removing them from the official unemployment count. In addition, among the numerous people who fail to claim benefits, especially social assistance benefits, to which they are entitled, will be many unemployed people. Take-up is especially low among ethnic minority communities (Leicester City Council 1988) who are also over-represented in the unemployment statistics (Arnott 1987). Immigrants subject to the 'recourse to public funds' rule are unable to claim means-tested benefits if they lose their job (NACAB 1990b; Lister 1990).

In a number of respects then the figures underestimate the true level of unemployment (see Hills 1987; Atkinson 1989). According to the standardized rate of unemployment used by the Organization for Economic Cooperation and Development (OECD), the unemployment rate in the United Kingdom peaked at 12.4 per cent in 1983 before slowly falling to 8.3 per cent in 1988. The OECD definition 'covers all people who are without work, are available for work and are seeking employment for pay or profit' (CSO 1990, chap. 4). This is a much wider definition of unemployment than that adopted by the British Conservative government during the 1980s. The Unemployment Unit, an independent research and campaigning organization, estimated that, according to its broader definition (working on the pre-1982 basis and taking into account some of the many changes to benefit regulations and other adjustments which have affected the official count), the real unemployment figure was more than one million higher than government figures. This produces an unemployment rate of 12.3 per cent of the workforce, compared to the government's figures of 8.6 per cent (Unemployment Unit/Youthaid 1991).

Although most of the changes to the official unemployment count led to a reduction in the total, many of the people who were removed did not necessarily cease to be dependent on the state for part or whole of their income. These include more than 700,000 people on government training and employment schemes. Thus the exclusion of the majority of 16 and 17 year olds from income support led to a reduction in benefit expenditure, but not of public expenditure, as they were supported by the Department of Employment through the Youth Training Scheme (YTS). The removal of men over 60 from the unemployment count actually increased benefit expenditure as they became eligible for higher social assistance payments. The advantage of this change to the Conservative government was that it reduced the unemployment count.

The second of Beveridge's necessary preconditions for the success of his social security plan was the payment of children's allowances. There were four main arguments behind this proposal. First, they would help to overcome one of the main causes of poverty identified in research studies undertaken for him, that of the mismatch between the family wage and family size. Second, because these payments are added to the disposable income of those in work, while being deducted from the means-tested benefits of those out of work, they help to maintain a differential between wages paid to people in work and benefits received by those out of work. Thirdly, it was felt they would help to increase the birth-rate. Finally, he argued that such payments acted as 'a signal of the national interest in children, setting the tone of public opinion' (Beveridge 1942, para. 413). Beveridge recommended that children's allowances should be paid for all children, except the first, on a non-contributory basis and regardless of income. He was opposed to means testing children's allowances:

> Little money can be saved by any reasonable income limit. In so far as it appears that children's allowances to all families irrespective of their means would mean giving money to prosperous people without need, this can be corrected by an adjustment of the rebates of income tax now allowed for children.
>
> (Beveridge 1942, para. 422)

The history of children's allowances in the United Kingdom has not been a happy one. The family allowance was introduced in 1945 at a rate nearly one-third lower than that recommended by Beveridge (Cmnd 9519, p. 64). It was increased only three times in the next thirty years before being abolished, along with tax allowances for children, in 1977. The legislation contained no requirement to increase child benefit in line with inflation along with other benefits and tax allowances. Consequently, it fell in value after its introduction. Child benefit was not increased in 1988, 1989 or 1990. By April 1990 it was worth just 58.7 per cent of the income support for children between five and ten compared to a peak of 71.4 per cent in 1984. In response to growing pressure from its backbenchers, the first post-Thatcher Conservative government conceded a £1 increase in benefit for the first child in a family to be paid from April 1991, and thereafter pledged to increase it in line with inflation.

The decision to increase child benefit marked a radical departure from the policy of the Thatcher administrations, whose commitment to child benefit during the 1980s was suspect, to say the least. The Review of Benefits for Children and Young People, one of the Fowler reviews of social security set up in 1983, rejected the means testing of child benefit only after substantial pressure from the Conservative Women's Advisory Committee and many MPs (see Lister 1989). But it was clear also that there would be no substantial increase in its value (Cmnd 9517 1985, p. 29). The 1987 Conservative Party Manifesto pledged that 'child benefit will continue to be paid as now, and direct to the mother'. The survival of child benefit in the cold public expenditure climate of the 1980s was attributed to the comma in this sentence (Lister 1989) but the tenor of the sentence enabled the government to justify not increasing its value.

During the third Thatcher administration, there were several intimations from government that child benefit was not regarded as an effective tool for tackling family poverty. Instead of increasing universal child benefit, the government preferred to 'target' help on the poorest families through means-tested family credit, a benefit for low-income families in work which replaced family income supplement (FIS) in 1988. Family credit reached just 285,000 families in 1989, approximately half of those who were eligible, compared to the 13.6 million families who received child benefit (DSS 1989). The financial advantages for the government of adopting such a strategy were considerable: each ten pence increase in child benefit costs £60 million compared to a total expenditure on FIS (in 1988) of £180 million. The disadvantage to poor families is similarly significant. Despite, in social security terms, a large-scale advertising campaign, and enhancing the take-up figures by changing the method of their calculation, the government has estimated that only half of the families eligible receive family credit. This means that nearly 300,000 of the poorest families are not receiving help. Only universal benefits reach *all* families in need; they do so because they go to all families.

Beveridge's third prerequisite for the effective prevention of poverty was the provision of free health care. The establishment of the National Health Service is widely accepted as one of the major achievements of the immediate post-war period. Although Beveridge argued that 'Restoration of a sick person to health is a duty of the State and the sick person' (1942, para. 427), his commitment to free health care was not entirely altruistic. He saw a free health service as a way of ensuring that as many people as possible were fit and able to work and therefore not reliant on benefit (Beveridge 1942, para. 437).

Over recent years a wealth of evidence has emerged showing the close link between low income and ill health (Townsend and Davidson 1982; Whitehead 1988). Despite the security that a national health service free at the point of entry has provided for people, it is clear that there remain great inequalities in the access which some groups in society have to health care and the service they receive from it, as well as in people's health chances. In addition, many people, including those on low incomes, are having to pay increased health charges such as prescriptions, and optical and dental charges. Poverty remains a contributing factor to ill health while at the same time ill health and disability are major causes of poverty (see Townsend and Davidson 1982; Whitehead 1988; Martin and White 1988).

FAILURE TO IMPLEMENT BEVERIDGE: THE DEMISE OF THE INSURANCE PRINCIPLE

The fact that Beveridge's prerequisites of full employment, children's allowances and comprehensive health care were only partially realized was an important contribution to the failure of the post-war social security system to achieve Beveridge's goal of the *prevention* of poverty. The failure of the British social security system to achieve the much more limited, but nevertheless important, goal of the *alleviation* of poverty effectively was due to other factors: first, the failure of successive governments to implement fully Beveridge's recommendations; second, their failure to address problems inherent in Beveridge's original proposals; and, third, the failure to amend provision in line with social and demographic changes.

Since 1948, the British social security programme has been moving away from the principle of social insurance towards social assistance, and yet no government has ever adopted any overt policy to do this. The demise of national insurance began as the result of omission and neglect; in the 1980s, it was the result of a policy of attrition.

Beveridge intended that the bulwark of his plan would be a scheme of compulsory social insurance into which people would pay contributions while they were in employment in order to receive benefits when they were not able to work. For those residual groups of people who would not be able to participate in, and therefore benefit from, an insurance-based system, a scheme of means-tested social assistance – called national assistance – was proposed 'for the limited number of cases' (1942, para. 19(x)) who would fall into this category.

Beveridge's espousal of the social insurance principle stemmed, on the positive side, from a belief that it implied a commitment by both giver and recipient. The creation of a national insurance fund, into which contributions were made and out of which benefits were paid, was expected to engender a sense of responsibility on the part of both the recipient *and* the government.

> The insured persons should not feel that income for idleness, however caused, can come from a bottomless purse. The government should not feel that by paying doles it can avoid the major responsibility of seeing that unemployment and disease are reduced to the minimum.
>
> (1942, para. 23)

On the negative side, Beveridge supported social insurance because it was preferable to the means test. He recognized 'the strength of popular objection to any kind of means test' (Beveridge 1942, para. 21) which had grown out of the hardship and misery caused by the application of the household means test in the 1930s (see, for example, Greenwood 1933). He was also opposed to the widespread use of selective benefits because they penalized the thrift of people who tried to save for harder times.

The inclusion of social assistance in the Beveridge plan was intended only to plug the limited and, it was thought, diminishing gaps in social insurance provision. Social assistance was to apply only to those born with a disability, deserted and separated wives (at that time a small minority), those disallowed insurance benefits because of misconduct, and those faced with an urgent or unforeseen emergency, as well as to provide a cushion for those with special needs above subsistence. Beveridge made a clear distinction between social assistance and social insurance and said that the former should be, and should be seen to be, inferior to the latter. The difference between the two systems was to be maintained, first, through the rules of eligibility (contributions versus the means test) and, secondly, by the additional controls on behaviour which would be a condition of receiving assistance but not insurance. These conditions built crucial stigmatizing features into social assistance, the long-term impact of which for social assistance recipients is discussed in Chapter 8. When Beveridge recommended building in these controls, he envisaged that they would affect relatively few people, as social assistance was intended to be a residual scheme. However, in the succeeding decades increasing numbers were affected, as more and more people became wholly or partially dependent on means-tested support. This was one of the key factors which gave rise to persistent and seemingly intractable problems for both the administrators and recipients of social assistance.

Up until 1979 all post-war governments, Labour and Conservative, publicly espoused a commitment to the insurance principle and the payment of benefits as of right rather than according to a means test. No government has ever formally suggested that the role of social insurance in income maintenance should be diminished and, in 1985, the Fowler reviews reiterated support for the insurance principle (Cmnd 9517 1985, para. 6.8). Though, as Minister for Social Security, John Moore (1987) had questioned the cost and efficiency of paying retirement pensions to all, the government moved quickly to quash rumours in 1989 that it planned to means test the retirement pension and was forced to introduce revised premiums in the income support scheme to stop such speculation.[1] As discussed above, proposals to means test child benefit were also shelved. However, despite party and governmental support for social insurance in public, the national insurance system has never provided security for the majority. Governments have failed to provide a truly universal and adequate system of social insurance. At best it has provided an inadequate income for its recipients; for increasing numbers of people it provides no income at all. As a consequence the balance between social insurance and social assistance has never been as intended; instead social assistance schemes have mushroomed and attempts have been made to adapt them to deal with numbers of people never envisaged at the beginning. There were two respects in which the inadequacy of the national insurance scheme led directly to a growth in reliance on social assistance: first, the relative levels of the benefits and, secondly, the scope and coverage of insurance benefits.

In *Social Insurance and Allied Services*, Beveridge stressed that the national insurance scheme should provide benefits which were adequate both in *amount* and in *duration*. Neither of these goals was implemented in the earliest or subsequent legislation. The flat-rate national insurance rates introduced in 1984 'fell short of providing an unambiguous national minimum' (Atkinson 1991), for reasons which Ernest Bevin made clear at the time:

(The government) rejected Sir William Beveridge's argument that benefit rates under the insurance scheme should be related to the cost of maintenance ... applicants who proved need would be entitled to obtain higher rates of assistance from the Assistance Board.

(Fraser 1984, p. 231, quoted in Atkinson 1991)

Consequently, the 1948 National Assistance Act made provision for partial compensation for the inadequacy of national insurance. As well as paying benefits to those not entitled to any national insurance benefits, the National Assistance Act allowed for social assistance to be paid in *supplementation* of national insurance benefits. It was assumed that this provision, which was included very much as an afterthought, would be a fairly minor function of the scheme (Deacon 1982).

However, when national assistance was introduced in 1948 the levels of benefits for many people, especially pensioners (who comprised the main group of beneficiaries), were higher than their national insurance entitlement. As a result, three-quarters of the assistance payments were made in supplementation of national insurance benefits. This could be justified at the beginning of the national insurance scheme because time was needed for the national insurance fund to build up. However, subsequent government action ensured that the gap between insurance and assistance payments did not close even though receipts to the national insurance fund exceeded payments from the fund in all but two years after its creation. In so far as the early post-war social security system strove to provide a national minimum it did so through means-tested provision, not as of right through the insurance system.

In subsequent years, governments continued to allow the pre-eminence of insurance to be eroded. In 1959, the Conservative government increased the rates of social assistance more than the rate of inflation. The official justification for this move was to improve the living standards of recipients. However, more importantly, this uprating in social assistance was made in preference to an increase in national insurance pensions, which would have been considerably more expensive (Walker 1983). Subsequently, further upratings and numerous additional special payments, which were added to the social assistance rates, widened the gap between the rates of the means-tested benefit and national insurance (see Chapter 3). When two new non-contributory national insurance benefits, invalid care allowance and severe disablement allowance (previously non-contributory invalidity pension and the housewife's non-contributory invalidity pension) were introduced, they were brought in at levels 60 per cent of the prevailing short-term national insurance rates, and so fell far short of social assistance, which most of the poorest new claimants would have been receiving already.

As a result of the inadequacy of the national insurance rates, the majority of people receive social assistance to top up these low rates. For example, in 1989, 77 per cent of pensioners receiving social assistance were also receiving the NI state retirement pension (DSS 1990, table A2.08). In the early 1960s, one-fifth of unemployed people were on social assistance; this increased to nearly three-quarters of men and over one-half of women registered as unemployed in 1989 (DSS 1991, table C1.07).

The second reason why social assistance has always been paid to more people than originally intended is that, contrary to Beveridge's recommendation, some of the major national insurance benefits are limited in duration. The most important of these is unemployment benefit. This benefit is paid for a maximum of twelve months regardless of the length of time that the person has been paying contributions. After that time recipients must turn to means-tested social assistance. In 1990, more than one-third of men and one-quarter of women on the unemployment register had been out of work for over a year, and therefore would have used up all their entitlement to NI unemployment benefit. In October 1989, the contribution rules for short-term NI benefits were made much stricter, which again excluded many people.

FLAWED FROM THE BEGINNING

While much of the blame for the failure of social insurance to meet the needs of the majority of people might be attributed to governments' failure to implement fully the Beveridge proposals or subsequently to protect the system adequately, there were also important flaws in Beveridge's original proposals: the shortcomings of insurance-based benefits and the level of benefits set.

Any contribution-based system of insurance will exclude those people who are unable to fulfil the qualifying criteria. People who cannot enter the labour market or whose participation in the labour market is interrupted have no opportunity to build up an adequate contributions record. The national insurance system has been unable to offer security to new and growing groups of people who are unable to build up a sufficient insurance record. This has always applied to people with severe disabilities – as we saw earlier the social assistance scheme was provided specifically for people like these – but increasingly it has affected also lone parents and unemployed people, including in particular young people and women. Young unemployed people, among whom there were unprecedented levels of unemployment in the 1980s, unable to enter the labour market, are unable to join the contributory system. In 1989, the Conservative government solved the 'problem' of their consequent reliance on means-tested benefits by taking the right to benefit away from the vast majority of 16 and 17 year olds. This merely postponed the problem until they were 18.

The original plan for social insurance made no provision for lone parents other than widows. However, the growth of lone parent families has been one of the most significant social changes in the post-war period. In 1966, 125,000 'women with dependent children' were in receipt of supplementary benefit (Walker 1983). Between 1980 and 1989, the number of lone parents on social assistance increased from 330,000 to 770,000 (Cm 1264 1990).

Neither did the insurance system make provision for carers or people's caring needs, an issue which has taken on growing importance in the closing decades of the twentieth century. A non-contributory benefit, invalid care allowance, paid at 60 per cent of the short-term national insurance rate, was introduced in 1976 for all carers except married women, to whom provision was extended in 1986 following a decision by the European Court. With growing numbers of older people, more people will be faced with caring costs by the next century, a need for which the national insurance scheme does not provide.

A further problem inherent in Beveridge's ideas was preference for levels of benefit which provided 'security of income up to a minimum' (Beveridge 1942, p. 130). The benefit rates which he recommended, and which are discussed at greater length in Chapter 3, were designed only to meet subsistence needs for food, clothing, fuel, light and household sundries. (Rent, along with special needs, was provided by additions to the basic social assistance rates.) To this he added a small 'margin' for inefficiency of 6 per cent of the total requirements (Townsend and Gordon 1989). While taking great care to provide a level of income sufficient to meet physiological needs, Beveridge did not allow for the costs of social participation (Veit-Wilson 1989) or for changes in living standards and expectations within society.

> People are not just physical entities they are social beings. As pressing as the physical need for survival are the social obligations of family, neighbourhood, employment and so on. Moreover many physical needs are themselves to some extent socially constructed... The problem with this subsistence approach is that it means, by definition, denying those reliant on the resulting income access to the resources necessary to play a full role in society, both economically and socially.
>
> (Walker 1990a)

Although, as discussed later, strict adherence to the subsistence principle was soon abandoned in favour of political expediency (Cooke and Baldwin 1984), the concept of a national minimum is deeply enshrined in the British social security system and has had a lasting effect on the benefits paid and the standard of living of benefit recipients.

Atkinson (1991, pp. 135–6) has argued that the adherence to the concept of a subsistence minimum rather than minimum rights (implicit in the social participation approach) has had important ramifications for the benefit scales and their structure.

> A minimum rights approach would suggest that (benefit rates) should be identical for men and women, as a matter of principle, and that a couple should receive the same as two individuals. This was indeed the case with

the old age pension of 1908, which was paid at the same rate to both men and women, and a couple received twice the amount for a single person. Notions of a subsistence minimum, on the other hand, pointed to lower benefits for women than for men and to a couple receiving less than twice the scale for a single person... Beveridge set the rate for a couple two-thirds higher than that for a single person, a relativity which has remained very little changed since that time.

This differential in benefit rates paid to single people and couples created the need for additional controls to be included in benefits administration. The rules concerning cohabitation or 'living together as husband and wife' have given rise to great concern and hardship. Such rules would be unnecessary if a couple received twice the benefit of a single person.

STAGNATION IN CHANGING TIMES

On publication of his report Beveridge was criticized (Abbott and Bombas 1943) for the provision made for women. Married women could not receive any benefit in their own right but only on the basis of the contributions of their husbands and no provision was made for lone parents, other than widows. More recently he has been criticized for the ethnocentricity of his proposals (Williams 1989). Undoubtedly both observations are valid. However, it could be argued that the Beveridge proposals were a product of their time. When he produced his report there were few lone parents, other than widows. Also he had access only to the 1931 Census, which showed that only a very small proportion of married women were in the labour market. This partly explains the tangential relationship he assigned to women in his plans for social insurance. His proposals were also drawn up before the growth in immigration in the 1950s and 1960s. Criticism might more validly be applied to the successive governments which failed to adapt social security provision to meet the changing position and circumstances of women, or the needs of an increasingly multicultural society.

Nevertheless, the problems faced by women in relation to the social security system can be traced back to the Beveridge proposals. Women form the main group likely to lose out in any contributory system because their access to the labour market is often limited by their caring responsibilities. In addition, married women were treated as the dependants of their husbands and their eligibility for national insurance benefits was conditional upon their husbands' contributions; they had no benefit entitlement in their own right. Those unmarried women who worked and paid contributions received inferior benefits because it was assumed they would not have responsibilities for dependants. Post-war governments were slow to redress this unequal treatment. Up until 1977, married women could choose whether to pay a reduced or full-rate NI contribution. The reduced contribution offered no financial protection, while the full contribution (equal to that paid by men) earned them benefits which were less generous than those received by men. The national insurance scheme continued to make provision for women whose marriages ended with the death of their husbands, but not for marriages that ended for any other reason (Pascall 1986).

Successive post-war governments failed to make good such inequitable treatment despite having the evidence of major social changes before them. Despite the steady growth in the numbers of lone parents in the post-war period to over one million in 1989 (Cm 1264), and despite the report of the Finer Committee on One Parent Families (1974), which recommended a benefit as right for this group, by 1990 approximately three-quarters of all lone-parent families were forced to live on social assistance (Cm 1264). Concerned by the rapid acceleration of lone parents on social assistance during the 1980s, the Conservative government determined that action should be taken. However, their efforts were confined to finding ways of encouraging lone parents to go out to work and of making fathers pay more towards the maintenance of their children (Cm 1264 1990; see also Brown 1989). There was no attempt to make benefit provision more adequate or secure.

The failure of post-war Labour and Conservative governments to respond to the situation of lone parents is the most glaring but not the only example of the social security system not being adapted to meet changing social and economic developments. The benefits system has been slow to adapt to increasing numbers of dual-earner families and to the increasing numbers of people in casual or part-time work. The benefits system distinguishes only between full-time and part-time work. The family credit scheme allows claimants to add together the hours worked from various jobs to meet the full-time work qualifying condition of 16 hours. However, the social assistance rules continue to penalize part-time work. Claimants have little financial incentive to work part-time as they can retain only a small part of their earnings, £5 or £15 (1991 rates) depending on status. It is not in social assistance claimants' financial interest to work unless they earn below the modest disregards level or until they can earn enough to lift themselves off benefit. Such rules make it difficult for benefit claimants to keep in touch with the labour market which, in the longer term, makes it more difficult for them to return to permanent full-time employment. Nor has either the social insurance or social assistance scheme been changed to meet the needs of the long-term unemployed, now over one million people, despite the fact that the national insurance system was originally designed to cope only with short spells of unemployment.

Thirdly, British social security has remained firmly ethnocentric. The DSS has done little to eliminate either institutional or informal discrimination. Qualifying residence rules which are applied to many NI benefits are most likely to affect people in ethnic minority communities. This means that they have to resort to the means-tested system, an option barred to many because of passport restrictions. The eligibility rules are insensitive to the lifestyles of some ethnic groups, for instance where family responsibilities or expectations take the claimant abroad for some time leaving dependants in this country. For many immigrants the right to social security is dependent on their immigration status. This leads to the informal practice of passport checking of any claimant, usually black, about whom an official may be suspicious (Ben-Tovim *et al.* 1986). Furthermore the 'recourse to public funds' rule, as Lister has pointed out, excludes those immigrants who are subject to it and 'creates uncertainty and anxiety for others' (Lister 1989a). The administration of benefits, including the introduction of lengthy application forms and discretionary rules which require good advocacy skills, has insufficiently considered the needs of people for whom English is a second language (NACAB 1990b; Arnott 1987; Gordon and Newnham 1985).

As the foregoing discussion confirms, British income maintenance provision has never conformed to Beveridge's ideal. The founding legislation and subsequent developments ensured that social assistance would play a significant and growing part in meeting the needs of poor people. The growth in dependence on social assistance during the post-war period occurred despite the professed commitment of both Labour and Conservative governments prior to 1979 to lifting people off these means-tested benefits. How then did social assistance come to play a major part in income maintenance provision and become such a major cause for concern in social security policy over four decades that it provoked frequent demands for reform? The answer is found, first, in the economic argument and then secondly, and only more recently, in the ideological debate.

THE COSTS OF SOCIAL SECURITY

In 1988–89 social security expenditure totalled £48.5 billion and was predicted to rise to £53.6 billion in 1990–91 (HM Treasury, January 1988). This represents approximately one-third of total public expenditure. The social security programme presents a particular problem to the Treasury. It is the only expenditure programme that is demand-led rather than budget-limited. Thus, overall expenditure is dictated, not by a fixed figure agreed at the beginning of the financial year, but by the number of people eligible to make a claim. Thus, as the number of claimants increases, for example following an increase in unemployment, so expenditure rises. While, or perhaps because, social security is the most expensive public expenditure programme, for reasons which are considered later in this chapter, it has never been the most revered part of state welfare provision; indeed, some aspects of it have been held in very low esteem by the general public and the press (see Chapter 8). The juxtaposition of these two factors has made it both an easy target for cuts and a low priority for additional expenditure.

It was under the Wilson and Callaghan Labour governments of the 1970s that social security, along with other areas of welfare provision, saw its most significant change of fortune. The economic crisis of that time led to cuts in welfare expenditure in many fields. Cuts to social security were made, albeit not explicitly (for example, in changing the basis of the uprating formula in 1975 from past to predicted levels of inflation), and any changes or improvements in policy which were sought had to be paid for by savings elsewhere in the system (see Walker 1983). The Thatcher administrations of the 1980s were far more explicit about their desire to cut social security expenditure and were successful in doing so. However, significant as any cuts in benefit are for claimants, the level of savings governments can levy is a tiny proportion of total social security spending. Cuts and savings can only be made at the margins of policy; the bulk of expenditure is beyond the control of the Department of Social Security and at the mercy of wider economic and employment policies. Thus, despite major cuts in parts of the social security and social assistance programme, overall expenditure continued to rise.

Given the relatively high level of expenditure, it is not surprising that concern with the cost of social security prevented many improvements in the British income maintenance programme. It was undoubtedly a key factor in the abandonment of Labour's ambitious plans to reform pensions provision in the 1960s (see Hall *et al.* 1975) and in the narrow focus of the review of supplementary benefit undertaken on behalf of the Labour government in 1976. However, it was the return to power of the Conservative Party in 1979 which marked the beginning of a new era, in which goals that had hitherto had only a subtle, unspoken influence began to dictate policy developments. While the Labour government made several covert attempts to reduce social security expenditure, the Thatcher administrations displayed no such coyness about their strategy. From the outset it was clear that social security would receive no special protection. In his first budget in 1980, Sir Geoffrey Howe, then Chancellor of the Exchequer, told the House of Commons that 'Social Security cannot be regarded as exempt from re-examination and entitled always to take absolute priority over spending on defence, the police, hospitals or schools – or over the need for proper control of public spending as a whole' (*Hansard*, vol. 981, col. 1463, 26 March 1980). The following day the Secretary of State for Social Services announced that it was 'inescapable that (the social security programme) must bear some share of the necessary economies' (*Hansard*, vol. 981, col. 1660, 27 March 1980). Similar sentiments prevailed in the 1985 White Paper on the Reform of Social Security: 'Social security accounts for one-third of public spending. It cannot be ring-fenced from the requirements of sensible management of the economy as a whole' (Cmnd 9691 1985, p. 2).

A number of legislative measures were introduced in the early 1980s which had the direct or indirect goal of saving money. In the first Social Security Act 1980, which was introduced in the year of their election, the government broke the link between the uprating of benefits and earnings. This has been a major source of savings since then: an estimated £10,000 million up to 1988–89 (Walker 1990). The same Act introduced major changes to the supplementary benefits scheme. While these changes were dressed up in the guise of increased efficiency and greater understanding for claimants and staff, they also managed to produce savings of £60 million. The new regulation-based system also offered the Secretary of State much greater control over expenditure. In such a system the Secretary of State could decide how generous or restricted regulations would be. This structure provided the framework, especially in relation to extra weekly and occasional payments, for the further deep cuts in single payments which were to be introduced in 1986 before their total abolition in 1988.

In its first term of office the Conservative administration defended its numerous social security reforms in terms of the advantages they offered to claimants. By their second term of office, the government saw less need to emphasize any such advantages. Other goals, most notably the need to control overall expenditure, had become more important. The 1985 Green Paper (Cmnd 9517 1985) was littered with references to the size of the social security budget. One of its three main objectives was that:

the social security system must be consistent with the overall objectives for the economy... Social security... is responsible for a major share of the current heavy tax burden on individuals and companies ... continued growth of this burden could severely damage the prospects for economic growth.

(Cmnd 9517 1985, p. 110)

Subsequently, there were numerous benefit changes, most of which saved money. Between 1979 and 1989, the social security budget suffered cuts which cumulatively totalled approximately £16.5 billion. Without them social security expenditure would have been one-third higher. Many, if not all of these cuts had an impact on social assistance: first, by reducing both national insurance and social assistance benefit levels and, secondly, by increasing the number of people consequently dependent on social assistance. The numerous changes to the unemployment count, discussed earlier, were a particularly important contributory factor as they not only reduced the number of unemployed people on the official count but also had a knock-on effect on the number of people eligible for social assistance.

FROM ECONOMY TO IDEOLOGY

Towards the end of the second Thatcher administration and during its third term, the government made claims about the success of its economic policy and the achievement of 'an economic miracle'. In this climate, the ground on which the social security debate was based began to shift. No longer did ministers justify changes in social security primarily by the need to reduce expenditure; instead they used ideological arguments to support their policy and thus the 'dependency culture' was born.

The seeds of this new emphasis were sown in the Fowler review. In the first volume of the Green Paper, *Reform of Social Security*, Norman Fowler set out his ideological agenda on poverty and social security. In this document the debate on the definition of poverty was addressed and the first salvo discharged against what had been the accepted definition of poverty. For over two decades, since the publication of *The Poor and the Poorest* (Abel-Smith and Townsend 1965), academics working in this field and even governments had come to accept that it was appropriate to consider poverty in relative terms – comparing the living standards of the worst-off with those of the rest of the community. While governments had refused to accept supplementary benefit as an official poverty line, in practice all outside commentators did so, facilitated by the production, until 1985, of low-income statistics which set out the number of people and households living on a range of incomes relative to the supplementary benefit scale rates (DHSS 1988a).

In the Green Paper, both the relative definition of poverty and the use of supplementary benefit as a poverty line were challenged:

> Various attempts have been made to measure poverty using a relative standard. A common approach is to count all families with incomes below the level of supplementary benefit as being in poverty and those with incomes between 100 and 140 per cent of supplementary benefit as being on the margins of poverty. There are, however, obvious drawbacks to this kind of approach. If the level of supplementary benefit rises relative to other forms of income, more families will be counted as being in poverty even if the real incomes of all families in the population are rising. For these and other reasons there is now no universally agreed standard of poverty.

(Cmnd 9517 1985, vol. 1, p. 12)

Shortly after publication of the Green Paper in June 1985, the government published, belatedly, the low-income statistics for 1983. Reflecting the concern expressed in the Green Paper, the then Parliamentary Secretary for Social Security announced:

> The technical assumptions in the low-income families tables have remained largely unaltered since the first analysis was undertaken. I have therefore set in train a technical review of the methods and assumptions on which the tables are based. Any improvements in measurement methods should be reflected in the future issues of the tables.
>
> (*Hansard*, 25 July 1986, col. 712, quoted in DHSS 1988)

The results of this review were published in March 1988 (DHSS 1988) shortly before publication of the much delayed 1985 low-income statistics (DHSS 1988a). The underlying thesis of the review was that the low-income statistics were flawed on a number of grounds but most significantly because they appeared 'to provide official endorsement of one specific approach to the definition and measurement of "poverty"'.

> The use of supplementary benefit *both* as the measure of low income *and* as one of the principal policy tools for helping those with low incomes creates the paradox that the higher the relative value of the benefit, the more people will be included in the tables (and the greater the apparent incidence of 'low income').
>
> (DHSS 1988, p. 10)

The changes which were proposed and implemented later that year with the publication of the 1985 figures were fundamentally different and incorporated a very different set of principles.

The first change in principle was implicit in the title of the new figures: 'households below average income'(HAI). The new figures were based on household income, rather than the benefit assessment unit (i.e. the people for whom benefit could be claimed). The justification for this was given in the report:

> One ambiguous feature of the (old) series ... is the use of the term 'family' to describe what are, in fact, administratively defined benefit assessment units – many of whom are actually adults living with other relatives, rather than self-contained families.
>
> (DHSS 1988, p. 10)

This introduces an extremely contentious principle back into the income maintenance programme – that of household income rather than individual income. One of the most unpopular aspects of benefit assistance before the second world war was the household means test, where the income of a wide range of relatives was taken into account when deciding whether or not financial help should be given. Since the war, benefits have been paid either on an individual basis, in the case of national insurance, or, in the case of means-tested benefits, on the basis of an 'assessment' or 'family' unit, which includes only the claimant, the partner and dependent children. To assume that other members of the family may be supporting 'independent' relatives is dangerous. Nevertheless, in 1988 the level of social assistance paid to people under 25 was cut because, the government argued, most would be living with their families (Cmnd 9517 1985).

The new figures do not compare incomes against the supplementary benefit/income support standard but were deliberately designed to be 'broadly independent of the various policy instruments which may affect low income (i.e. social security benefits)' (DHSS 1988, p. 15). Instead the figures concentrate only on the distribution of income, and where different groups fall in the hierarchy of income distribution. Despite generating a plethora of tables, the revised statistics offer no information on actual living standards or the amount of money people have to live on. Information on the distribution of income – which groups fall in the bottom quintile of income distribution, and incomes of the worst-off relative to the average – provide no hard information on actual levels of income. The House of Commons Select Committee on Social Services (1988) were so concerned at the loss of such basic information on actual standards of living that they themselves commissioned the Institute for Fiscal Studies (IFS) to produce figures calculated on the old basis (Social Services Committee 1988; Johnson and Webb 1990).

TARGETING OR SCAPEGOATING?

As well as redefining the measurement of poverty and thus reducing if not eliminating the problem, members of the Conservative government, including the then Prime Minister, Margaret Thatcher, launched a sustained attack on social security claimants: first, on the familiar front of fraud and abuse and, secondly, on the new issue of 'welfare dependency'.

Government policy is made not only within the context of the prevailing economic climate but also within a wider social and political context. Social security, certainly as much as, and probably more than, other areas of welfare policy, is affected by outside factors. One of the persistent concerns in the field of social security is that of fraud and abuse. This has been an influential consideration in both Conservative and Labour governments since the 1930s (Deacon 1976; Golding and Middleton 1982). Governments have been quick to respond to allegations of abuse in the system. The Heath government set up the Fisher Committee in 1972 to look at this question (Cmnd 5228 1973); the Callaghan government introduced special initiatives (fraud awareness packages) in response to one of the most vitriolic press campaigns against the social security system and claimants in 1976. The setting up of the review of supplementary benefit in 1976 was linked to this issue, and the tackling of fraud and abuse was one of three objectives set for this area of policy in the first Queen's Speech of the first Thatcher administration. The 1980s was marked by a succession of measures designed to increase control within the system. These included setting up regional fraud units and, in 1982, the 'Oxfraud incident' during which hundreds of homeless people were arrested after reporting to a fake social security office (Franey 1983; see also Smith 1985 for broader discussion on this issue).

The welfare dependency debate was picked up with considerable enthusiasm by Norman Fowler's successor as Secretary of State for Social Services (later Secretary of State for Social Security), John Moore. In two important and well-publicized speeches he set out his thesis on the dependency culture and then challenged the conventional debate on poverty claiming that critics would find 'poverty in paradise' (1989). Many saw this second speech as an attempt to redeem his waning reputation after the break-up of his Department. In this respect he failed; he was sacked just two months later (in July 1989). However, the philosophy underlying the speech continued to influence the development of the Conservative government's social security policy.

The 1980s became the decade of the 'dependency culture'. Proponents of this thesis maintained that people were encouraged to remain dependent on the state by the very policies which had been put in place to assist them (Moore 1987). The views underlying this philosophy can be seen in the treatment of various groups of claimants during the 1980s. First, and most obvious, was the treatment of the unemployed. As discussed earlier, a series of measures to cut and restrict benefits to the unemployed were introduced. The value of benefits was reduced for some and a series of measures, including an 'availability for work test', introduced to ensure that unemployed claimants were taking all possible steps to find work (see Atkinson 1989; Andrews and Jacobs 1990).

The next group to receive attention was elderly people. During the 1960s poverty had been seen primarily as a 'pensioner problem' (Abel-Smith and Townsend 1965; Hall *et al.* 1975) and the introduction of supplementary benefit in 1966 had been intended to overcome the resistance of elderly people to claiming their benefit entitlement. However, the 1980s saw the emergence of a new group: the 'WOOPIES' – well-off older people. Originally identifed by the marketing industry as a new target group for advertising, the concept was seized upon by the government as a justification for re-examining provision for people over retirement age. Ministers began to talk increasingly of the growing numbers of affluent retirement pensioners. Their existence, it was argued, provided justification for concentrating resources on the minority of older people who were not sharing in this affluence by transferring resources from the national insurance retirement pension to means-tested social assistance. In a well-publicized press briefing in 1988, the Chancellor of the Exchequer, then Nigel Lawson, argued for a reduction in the state NI pension as only a 'tiny minority' of older people 'genuinely' experience 'difficulty making ends meet' (quoted in Walker 1990). In fact while, according to the HAI figures, people over retirement age formed a smaller proportion of all people living in or on the margins of poverty in 1985, they remained almost static in number. Thus, although the number of retirement pensioners benefiting from occupational or other private pensions increased, there were no fewer *poor* pensioners. In 1987, people over retirement age formed the largest group of people living on incomes below supplementary benefit level (26 per cent). Though pensioners accounted for only 12 per cent of the poorest one-tenth of people in 1987, compared to 26 per cent in 1979, this happened not because older people suddenly became better off, but because younger people were made worse off (see Walker, A. 1986; Walker 1990). Inevitably, given that their incomes remained little changed in real terms, the 1988 HAI figures showed an increase in the proportion of older people in the bottom decile of the income distribution (DSS 1990).

Another group singled out for special consideration was young people. In the face of rising numbers of unemployed young people leaving home in the 1980s, the government sought to prevent those on social assistance living in commercial board and lodging accommodation. After several false starts, it was eventually successful and this type of accommodation was closed to young people on benefit. In 1988, cuts were made in the level of benefits to the under-25s and benefit as of right was withdrawn from 16 and 17 year olds. All these steps were justified in the name of family responsibility: that young people should look to the labour market or their families for support and not the state. The result was increased poverty and homelessness among young people (Kirk *et al.* 1991). In the summer of 1991, the Conservative government announced that it was spending £3 million on a housing initiative for young homeless people. In the announcement, the Minister of Health, Virginia Bottomley, said that the role of social security needed to be re-examined in this area. Up to the time of writing no announcement has been made regarding any future action.

By the end of the decade, a new group was the focus of government attention. In 1989 the government announced a review of benefits paid to lone parents. In 1990 the new Secretary of State, Tony Newton, abandoned this review but in response to a speech by Margaret Thatcher (1990) legislation was introduced to increase the amount of support obtained from fathers after separation and to increase powers to collect this money (Cm 1264 1990).

All these initiatives had the same end result. Whether they concern unemployed people presented as being unwilling rather than unable to work, pensioners not really being poor any more, parents not taking responsibility for their young people or fathers not taking responsibility for their children, the promulgation of such arguments is designed to reduce pressure on government for improved state support for the poor. By making subtle, and sometimes less than subtle, attacks on people living on state benefits, the Conservative government seemed to be determined to undermine the credibility of these people. Do they really deserve help? Do they need help? Are they 'genuinely' poor? In such a climate, it is easier for cuts to be made within the benefits system and much harder to defend the interests of poor people against the weighty government machine.

CONCLUSION

This chapter has explored the ways in which post-war governments have managed poverty from a top-down policy-making perspective. Government action on poverty has been confined to a policy of alleviation rather than prevention. Beveridge's goal of making 'Want under any circumstances unnecessary' (1942, para. 17) has not been achieved, partly because of important flaws in his design regarding the insurance principle and the concept of a national minimum, but also because successive governments failed to implement fully key elements of his proposals, especially relating to the adequacy of national insurance benefits, or to adapt social security provision in the face of changing social and demographic trends.

The slide from a rights-based national insurance system to a means-tested scheme occurred first as governments neglected national insurance. It continued as improvements in social assistance were implemented in preference to improvements in the national assistance scheme because they were cheaper. Such policies of benign neglect and short-term political expediency were replaced in the 1980s by an ideological preference for selective provision.

In the 1980s, the management of poverty extended beyond a concern with the method of paying benefits. The Conservative government abolished the term 'poverty' from the official vocabulary of the DSS. It changed the official statistics to prevent any comparison being made between past and present levels of poverty. As well as seeking to abolish poverty by semantics and statistical manoeuvring, the government orchestrated a campaign of hostility against benefit claimants. Frequent attacks were made on their honesty and integrity. This 'social construction of stigma' (Walker 1990) made it easier for the government to justify a benefits policy which penalized many benefit recipients. In so doing, it displayed more concern for managing or controlling the poor than with tackling the causes of poverty.

This and the preceding chapter have sought to provide the context of post-war social security policy and the reasons for the growing significance of social assistance within it. The rest of this book looks at the impact of that policy on benefit claimants and explores, from the bottom up, the ways in which recipients manage their poverty.

NOTE

1   Following a briefing with Nigel Lawson in 1989, the Sunday newspaper journalists reported that the retirement pension would be means tested. Lawson moved quickly to deny this and said that what he had been referring to was a new higher premium for older pensioners.

3 The adequacy of benefits
How much is enough?

As the previous chapter has shown, the British social security system developed in a way which was both quite different from that proposed by Beveridge and contrary to the stated objectives of successive governments. As the national insurance system failed to provide comprehensive support for the majority, increasing numbers fell outside its scope; for those who fulfilled the eligibility criteria, it failed to provide an adequate income. As a result social assistance was forced to play a growing role in British social security policy in the post-war period. That has presented persistent and seemingly intractable problems for this aspect of income maintenance provision.

The second major factor which led to problems for social assistance stemmed from the low level of benefits. The previous chapter established that social assistance rates for many people were higher than national insurance rates. It was also established that social assistance rates have been interpreted by commentators as the official definition of the minimum standard of living to be provided to claimants, and sometimes, wrongly, as the minimum level 'necessary' to meet basic needs. However, the history of the post-war development of social security shows how successive governments gradually abandoned the subsistence principle and the determination of benefit levels failed to take into consideration the actual living standards of benefit claimants.

Given that adequacy of benefits is central to any income maintenance programme, it is perhaps surprising that governments have spent so little time addressing the question. While many claims have been made on behalf of successive governments that the level of benefits is adequate, no evidence has been presented to substantiate these claims. Most of the empirical evidence that has been published over the past two decades has shown that benefit rates are too low. Nevertheless, a key assumption on which the reforms enacted in the Social Security Act 1986 were based was that the level of benefits was broadly satisfactory. The proposals were designed, therefore, only to ensure that resources were targeted effectively towards those groups in greatest need:

> At its most basic, the social security system has done much to ensure that absolute deprivation such as existed before the Second World War cannot return.
>
> (Cmnd 9517 1985, para. 4.2)

> The living standards of those most dependent on social security benefits can ... be seen to have improved substantially over the post-war period and in this respect a prime objective of the social security system has been achieved.
>
> (para 4.4)

Consideration of the question 'how much is enough?' (Cooke and Baldwin 1984) is crucial in determining whether social security provision can and does provide a solution to poverty – at least to the poverty of those dependent on state benefits. In practice, British social security policy has tried, at best, only to alleviate poverty, while attempts to prevent it in other policy areas, such as employment and training measures and some local anti-poverty strategies, have been inconsistent and, as the figures show, ineffective. What has been increasingly called into question is whether social security has achieved even the more limited goal. Has social assistance policy succeeded in alleviating poverty, or has it in fact been a major cause of it? This chapter looks at how far the concept of 'adequacy' has been taken on board by governments and how far it has been, or can be, taken into account in the setting of benefit rates. The next two chapters look at the actual standard of living of recipients of social assistance.

THE DETERMINATION OF BENEFIT LEVELS

Beveridge went to considerable lengths to calculate appropriate rates of benefit, which were to be paid at an adequate but subsistence level (see Chapter 2). When determining the main benefit rates, Beveridge drew on various official data and the surveys of Seebohm Rowntree (1901, 1941) and discussed the basis of his calculations at some length in his report (1942, paras 217–23). It has been argued that this was the last attempt to test empirically the adequacy of base rates (Andrews and Jacobs 1990). The rates he recommended were intended to cover the barest essentials: the cost of food, clothing, fuel, light and household sundries, with a very small addition to cover inefficient spending. Such an approach inevitably leads to generalizations about the expenses faced by a diverse range of people, from single, young people to people with disabilities; from couples with young children to older people.

Beveridge took three factors into account in drawing up a schedule of proposed scale rates. First, he assumed that the costs for men and women would differ primarily because of their different dietary requirements. However, he did not take into account other differences that might exist within groups, for example whether people were very active or led sedentary lives (Townsend 1979). Secondly, in order that the main benefit rates could be maintained at a 'subsistence' level, Beveridge proposed that social assistance should make additional payments for housing costs and any special needs which would take expenditure above subsistence level. Thirdly, in setting the benefit rates, Beveridge added just 6 per cent of total requirements to allow for the fact that people's expenditures might not be as rational in practice as policy-makers might demand in theory.

The foregoing calculations, particularly that for food, assume complete efficiency in expenditure, i.e. that the unemployed or disabled person buys exactly the right food and cooks and uses it without waste. This assumption is clearly not likely to be realized. Some margin must be allowed for inefficiency in purchasing, and also for the certainty that people in receipt of the minimum income required for subsistence will in fact spend some of it on things not absolutely necessary.

(Beveridge 1942, para. 221)

Housing costs were not included in the calculations for either social insurance or the basic social assistance scales. The 'problem of rent' (Beveridge 1942, p. 76) arose for three reasons: rent varied according to region; it was related to family size and it was one expense which a family could not reduce in the short term. Beveridge argued that as the underlying cause was the maldistribution of work caused by different levels of prosperity throughout the country, the answer had to be found in policies outside the social security system. The failure of governments to do this led to a massive growth in the number of people receiving help with their housing costs in the post-war period. Help with mortgages has been provided only to those in receipt of social assistance, and that help was cut back in 1986, despite the Conservative government's promotion of owner-occupation. The restriction of help with rent, and later rates, only to people on social assistance led to calls for similar help to be provided for other poor tenants. A separate national scheme of means-tested rent and rate (later poll tax) rebates was introduced in 1972, administered by the local authorities. The assistance provided for rent and rates by the local authorities and the then supplementary benefits scheme were combined into the housing benefit scheme in 1982/83. At its peak in the early 1980s, housing benefit was paid to one in three households. Since then it has suffered some of the most savage cuts in the social security programme.

While the method and results of Beveridge's calculations may be criticized (see Chapter 2), he did at least make an attempt to substantiate the level of benefits proposed. No subsequent review of any aspect of social security has attempted such an undertaking. Successive governments have been reluctant to provide empirical evidence to justify the level of benefits they have set. They refused to break down weekly benefit rates by anticipated expenditure or needs on the grounds that, while such payments were expected to cover all essential expenditures, it was up to individuals to decide how to spend the money. Such a response merely ducks the true issue: that to conduct such an exercise would prove that the benefit rates are too low for many people in many situations. Atkinson (1991, p. 121) argues that determination of the benefit levels has been characterized, deliberately, more by ambiguity than by clarity as the stated goal of achieving a national minimum has conflicted with other imperatives, such as the need to control overall expenditure and the avoidance of disincentives:

> The compromise is often left implicit rather than made explicit, governments hoping that a blurring of the goal (a national minimum) with the instrument (a level of benefit) would leave the impression that the objective had in fact been fully achieved.

In their attempt to translate benefit rates into goods and services which claimants could actually buy, Bradshaw and his colleagues (1987) found that the results were 'absurd'. For example, the budget allowed (at 1986 rates) expenditure of 94 pence per week on clothes:

> (A mother could) afford one coat lasting 15 years, three pairs of knickers every year, one pair of shoes every one and a half years and a handbag every 10 years....
> The full budget ... shows that the living standards of families on SB ... is harsh: the food component is short on calories and even that diet is only achieved with the most determined of self control ... it is achieved at the expense of expenditure on other commodities ... the family cannot afford a holiday away from home ... cannot afford a newspaper every day and has no money for books and magazines, never go to the cinema, cannot afford to buy bicycles or run a car, cannot maintain a garden, can afford one haircut a year, and so on.
> (Bradshaw, Mitchell and Morgan 1987, p. 174)

In the past, several people, including a member of the Supplementary Benefits Commission (SBC) and an MP, tried to live on the social assistance rate of benefit. Such experiments do not reflect the true experiences of real claimants as they ignore most of the factors which go to make life on benefit so precarious. Usually lasting only a week, such short-term experiments cannot portray the sheer drudgery and worry of living on a low fixed income week after week. The subjects lived alone without children, who, as is described in Chapter 4, make predicting and planning expenditure so difficult; there was no birthday or Christmas that week – the life events which are a source of worry, not joy, for poor families; and the giro arrived on time and was paid at the right amount. Despite these advantages, the protagonists, including the Conservative MP, could not make their money last out the week.

None of the innumerable changes to social assistance which have been made since the introduction of a national scheme in 1948 followed or were 'accompanied by any rational assessment of the efficacy of the various schemes' (Walker 1983, p. 25). Most significantly, neither of the two major reviews of supplementary benefit, the first set up by the Labour government in 1976 and the second by the Conservative government in 1983, examined in any depth whether benefit rates were adequate.

The 1976 Labour government review of social assistance looked at, and quickly dismissed, the issue of adequacy. Only three pages in the 127-page report were devoted to a discussion of this key issue. What discussion there was centred on the difficulty of deciding just what is adequate and concluded that 'There is no single objective criterion by which the "right" level of scale rates can be fixed for all time' (DHSS 1978, p. 38). The review team, therefore, made no further attempt to reach a firm conclusion on the level of the rates, although many of the proposals had the impact of increasing, or more often reducing, the amount of benefit which would be paid. The review team made no recommendation to increase social assistance levels generally; to have done so would have exceeded their no-cost remit. However, they did conclude in the report that many people on social assistance did face real difficulties (DHSS 1978, p. 38):

> There can be no real doubt that many claimants, particularly families with children, have little, if any, margin in managing their financial affairs.

Despite making this statement in the report, one member of the review team revealed how unaware he had been, while preparing and writing the report, of the true circumstances of claimants by admitting that it was only during the public debate which took place *after* the publication of their report, *Social Assistance*, that he discovered how 'finely pared life on benefit was' (quoted in Walker 1983).

The review of supplementary benefit set up in 1983 by the Conservative government once again failed to make any serious attempt to examine how adequate the benefit rates were in terms of the standard of living they afforded claimants. The Green Paper, *Reform of Social Security* (Cmnd 9517 1985), adopted the earlier review team's defeatist approach:

> There have been many attempts to establish what would be a fair rate of benefit for claimants. But it is doubtful whether an attempt to establish an objective standard of adequacy would be fruitful.

As Cooke and Baldwin have pointed out, the 1983 review of the supplementary benefits scheme considered only 'the basis on which support for the main groups covered by the scheme should be *structured*, and the extent to which the existing scale rate *structure* remains appropriate' (my emphasis) (1984). Thus, like *Social Assistance* before it, the 1985 Green Paper, which provided the fullest explanation of, and justification for, changing the supplementary benefits scheme, was concerned only with structures, not with levels of benefit. It was not until the White Paper had been published, some six months after the Green Paper, that some illustrative figures on the level of benefits to be paid were provided in a technical annex (Cmnd 9691 1985). It was not until after the announcement in November 1987 of the April 1988 benefit rates (the date of the introduction of the new scheme) that the actual effect of the new scheme on real people could be considered and calculated. This lack of concern for the effect on individual claimants was characteristic of the Conservative government's attitude to social security and indeed other aspects of policy. Global figures and total costs were bandied about with no consideration of how that overall budget was broken down, or whether that budget was sufficient to run a school, meet all a hospital's needs or provide a social security claimant with a decent standard of living.

Levels of benefit are determined more by what a government is prepared to dedicate to a specific budget heading than by how that expenditure itself breaks down. An increase in overall spending, such as happened in social security during the 1980s despite numerous benefit cuts (see Chapter 2), did not necessarily mean that benefit recipients were better off (see Hills 1987). It is more likely that this, not any methodological difficulties, is the real reason for governments' reluctance to test benefit levels empirically. As Bradshaw and Holmes (1989, p.132) argue:

> While the setting of income support levels may be largely a matter of subjective judgement, since these are based on a variety of political and other considerations, it is wrong to suppose that it is impossible to discover what levels of personal incomes and other resources are required for participation in normal British society.

The claim in both the Labour and Conservative supplementary benefit reviews that it is impossible to determine an objective measure of adequacy is disingenuous. Of course it is difficult to establish 'an objective standard'. Any standard which is set will have its supporters and its detractors. But establishing a standard would focus a debate on what, as a society, we believe is a decent standard of living for those drawing state benefits. It requires politicians to hoist their colours to the mast, but that is precisely what politicians and governments have not wanted to do. They have preferred to hide behind obfuscation than to try to justify empirically the level of benefit rates. It was for this reason that the two major reviews of social assistance totally abdicated their responsibility for shedding light on this fundamental issue. Both enquiries largely ignored the human impact of social assistance provision.

What justification can any government have for frequently maintaining that benefits are adequate without addressing the central issue of the quality of life afforded to people living on state benefits? If a government had been prepared to take this fundamental concern on board then the pressure for an increase in benefits would have been irresistible. Ignoring this issue has meant that the various benefit changes, especially in 1980 and 1988, left many people even worse off.

ARE BENEFITS ENOUGH?

Recognition of the low level of social assistance was made by both the non-governmental agencies responsible for the administration of social assistance: between 1948 and 1966 the National Assistance Board (NAB) and, between 1966 and 1980, the Supplementary Benefits Commission (SBC). Since 1980 responsibility for social assistance has rested with the Department of Social Security (previously the Department of Health and Social Security), which receives advice from the independent Social Security Advisory Committee (SSAC) on virtually all aspects of the social security system, including social assistance policy. All three bodies, NAB, SBC and SSAC, commented on the meagre level of social assistance payments. For example, in its evidence to the Royal Commission on the Distribution of Incomes and Wealth in 1977 (DHSS/SBC 1977, p. 28), the SBC reported that:

> the supplementary benefits scheme provides, particularly for families with children, incomes that are barely adequate to meet their needs at a level that is consistent with normal participation in the life of the relatively wealthy society in which they live. This impression is borne out by the extent to which we find it necessary to make use of our discretionary powers to provide more than the minimum levels of benefits determined by the scale rates.

This sentiment was later reiterated rather more cautiously by the SSAC (1982, para. 3.21).

Arguments are sometimes advanced that even the poorest in the community cannot be spared the impact of falling living standards. Such arguments imply that there is some fat to be cut, which is not a view we share. Present supplementary benefit rates come too uncomfortably close to subsistence levels to offer any scope for cuts.

Since the war, a number of studies have shown the many problems faced by people on benefits. Abel-Smith and Townsend's study, *The Poor and the Poorest* (1965), as well as government enquiries (Cole with Utting 1962), provided early indications of the persistence of poverty. Townsend's study, *Poverty in the UK* (1979), showed the meagre standard of living of social assistance claimants. The persistence of this trend even after the introduction of supplementary benefit in 1966 was shown in the SBC's evidence to the Royal Commission on the Distribution of Incomes and Wealth (DHSS/SBC 1977). A number of studies, some commissioned by the DSS (Berthoud 1984; Walker with Dant 1984; Cole-Hamilton and Lang 1986; Mack and Lansley 1985), produced evidence to show that, after the major supplementary benefit reforms made in 1980, claimants still had very great difficulty in managing. And, most recently, evidence is emerging to show that implementation of the Social Security Act 1986, with the replacement of supplementary benefit by income support, has not helped even those groups that were targeted for extra help by the government and has left many people even worse off than before (Social Services Committee 1989; Noble *et al.* 1989; Bradshaw and Holmes 1989).

The Conservative governments' assertions during the 1980s that benefits were adequate were based on two grounds: that overall expenditure on social security had increased and, secondly, that the value of benefits had improved. With regard to the first proposition, it is true that social security expenditure now forms the largest item of public expenditure (see Chapter 2) and that it has grown substantially. The total social security budget has more than quadrupled in real terms since the war (Cmnd 9517 1985, fig. 1). Expenditure on social assistance increased even faster, growing from £246 million in 1966 to £8,068 million in 1988 (DSS 1989). However, even this vast increase in overall expenditure did not necessarily mean that individual claimants became better off. In fact, as Hill (1990, p. 56) has pointed out, a paradox emerged:

... between 1979–89, a considerable number of cuts were made to the social security system, with the consequence that the deal it offered to claimants, or would-be claimants, markedly deteriorated, whilst at the same time overall public expenditure on social security grew rapidly.

The main reason for the increases in social security spending generally has been the increased number of claimants, in particular the number of unemployed people. On the more positive side, the introduction of new disability benefits in the early 1970s (mobility allowance, attendance allowance and, as it later became, the invalid care allowance) as well as benefits for people in work, family income supplement (now family credit) and the extension and rationalization of local rent and rate rebate schemes, brought new people within the ambit of social security and increased expenditure. In the 1980s, the Conservative government's policy of phasing out subsidies to local authority tenants led to an increase in rents which in turn led to an increase in housing subsidies provided by the social security system (see Hills 1987). The increase in social assistance spending has also resulted from a growth in some claimant groups, such as unemployed people and lone parents, an increasing proportion of whom are not covered at all or not covered sufficiently by the national insurance scheme. Thus, although more money has been spent on the social security programme, even after taking into account the substantial cuts made to the programme discussed in Chapter 2, it has been spread among far more people. During the 1980s individual gains were modest and many more people became worse off. The DHSS estimated that two-thirds of the increase in benefit expenditure between 1979 and 1987 has been due to the increased number of claimants and only one-third due to improvements in benefit levels (Hills 1987). Even this improvement in the value of benefits is unlikely to be repeated during the 1990s unless a decision is taken to increase benefits more than the rate of inflation. The increase in the 1980s followed the more generous uprating policy which applied prior to the 1980 uprating (in line with prices *or* earnings, whichever was higher; subsequently, benefits have gone up in line with prices only) as well as one-off increases for some children, which were introduced as part of the 1980 supplementary benefit reforms.

The second defence which the Thatcher governments made of the level of benefits was based on the improvement in their value since 1948. This point was made in the 1985 Green Paper on the Reform of Social Security (Cmnd 9517 1985, para. 4.2):

> The levels of major benefits like pensions and supplementary benefit have more than doubled in real terms since the War and more than kept pace with the take-home pay of the average earner.

Historical trends may be interesting but in fact they reveal little about whether current benefit rates are sufficient. First, comparisons of figures alone do not reflect changes in living standards. For example, the lifestyle afforded to the poor by Seebohm Rowntree in his pioneering work on poverty in 1899 allowed only for the 'maintenance of physical efficiency', and allowed nothing for 'the maintenance of mental, moral or social sides of human nature' (Mack and Lansley 1985, p. 17):

> A family living upon the scale allowed for must never spend a penny on railway fare or omnibus. They must never go into the country unless they walk. They must never purchase a halfpenny newspaper or spend a penny to buy a ticket for a popular concert. They must write no letters to absent children, for they cannot afford to pay the postage. They must never contribute any thing to their church or chapel, or give any help to a neighbour which costs them money. They cannot save nor can they join a sick club or trade union, because they cannot pay the necessary subscriptions. The children must have no pocket money for dolls, marbles or sweets. The father must smoke no tobacco and drink no beer. The mother must never buy any pretty clothes for herself or her children, the character of the family wardrobe as for the family diet being governed by the regulation 'nothing must be bought but that which is absolutely necessary for the maintenance of physical health'.
>
> (Rowntree 1922, quoted in Mack and Lansley 1985, p. 17)

In later work Rowntree used a higher standard because 'ideas of what constitutes "obvious want and squalor" have changed profoundly (since 1899)' (quoted in SSAC 1989, para. 8.29). Caution has to be exercised when using this 'basket of goods approach' (Bradshaw 1987) to compare benefit levels over time. It is not sufficient only to increase prices in line with inflation, it is also necessary to adjust what goes into the basket as what is available and what is desirable changes. As a society becomes more affluent many cheaper goods disappear, and the poor may not be able to buy the cheaper cuts of meat or, especially in a hypermarket society, the small quantities of goods which they can afford (Atkinson 1991).

As discussed earlier there is no doubt that Beveridge took considerable trouble to determine an appropriate benefit level using the empirical work of Seebohm Rowntree and others to assist him. However, as discussed in Chapter 2, he was criticized for allowing only for bare physical needs and not for the costs of meeting social needs and obligations. Beveridge's subsistence definition of need is in marked contrast to the 'essentials' of living in the 1980s which were identified by the respondents of a national survey carried out by London Weekend Television and *New Society* (Mack and Lansley 1984). The list included heating, indoor toilet, damp-free home, bath, beds for everyone (indicated by over 90 per cent of respondents), access to public transport, warm waterproof coat, three meals a day for children (mentioned by over 80 per cent), self-contained accommodation, two pairs of all-weather shoes, refrigerator, toys for children, carpets (over 70 per cent), roast joint once a week, washing machine, new, not second-hand, clothes, hobby or leisure activity, presents once a year, and a holiday (over 60 per cent).

The second reason why it is necessary to be cautious when using historical bases to determine whether modern rates are adequate is that those original rates might not have been sufficient in the first place. There was some concern that the rates introduced in 1948 had not taken sufficiently into account the changes in prices which took place in the six years between introduction of the new social security programme and 1942 when the Beveridge Report was published. Exact measurement was complicated by the existence of food and other subsidies as well as the system of rationing which continued after the end of the war (Cooke and Baldwin 1984). Most importantly, as discussed earlier, political expediency won the day and the benefit rates that were introduced by the Labour government in 1948 were not in line with Beveridge's recommendations (Deacon 1982). The adult rates were set higher and the children's rates lower than recommended. Thus, at the outset the link between subsistence and assistance was weakened:

> With the level of assistance detached from its original subsistence basis, the question of whether or not assistance was 'adequate' became unanswerable by appeal to any clearly determined standard. In this sense, what had always been 'to some extent a matter of opinion' had become even more so by the time national assistance came into being.
>
> (Cooke and Baldwin 1984, p. 10)

The lack of any scientific basis for the determination of benefit rates was weakened still further by the various uprating policies which have been adopted in the last 40 years. Before 1966 there was no precedent or legal requirement to increase benefits on a regular basis. Deacon and Bradshaw (1983) described the policy on upratings between 1948 and 1965 as one of 'total confusion' with ten upratings of national assistance and six of national insurance during that period. Generally, national assistance upratings were favoured over the more expensive policy of uprating national insurance rates. Thus prior to the 1959 election the Conservative government increased the real level of national assistance by 11 per cent despite stable prices. Their stated justification was that they wished national assistance recipients to share in the rising prosperity of the country. In fact they favoured this option because it was cheaper than increasing the national insurance rates (Walker 1983). Deacon and Bradshaw (1983, p. 100) argue that only the 22 per cent increase in insurance rates which took effect in February 1955 represented a genuine attempt to reduce dependence on national assistance.

Since 1965 most income maintenance benefits have been increased annually. There were two exceptions: in 1975, because of the particularly high inflation rate, two upratings were made, and between 1985 and 1987 there were shorter periods between upratings as the annual uprating date moved from November to April. In 1971, some coordination was introduced to the uprating of social assistance and national insurance rates and since then they have been reviewed at the same time and, generally, on the same basis. Between 1975 and 1980 pensions and other long-term benefits were uprated in line with either earnings or prices, whichever had risen most quickly, while short-term benefits such as unemployment and sickness benefits were uprated in line with prices. A similar formula was applied to social assistance with the result that long-term rates rose broadly in line with earnings and the basic rates rose broadly in line with prices. By the time the Conservative government abolished the dual uprating formula in 1980 by ending the more favourable link with earnings, the gap between the long-term and basic rate for a married couple was £8.85. By the time the long-term/short-term distinction was abolished, along with supplementary benefit in 1988, the gap was £12.50 for a married couple. The long-term rate of benefit had been consistently 25 per cent higher than the basic rate. After 1988, long-term benefits stopped pulling away from short-term benefits because they too were subject to the less generous uprating formula. However, the trend for earnings to rise faster than prices continued in the 1980s. Had the Conservative government not scrapped the link between benefits and the increase in earnings the retirement pension for a couple would have been £17.60 (25 per cent) higher than in fact it was in 1990.

Increasing benefits in line with earnings means that, as long as earnings rise faster than prices, benefit recipients see a real improvement in their standard of living. Uprating only in line with prices means that claimants can only hope to see their current standard of living maintained; it will never improve. Although at each benefit uprating, government spokespersons maintain that the increases ensure that the living standards of those on benefits are protected, an increasing body of evidence has emerged to cast doubt on that assumption. It is now clear that increasing benefits in line with the retail price index (RPI) does not fully protect claimants against price inflation. The RPI is an unreliable indicator of the increase in the cost of living of poor people. People on the lowest incomes spend a higher proportion of their income on basic expenses, like food and fuel. Bradshaw and his colleagues calculated, on the basis of 1986 benefits levels and Family Expenditure Survey expenditure patterns, that the average expenditure (excluding housing costs) of a family with two children on fuel, food, clothing and footwear was 63 per cent higher than that of a similar family on supplementary benefit (1987, p. 178). However, such expenditure accounted for only 40 per cent of the total spending of better-off families compared to 62 per cent of the total spending of families living on benefit. These basic, essential expenditures have tended to increase faster than luxury goods (Johnson and Webb 1990). It has been estimated that for a household consisting of two adults and two children the weighting of the RPI corresponds to the expenditure pattern of a household about three-quarters of the way up the income distribution scale (Muellbauer (1977) reported in Cooke and Baldwin 1984; see also Williams 1977). The pensioner index calculated by the DSS is approximately one-half of one per cent higher than the RPI index on which the annual benefit upratings are based.

It is clear, therefore, that increases based on the RPI do not adequately protect low-income families against price inflation and the result is a real drop in their standard of living. Claimants' spending power has also been diminished as they have been expected to meet new expenses. The cuts in single payments which were introduced in 1980 and again in 1986 (see Chapter 6) meant that many claimants had to meet the cost of lump sum items such as clothing and furniture for which previously they would have been eligible for a grant. The abolition of single payments in 1988, to be replaced largely by loans from the social fund, and the replacement of extra weekly additions paid according to individual need by broad-based premiums, means that claimants have to meet, out of their weekly benefit, many expenses with which they might previously have received help.

The income support scheme required claimants to meet further new expenses: water rates and a proportion of the poll tax (previously the general rates). In April 1990, the House of Commons Select Committee on Social Services reported that the 20 per cent contribution to the poll tax and the full payment of water rates meant that the basic rate for a married couple moving from supplementary benefit to income support in April 1988 fell by over 5 per cent in real terms relative to the retail price index (excluding housing costs) (Social Services Committee 1989).

Far from improving provision for those dependent on social assistance, the introduction of income support led to a real cut in disposable income. The Disability Alliance calculated that actual expenditure on the three main means-tested benefits – income support, family credit and housing benefit – was £245 million lower in 1988–89 than it would have been under the old system: this figure does not include the savings made by the abolition of single payments (Disability Rights Bulletin, Summer 1988). Bradshaw and Holmes (1989) estimated that of the 43 families in their study conducted before April 1988, 20 would be worse under income support calculations. This high proportion of losers is particularly disconcerting given that the sample was made up of families with children – the group on whom the changes were supposed to be targeted.

FROM 'LESS ELIGIBILITY' TO 'WHY WORK'

Any discussion on the level of benefits must take into account the relationship between incomes in and out of work. The relationship between rates of benefits and wages is a crucial one, as governments are always concerned that benefits should not be so generous as to discourage people from taking jobs.

> The social security system discriminates systematically against the longer-term unemployed and the old Poor Law 'less eligibility' principle (often translated into the language of 'why work?' and (primarily male) work incentives) is a more important influence on benefit levels for the unemployed than is need.
>
> (Lister 1989a, pp. 216–17)

The strategy of successive governments, therefore, has been to maintain a gap between benefits and low-paid work. During periods like the 1980s when low pay was, with unemployment and retirement, one of the three main causes of poverty, government impetus to keep down benefits for the unemployed (with the consequential knock-on effect to benefits paid to other groups) is sharpened. In 1987 (the latest year for which figures are available) over one-quarter (2.7 million) of those living on incomes below 50 per cent of average income were in full-time work. Of those living *below* SB levels, 9 per cent were in full-time work and 11 per cent were self-employed (Oppenheim 1990). In 1989, over 4 million part-time workers (78 per cent of the part-time workforce) were low paid, as were nearly 5 million full-time workers (29 per cent of the full-time adult workforce). As Oppenheim points out: 'This makes a staggering total of 8.88 million low paid workers in Britain, or 41 per cent of the adult workforce in 1989, 71 per cent of whom were women' (1991, p. 70). Because of discrimination in the labour market, people from racial minority groups are also over-represented among the low-paid. The lower the wages paid and the greater the prevalence of low pay, the harder it is to get increases in benefit levels. The result is that, to maintain the gap between wages and benefits, the living standards of those dependent on benefit must fall further behind those of the rest of the community.

While rejecting the notion of relative poverty, which is implicit in comparing the standards of living of one group with another, the Conservative government's Green Paper on the Reform of Social Security (Cmnd 9519 1985) maintained that SB recipients were closing the gap on those in work. Comparing the ordinary supplementary benefits scale rates, plus an allowance for rent, with average earnings, net of NI and tax, but including child benefit, it concluded that the former increased as a proportion of the latter between 1948 and 1984 from 29 per cent to 40 per cent for a single householder, from 42 per cent to 54 per cent for a married couple and from 50 per cent to 67 per cent for a couple with two children. More recent independent analysis has challenged this claim. For example, Hills argues that this calculation ignores the impact of indirect taxes which hit low-income families particularly hard in the 1980s (Hills 1990). Assessing the worth of supplementary benefit rates over the first two Thatcher administrations, Piachaud (1987, p. 22) concluded there was little room for self-congratulation:

> There have been shorter periods when, as social security ministers have argued, SB levels have kept pace with average incomes, but there have been other spells when they have fallen behind more. The overall picture since the Conservatives took office is of those dependent on SB falling further behind the rest of the population.

Between 1978 and 1987 personal disposable income per capita rose by 14 per cent in real terms, but supplementary benefit rose by only 5 per cent (Piachaud 1987, p. 22):

> Thus, compared with incomes in general, SB levels have fallen considerably − for a couple on the ordinary rate from 61 per cent of personal disposable income per capita in 1978 to 53 per cent in 1987.

The less generous uprating formula used since 1980 will ensure that the value of benefits against earnings will fall further in the future. Still more recently, and using the Conservative government's Households Below Average Income (HBAI) statistics, the IFS also concluded that the gap between those in work and those out of work had widened as average earnings had risen much faster than inflation.

> It is immediately clear that while the real value of the supplementary benefit scale rates actually increased a little over the period, average earnings increased much faster. This implies that as well as the numbers on and around the supplementary benefit line having increased considerably, the level of income represented by that line has fallen significantly in relation to average earnings. Thus, although people appearing in the tables in 1987 were no worse off than those appearing in 1979, they were much further behind the rest of the population.
>
> (Johnson and Webb 1990, p. 19)

Comparisons with earnings allow the increases afforded to one group to be seen against those gained by others and provide evidence of levels of inequality but, again, do not have anything to say about whether benefit levels are actually enough. This comparison is further complicated by evidence on the ten years from 1979 which shows that the gap in earnings between the well-paid and the low-paid widened so that it was greater than 100 years previously (Byrne 1987). There is, therefore, the danger that 'average' earnings and 'average' wage rises are misrepresented as minimum figures. In reality many poorer workers have seen their wages fall as they received the smallest wage increases and benefited least from tax changes over that period (see Walker and Walker 1987; Hills 1990).

CONCLUSION

The issue of 'how much is enough' should be central to any social security programme designed to tackle poverty. In practice, this question has played a secondary role, particularly since 1975, to governments' concern with overall social security spending and the perpetuation of the 'less eligibility' principle. Unlike Beveridge, post-war governments have consistently refused to spell out in detail the expenses which benefits are supposed to cover, for the very good reason that the rates have never been based on any empirical assessment of need; secondly, to do so would expose the myth maintained by governments that benefits are adequate.

The question of 'how much is enough' is of course linked to perceptions of poverty. The answer will be influenced by whether one takes an absolute or relative position, whether one feels the causes are individual or structural, and whether one wishes to ensure that those dependent on state benefits receive the minimum necessary for existence or whether they should be enabled to participate in the life of the rest of community. The following chapter looks at some of the evidence available to illustrate whether social assistance benefits are enough.

4   Living in poverty

The last chapter examined the factors which affect governments' determination of the levels of benefit rates, in particular social assistance rates. Regardless of the measure used and the claims for objectivity that are made, all include a measure of subjectivity; all vary according to what the advocate considers to be an appropriate standard of living for those existing on state benefits. Decisions on whether benefits are adequate are taken in the light of individual perceptions and political values. For example, in its first term of office the Thatcher government declined to make improvements in the social security system on financial grounds. It was later argued that to make benefits more generous would merely increase the problem of the 'dependency culture'. Such a view reflected a particular political ideology and not the growing body of evidence, including the findings of a literature review on poverty conducted on behalf of the DHSS/SSRC Joint Working Party on Transmitted Deprivation, which reached a contrary conclusion:

> Notions about the improvidence and extravagance of the poor die hard and complacency about the current income maintenance system is wide-spread. The sober evidence assembled in this review should help to dispel ideas that the poor have only themselves to blame for their difficulties, or that living on social security is an easy ride.

> (Ashley 1983, p. x)

This chapter and the next examine some of the empirical evidence which has been collected on the standards of living of benefit recipients. This information has been garnered from interviews with claimants themselves and, in contrast to the official perspective considered in Chapter 2, concentrates on claimants' own views of their situation. No one understands a service better than the service users and yet, in welfare services in particular, they have been least heard and, if heard, least influential. Claimants, and more frequently their advocates, were able to participate in the civil service review of supplementary benefits only *after* completion of the final report in 1976

(DHSS 1979; Walker 1982). On that occasion, it was the review team, comprised of civil servants working to a tight remit, which set the agenda for debate so that, during the period of public consultation which took place after publication of their report, discussion inevitably focused on their concerns, which were quite different to those of claimants (see Walker 1983). The pattern repeated itself in the Fowler social security reviews published in 1985. The views of claimants were not specifically sought out, though, like all members of the public, they could respond to the Green Paper, *Reform of Social Security*, when it was published at a cost of more than £20 (Cmnd 9517–9 1985).

In presenting claimants' views of social assistance in this and subsequent chapters, a major source of the data is material collected as part of a local study of over 400 claimants conducted between 1981 and 1983 in Leeds (Walker with Dant 1984), supplemented and updated by other research on the living standards of the poor. It would be a welcome criticism of this data if it was found not to reflect the situation today. Unfortunately, although it does pre-date the major changes in social assistance which took place in 1988, that is not the case. There is a growing body of evidence available to show that the lives of people on social assistance at the start of the final decade of the twentieth century is still very meagre. A number of respected bodies, including the House of Commons Social Services Select Committee, and independent research have shown that the 1986 Social Security Act left many claimants worse off than under the supplementary benefits scheme (Social Services Committee 1989; Noble *et al.* 1989; Becker and Silburn 1990).

This chapter considers the diversity of needs and circumstances of claimants. It then compares people's standard of living before and after claiming social assistance and examines how far claimants are able to meet those costs which account for the bulk of their spending: fuel, housing and food, as well as clothing and footwear (the last two items are one of the most frequently reported unmet needs in studies of social assistance recipients). The next chapter considers how claimants manage their poverty and the strategies they adopt to keep their heads above water. In the light of the views put forward by claimants, it is for the reader to decide whether the standard of living of this group of citizens is acceptable in Britain in the 1990s.

THE DIVERSITY OF NEED

The term 'social security claimant' subsumes under one common umbrella a plethora of people and circumstances. Studies which purport to present the standard of living of claimants must take into account this heterogeneity. For statistical and administrative purposes, the DHSS divided supplementary benefit claimants into four main groups: lone parents, pensioners, sick and disabled people, and the unemployed. The obvious differences between these officially defined groups of claimants were reflected in the different levels of benefits which each group received. Thus, pensioners received the higher long-term rate of benefit from the outset of a claim; lone parents and those classed as sick or disabled moved on to this rate after serving a qualifying period (two years up to 1980 and one year after November 1980). The unemployed remained on the lower basic rate of benefit regardless of how long their claim lasted. While getting rid of this particular iniquity of the supplementary benefit scheme, income support introduced a new set of differentials.

The first relates to personal allowances (previously called scale rates). These vary, understandably, between single people and couples, though as the latter is less than double the former, it is clear that in government circles the belief that two can live more cheaply than one still prevails. More contentiously, personal allowances also differ according to age. Single people between the ages of 18 and 25 receive a rate of benefit 22 per cent lower than that paid to people over 25 (1991/92 rates). The second differential results from the payment of premiums. When income support was introduced in 1988 the following premiums were paid: family premium, lone-parent premium, disabled child premium, disability premium, severe disability premium (paid only in addition to the disability premium) and the pensioner and higher pensioner premium. The enhanced pensioner premium for 75–79 year olds was introduced in October 1989 and a carer premium in October 1990. There is no premium for unemployed people, who consequently receive a lower rate of benefit than other groups. The system of payment of premiums, which are awarded automatically according to tightly prescribed criteria laid down in the law, effectively creates different rates of basic benefit for different types of claimant. The principle of one rate of benefit for all inherent in national provision has, therefore, been abandoned. The issue of how far premiums are adequate and a true reflection of the needs and costs of particular groups is discussed in Chapter 7.

People who have been on benefit for a prolonged period face particular problems. However, this does not mean that those on benefit for a short time face less difficulty than long-term claimants, as some writers have argued (see, for example, Berthoud 1984). Even a short spell on benefit on a reduced income can have a long-term impact on family finances. In the Leeds survey of supplementary benefit claimants, one family fell behind with the rent in order to prevent disconnection of their telephone while they had been on benefit for a short time. A lone parent, who had claimed supplementary benefit for about three months while off sick from work, fell behind with several bills in this short time. She was interviewed many months after she had returned to work but she was still in debt. With increasing numbers of people in low-paid employment, this is a problem faced by more and more people. It is extremely difficult for such people to make good the debts which might have accumulated while on benefit. The problems incurred while claiming may take many months to clear.

In addition to differences between groups of claimants, there is also enormous diversity *within* groups. Insufficient attention has been paid to this in the determination of benefit provision. Just as there is no 'average' person, so there is no 'average' claimant. Individual situations differ. Some have the support of a family, emotionally and socially even if not financially; some live in good quality accommodation, others do not; some are without a home at all; some live independently, others with relatives or another family; some have the support of a partner, others do not; some are good managers, others are not. What is certain is that claimants, social security staff and wider society tend to be more unforgiving of the poor. The poor are expected to be efficient and rational spenders. When they are not they are accused of not being poor at all or of bringing their poverty upon themselves because of their own fecklessness. The poor are not allowed to make mistakes (Moore 1989).

PAST EXPERIENCES AND FUTURE EXPECTATIONS

One measure of how well off claimants feel is to compare their standard of living on benefit with that experienced before becoming a claimant. In this way the widespread concern of successive governments (see Chapter 3) and of wider society (see Chapter 8) that benefits should not offer recipients a better standard of living than they could achieve when in work can be examined. The balance between income received while on benefit and income received when not on benefit is one of the most significant, negative factors which have influenced the determination of benefit levels by successive governments. Concern has tended to be confined to those below retirement age and to unemployed people in particular.

Concern about the 'why work' syndrome heightened during the 1980s (Walker 1987) despite a growing body of evidence that the benefits system does not have a disincentive effect on people's desire to find work. In their review of the British evidence on this, Atkinson and Micklewright (1985, p. 240) concluded that 'there is no firm evidence of a quantitatively large disincentive effect'. Enquiries into this issue by independent researchers, and by the SBC, SSAC and the first SB review, all concluded that benefits did not have any significant impact on people's willingness to take full-time work (DHSS 1976; Berthoud 1984; Moylan *et al.* 1984; Heady and Smyth 1989). The DHSS cohort study of unemployed people conducted in 1978 found that 'for the vast majority of the men net earnings exceeded unemployment-related benefits. For half of them net earnings exceeded unemployment-related benefits by at least £20 per week (1978 prices, about £33 in March 1983 prices)' (Moylan *et al*. 1984, p. 64). For only 6 per cent did unemployment-related benefits exceed net earnings. Going on to look at the distribution of the benefit/earnings ratio (the level of benefit entitlement compared to earnings), the study again found that people became substantially worse off once they went on to benefit.

> For almost half of the men unemployment-related benefits replaced less than half of earnings. For a further two-fifths unemployment-related benefits replaced no more than 80 per cent of net earnings. In the remaining one-sixth of cases unemployment-related benefits were equal to more than 80 per cent of net earnings.
>
> (Moylan *et al*. 1984, p. 65)

In addition, the authors argued that, as many people had not claimed the means-tested benefits to which they were entitled when in work, the gap between income in work and out of work was narrower than it should have been.

An OPCS survey conducted on behalf of the DHSS in 1983 and 1984 also found that income fell once people became unemployed. They found that the average disposable income of families whose head had previously been in full-time work was 59 per cent of what it had been before signing on.

> Most families experienced a rapid and substantial reduction in their material living standards as a result of the head of the family's loss of work.... The areas in which the families ... (experienced) major reductions in their material living standards were food, clothing, and entertainments. Nearly all the reduction in these areas of consumption appears to have taken place in the first three months of unemployment.
>
> (Heady and Smyth 1989, p. xvii)

It is not only unemployed claimants who suffer a drop in their disposable income once they claim benefit. The Leeds survey found that most people had suffered a deterioration in their standard of living when they claimed social assistance (see Table 4.1).

Overall, more than three-fifths of the people interviewed said that their standard of living was a 'little worse' or 'very much worse' on benefit than it had been before. The group most likely to be poorer were the unemployed; four out of five in this group said that their situation had deteriorated. Among the other groups, three out of five lone parents and a similar proportion of sick or disabled respondents, and just over two out of five of those over retirement age, also felt they were worse off. Most people reported a number of adverse changes in the way they lived and in the quality of their life. These

Table 4.1 Claimants' standard of living on supplementary benefit compared to that before

	Unemployed %	Sick & disabled %	Lone parent %	Pensioner %	All %
Better	2	16	18	17	13
Same	11	14	13	34	18
Little worse	16	20	12	22	18
Very much worse	64	39	51	22	44
Could not say	8	11	6	5	8
Total	100	100	100	100	100
N =	110	94	127	100	431

included a lack of choice in the sort of food or clothes they could buy, the struggle to manage from day to day and from one bill to the next, and a withdrawal from social activities because they could not afford to go out.

> (We've had to give up) going out with the family. No holidays. No socializing. No new clothes.
>
> (unemployed claimant with children)

> I have to try harder to manage and I'm waiting all the time for the next payment. I don't eat the best sort of food.
>
> (pensioner)

> We were both well then. We lived. We went out, had more clothes, footwear, more holidays ... impossible now. We had a car. Apart from food you do without everything what is part and parcel of life. What life is all about. I've grandkids ... can't treat them. Loved to take some interest in his (grandson's) football ... can't buy him boots and things, you can't because of the money.
>
> (man unable to work because of
> illness and receiving dialysis treatment)

> Worse because (I) can't do what I want to do. I'm not complaining honestly. Now when you get laddered tights you cut the legs off and wear two pairs. My daughter buys me fruit and things. She knows I can't; ... (she) bought a Birds trifle because I used to have them and can't afford them now ... bottles of pop, silly things like that. She's young, needs the money herself.
>
> (woman with a chronic illness)

> It's all altered so gently, so many different ways. A little bit of everything. Can never *plan*. Just plan to keep things going.
>
> (lone parent)

(worse off) and I wasn't so well paid, worked in a mill. Could manage ... to save, have holidays, buy curtains ... can't do anything now. I'll just exist when my money's (savings) done.

(unemployed woman)

Some claimants reported that their standard of living had not changed or had even improved after claiming social assistance (see Table 4.1). The majority of these, especially in the former category, and many of those in the latter had previously been in receipt of a national insurance benefit only and had not been getting the supplementary benefit or other benefits to which they were entitled. For example, two-thirds of the pensioners who said they were better off on supplementary benefit had previously received the retirement pension only. Government figures show that failure to take up means-tested benefits accounted for 42 per cent of the families (810,000) whose incomes were below SB level. Fifteen per cent of the families below this poverty line were failing to take up SB (Oppenheim 1990, p. 25). One of the major problems with social assistance has always been its poor take-up record. Government statistics show that the caseload take-up of supplementary benefit in 1985 (the latest year for which statistics are available in 1992) was 84 per cent. This means that 840,000 people were eligible but not claiming this benefit. The average amount unclaimed was £12.60 per week, saving the government some £550 million per annum (DSS 1989, table 48.01).

An improvement in income for some claimants once they claim social assistance can occur because they are recategorized under the rules of the system. Thus, on reaching 60, an unemployed claimant is relabelled a pensioner claimant and benefit increases. In the last year of the supplementary benefit scheme a married couple's benefit would increase by 30 per cent once they moved from being classed as unemployed to being retired. Under the income support system, weekly income would go up by 31 per cent (1991/92 rates).

The people most likely to be better off once claiming benefit are lone parents. Nineteen out of 20 lone parents on social assistance are women. For them, claiming benefit offers, often for the first time, an independent source of regular income. Hence Pahl found that between one-fifth and one-third of women in her study were better off once they had left their husbands (Pahl 1983). As Lister has pointed out (1989, p. 13), social security, with all its imperfections, has many advantages over being reliant on a partner.

Even dependency on means-tested income support, with all its inadequacies and indignities, can for some women be preferable to dependence on an individual man. It may not be totally reliable; the rights it gives are being eroded; and claiming it can be a humiliating process (especially for black people); but at least the relationship between the State and the woman claimant is a more impersonal one and provides some enforceable rights and some sense of control over the money once received...

Reporting on a study conducted in 1966, Marsden said that the lone parents he interviewed 'preferred the regular income from the National Assistance Board to the uncertainties of budgeting during marriage' (Marsden 1969). For some of the lone parents interviewed nearly twenty years later in Leeds, the fact that they *knew* benefit would arrive regularly and the security which that knowledge provided was as important as the actual amount of money received.

> I'm better off because I have a set amount of money coming in each week. My husband boozed it.

> ... was with my husband. Now I have the money to spend on the house. When he was here I didn't get it.

> Because I know it's regular every week. It's more money than maintenance.

Social assistance, like other means-tested benefits, is based on the family as the unit of assessment whereas national insurance is based on the individual. This means that where a man and woman are married or 'living together as husband and wife' (Social Security Act 1986, Section 20(11)) the incomes of both are taken into account and they receive the benefit rate for a couple of £62.25 (if over 18, April 1990 rate), not double the single person's rate of £39.65. The family's benefit, which covers both adults and any children, is paid to one partner. The Social Security Act 1980 allowed the woman to be the claimant if she met certain conditions. The Social Security Act 1986 allows either the man or the woman to be the claimant for income support in all circumstances. The Conservative government, like the Labour government which preceded it, made these (and other) moves towards the equal treatment of men and women in the social security system slowly and reluctantly and, in the final event, only at the behest of a European Community directive. Despite the fact that the law now allows couples to choose who will be the claimant, in practice it is far more likely that the man would assume this role as it is the man who is most likely to have full-time work and the higher earnings (Millar 1989). In many families there is great resistance to the woman taking on the claimant role (McKee and Bell 1985).

The Leeds study (which took place when it was only possible for a minority of women to act as the claimant) revealed that the payment of the whole family benefit to the male partner caused two particular problems for women. (Obviously these problems could arise for men too in the more limited number of cases where the woman acted as the claimant.) The first problem was financial. The claimant might mis-spend the money and not give sufficient cash to his partner. Secondly, a woman would suffer additional embarrassment and difficulty if the relationship broke down temporarily or permanently. If a woman is left by her claimant partner, then she has to make a fresh claim. On doing so, she might be treated with scepticism and suspicion, and her distress exacerbated, as she has to prove that the separation is genuine. One woman in the Leeds study, whose husband had walked out for several weeks on two separate occasions, explained her problem:

> I can't get the money ... it goes to my husband and he keeps clearing off (Last time he went) they were a bit clever with me. They more or less said you *should* know where he is ... (and) said they couldn't pay out till they knew where he is. How do I know? ... Then he comes back, new statement all over again. I asked about my last payment (which was) stopped because he'd come back... 8 days with no money. Dreading going down there again (her husband had since disappeared again without warning).

The joint assessment of couples creates particular problems for some ethnic minority families when, for example, the husband goes back to the family's country of origin for a prolonged stay to meet family commitments. In such cases, it is difficult for the remaining partner to get benefit. The payment of social assistance to each partner in a couple on an individual basis was rejected by the 1976 supplementary benefits review team because it would have brought many more women on to benefit and would have been very expensive. The 1985 Fowler review did not even discuss this option in the resulting Green Paper, *Reform of Social Security* (Cmnd 9517 1985). A more modest alternative to the payment of a couple's benefit to one partner was suggested by some of the women in the Leeds research, some of whom were still living with partners. They suggested that each partner should receive *half* the family benefit. By making separate payments to each partner in a couple, both could count on a regular income. Thus each could count on having some money regardless of the behaviour of the other.

Despite these few exceptions, for the majority of claimants, going on to benefit means a drop in income. This does not necessarily mean, of course, that they are 'poor'. To make judgements about poverty it is necessary to look at people's standard of living once on benefit. At the time of the Leeds survey the basic weekly benefit for a couple with two small children, where the claimant was registered as unemployed was £53.55 (after rent) compared to average gross earnings of £112. In April 1991, a similar family would have received £75.15 in income support (excluding housing costs), out of which they would have had to pay their water rates and 20 per cent of their poll tax (previously general rates). This compares to average gross earnings of over £200 and average household expenditure of £204 (CSO 1991). The income gaps between those on benefit and those of the rest of the community are wide and widening (see Chapter 3).

IS SOCIAL ASSISTANCE ENOUGH? THE CLAIMANT'S VIEW

Politicians and others might pontificate about whether or not benefits are adequate but the people who know best whether that assertion is true are those who have to live on them. It might be argued that it is unrealistic to leave the definition of adequacy to claimants as, free from resource constraints, they will not try to differentiate between 'needs' and 'wants'. However, the following discussion confirms the conclusion made by Runciman (1972, p. 10) almost 20 years ago, that poor people actually have very modest aspirations. They are looking for a little extra to ease the burden, not a huge increase which would allow a lavish change in lifestyle.

> It has become a commonplace that steady poverty is the best guarantee of conservatism: if people have no reason to expect or hope for more than they can achieve, they will be less discontented with what they have, or even grateful simply to be able to hold on to it.

In the Leeds study, the majority of people we spoke to did not think that their benefit was sufficient to meet their day-to-day expenses: 49 per cent of the pensioner group thought that benefit was inadequate compared to 74 per cent of the lone parents, 71 per cent of those classed as sick or disabled and 86 per cent of the unemployed group. The national PSI study also found high levels of dissatisfaction with the level of benefit: 3.5 out of 10 pensioners were dissatisfied, 5.9 out of 10 lone parents and 7 out of 10 couples with children (Berthoud 1984, table 11a). In both the PSI and the Leeds studies, which were conducted under the same DHSS initiative, the majority of claimants expressed problems managing on their weekly benefit. In the PSI study, 69 per cent of householders interviewed said they were 'just getting by'; a further 16 per cent said they 'were getting into difficulties'. Only 12 per cent said that they were 'managing quite well'. In both surveys, it was those below 60, particularly unemployed people, who experienced the greatest difficulty. Among the Leeds respondents over one-third of the unemployed respondents and over one-quarter of lone parents said they were 'getting into difficulties' compared to 5 per cent of pensioner respondents. Although the majority of respondents in all groups claimed that they were 'getting by', a closer examination of their situation shows this was barely the case (see Chapter 5). Many respondents merely preferred to give this answer to avoid the embarrassment of admitting either to the interviewer or to themselves that they could not manage.

Does this dissatisfaction with benefit levels and the inability to manage reflect that claimants' aspirations are unrealistically high? Do claimants expect too much? This does not seem to be the case. The Leeds study found, as Runciman has argued, that people have very modest aspirations. This point was illustrated when respondents were asked to speculate on how they would spend an extra £5 per week (see Table 4.2).

In all groups of respondents, approximately two-thirds of people mentioned expenditures which were in fact basic items supposed to be covered by weekly benefit. One person said: 'I'd probably go to Tesco'. Extra income would serve mainly to ease the pressure on tight weekly budgets, or perhaps improve a limited diet. This option was taken by one married couple in particular. Throughout their interview they said how they had had to cut down on food, which was all the more serious because they thought this had prevented the husband from regaining weight lost through illness. The wife said:

> I haven't had a joint in nine months (when they came onto benefit). Yorkshire pudding, peas and potatoes ... I'd go out and buy a joint of meat ... and put £1 away.

Most respondents said they would use the money for essential expenditures.

> I'd put it into the bank until I have enough money to take the children on holiday. It would also buy Christmas presents.

Several people said they would save the money. The desire to save was strong, not because claimants did not need the money each week but because the lack of any money to fall back on in case of emergency or to meet bills led to a deep sense of insecurity and worry. A small number of claimants said they would spend the money on a 'luxury'. However, on examination the

Table 4.2 How claimants would spend an extra £5 per week

	Unemployed %	Sick & disabled %	Lone parent %	Pensioner %
Buy food or other essential item covered by scale rate	33	33	36	44
Buy clothes	32	31	34	30
Pay bills	17	15	11	15
Save it	16	27	19	11
Spend it on a luxury	8	6	6	11
Other	23	17	18	9
Don't know	2	2	3	8
N* =	108	98	128	100

term 'luxury' had a rather more modest connotation than the word might normally imply. This again underlines the modest, or realistic, aspirations of people living on benefit:

> I'd give my children treats as other children with earnings get; get meat, fruit for a start.
>
> (lone parent)

> Buy some socks, knickers for the kids, some sweets.
>
> (lone parent)

> Get some things we've had to do without. Luxuries – piece of beef – owt like that – haven't had a piece of beef for ages.
>
> (unemployed respondent)

> Difficult, there's so much. Possibly spend it on paint and wallpaper. I'd take the girls out occasionally. We never go out as a family.
>
> (unemployed man)

> I'd go riding about on buses and see a bit of life, and treat myself to a drink now and again.
>
> (pensioner)

> Night out now and again. A trip to the cities which you can't afford to do. Can get there but nothing to spend. Can't afford a day out at the seaside.
>
> (pensioner)

GETTING THROUGH THE WEEK

One of the common measures used to assess whether people can manage on their income is to examine whether they can make their money last from one pay day to the next (see Berthoud 1984; Walker with Dant 1984). Striving to achieve this was a constant preoccupation for many respondents in the Leeds survey. Many, especially those under retirement age, were unable to make their money stretch (see Table 4.3).

Table 4.3 Proportion of claimants who ran out of money before their next pay day

	Unemployed %	Sick & disabled %	Lone parent %	Pensioner %	All %
Regularly	69	44	56	22	48
Sometimes	18	21	29	22	22
Never	13	35	15	56	30
Total	100	100	100	100	100
N =	110	100	128	100	438

The difficulty of managing is exacerbated for unemployed people, the vast majority of whom reported that they ran out of money regularly; unlike other claimants, their money was and is paid fortnightly, and by giros which are more vulnerable to delays than the order books given to other groups of claimants.

The Leeds survey found considerable disparity between different groups of claimants in their ability to make their money last (see also Berthoud 1984). One explanation is that social assistance payments vary between groups of claimants. A second factor stems from the family circumstances. Most claimants over pension age live alone or with a partner, with no dependants. Their weekly expenditure and consumption of food is therefore predictable. They can cut down if they see difficulties ahead. People with children, including those classed as non-dependants by the DSS, cannot be so certain. For example, in the Leeds study one lone parent interrupted her interview to admonish her children for eating too much bread. She broke down in tears when she noted the speed with which they had finished a bottle of orange squash. An adult living alone can predict how long a loaf of bread will last, parents with children cannot. In addition, having children generates extra unpredictable expenses. Besides the growing burden being placed on parents to meet certain school costs (Bull 1983), the sudden requests for money for a school trip, for the school play, the school photograph or, ironically, for a charitable collection, are a frequent cause of concern for families on a low fixed income.

Among those respondents in the Leeds study who said they did not run out of money were some who found that, having bought the week's shopping, and perhaps put aside for bills, they would simply have no cash available for the rest of the week. Thus, for some respondents there would be no heat after the last 50 pence had been put in the meter, or, if they had a slot television, no more television. Others would survive on the most basic food. The following lone parent was not alone when she said that she did not run out of money...

... but some weeks we've had egg and chips on Sunday.

PLANNING AHEAD

Claimants not only have to meet day-to-day expenditures but also have to plan ahead for occasional expenses such as bills, clothing, Christmas and birthdays or just to provide for the unexpected. When the weekly budget is stretched it is particularly important, and yet particularly difficult, for people to set money aside (see Ashley 1983 for further discussion of this). Less than half the pensioner respondents in the Leeds survey said they managed to put some money aside. Those under pension age did so far less often, with almost two-thirds of the unemployed and more than half of the sick and disabled and lone parent respondents never managing to save. In the PSI study (Berthoud 1984) 43 per cent of all claimants and 74 per cent of couples with children never managed to put money aside. The difficulty apparent in saving needs to be borne in mind when considering the system of social fund loans introduced in 1988. When applicants receive a loan from the social fund they have repayments deducted at source from their benefit. What they are unable to save for in advance, they have to pay for in arrears. They can only do this by going without or cutting down on other essential expenditure. This was the option spelt out by one Leeds respondent:

> I'm a fellow who won't get into difficulties. When it comes time to buy shoes and clothing will just have to cut down on something else. Don't buy meat. Need some money at the back of you.

THE FEAR OF BILLS

Evidence collected in 1981/82 after the implementation of the 1980 SB reforms showed that households had greater difficulty managing than non-householders. Life on benefit is not easy for non-householders but their hardship is often less tangible in that they are less likely to bear responsibility for meeting household bills. To reflect this distinction, householders under both the national assistance and the supplementary benefit schemes received a higher rate of benefit than non-householders. Income support makes no such distinction. All claimants receive the same personal allowances whether they are running an independent household or living within someone else's. As discussed in Chapter 3, low-income households spend a higher proportion of their income on necessities such as food, housing and fuel. In 1988 these three items accounted for over one-half the expenditure of households with an average weekly income of under £150, compared with two-fifths of the expenditure of all households (CSO 1991, p. 101). It is inevitable, therefore, that many householders on benefit will face financial difficulty. The income support structure, and in particular the lower rates of benefit which are paid to single people under 25, makes it very difficult or impossible for some people to live independently. This discrimination against the under-25s, together with the loss of benefit as of right to 16 and 17 year olds and changes in payments for board and lodging, has contributed to the problem of homelessness among young people (Andrews and Jacobs 1990; Kirk *et al.* 1991).

Bills, or more accurately the fear of bills, cause constant concern for claimants. People go to great lengths to avoid them. In the Leeds survey many people preferred slot meters for fuel and many had slot television, even though this was a more expensive way to pay. They were more likely to use weekly paid catalogue clubs for clothing and household items, despite the fact that they often offered a more limited choice and might be more expensive. They paid for their television licence or telephone bills in advance by buying special stamps, even though it would have been financially advantageous to put the money into a savings account to earn interest. There were several instances of people cancelling milk deliveries because of the fear of the bill at the end of the week.

In the Leeds survey approximately half the householders in each group said that they worried about the regular household bills. The bills which caused greatest anxiety in both this and the PSI study were fuel bills. In the Leeds study one-third of respondents identified gas and electricity as the bills which they most worried about; rent was the second most frequently mentioned (this was before the introduction of housing benefit when local authority rent and rates were paid direct to the landlord, not via the claimant). A great many respondents tried to avoid the problem of high bills by cutting down on their heating. Consequently, 25 per cent of people interviewed said that they had gone cold almost all the time during a particularly cold part of the previous winter; a further 16 per cent said they did so now and again; 10 per cent and 25 per cent respectively said they went cold all the time or now and again at other, less cold, parts of the winter.

Under both the supplementary benefit and the income support schemes (the latter on a rather more restricted basis), direct deductions could be made from benefit to meet some key bills. These deductions have been made most commonly for rent and fuel arrears. Since 1990 they have also been made for poll tax arrears; up until 1988 deductions could be made to help claimants save for clothing. In 1988, 3.7 per cent (152,000) of claimants were having deductions made to cover gas, and 3.9 per cent (166,000) had deductions for electricity.

In the Leeds survey, it was found that direct deductions lifted a great deal of worry off claimants' shoulders. Some people liked the fuel direct system, even though it left them with less money to manage on each week, because it relieved them of the worry of whether they would be able to afford the bill at the end of the quarter. Tomorrow's bills had to take second place to today's needs. Of all the respondents who were having deductions made from their weekly benefit, all but five said it was a helpful arrangement. One woman who had deductions for both electricity and rent was extremely upset that the DHSS would not also pay her gas bill (because it would have left her with less than the minimum proportion of her benefit in hand). The rules have now been changed to allow claimants to elect to have as much as necessary deducted from benefit. While direct deductions do play an important part in reducing anxiety, they do not provide any additional help with the cost of fuel. Since the fuel crisis of the early 1970s, social assistance policy and then legislation has gradually restricted the amount of additional help which can be made with the cost of fuel. Though direct deductions are an effective way of preventing disconnection for many, they do not solve the underlying problem of why the claimant got into difficulty in the first place. Because they reduce weekly disposable income, they can lead to problems elsewhere in the household budget.

Rent is another expense that is frequently mentioned by claimants as giving cause for concern, even though the majority get their rent paid in full by housing benefit (before 1982 this was paid as part of their supplementary benefit). Two groups of social assistance claimants face difficulty with housing costs. The first are the growing number of people with mortgages on social assistance. During the lifetime of supplementary benefit the proportion of householders with mortgages grew from 3.5 per cent in 1967 to 9 per cent in 1987 (DSS 1989, table 34.58). The second group, which includes both owner-occupiers and tenants, are those householders who have non-dependants living with them. The size of the deduction from both social assistance housing costs and housing benefit which is made for each non-dependant in the household has grown significantly. Between 1983 and 1990 the higher level of deduction grew from £4.70 to £13.50. The lower level also doubled from £2.20 to £5.70. This means that where claimants have, for example, grown-up children living in the household, they receive relatively little help with their housing costs. This presents particular problems if the non-dependants do not make an adequate contribution to the household expenses. One respondent in the Leeds survey had asked the local authority to provide her with alternative accommodation as her grown-up sons would not make good the non-dependant deductions.

Since 1988 claimants have had to meet some new bills. All claimants have to pay 20 per cent of their poll tax (previously rates). With the introduction of income support in April 1988, claimants ceased to receive benefit to cover the actual cost of their water rates. The personal allowances were increased by £1.00 to offset this expense, but for many claimants this was less than the amount they paid. Although these bills have an advantage over fuel bills in that it is known how much they will be, research evidence shows that many claimants have difficulty meeting them (SSRC 1991). The local authority associations have pressed to have the 20 per cent contribution abolished. It is disproportionately expensive to collect (collection costs are greater than revenue collected) and accounts for a sizeable proportion of those unable to pay their poll tax bills because of hardship. The difficulty which people have meeting these unavoidable bills is closely linked with the kind of debts which claimants accumulate (discussed in the following chapter).

THE 'FLEXIBLE DIET'

Food is obviously the most essential and immediate item in a family's expenditure, so the greater the proportion of income which goes on this, the less there is to pay for other goods and services. Bradshaw, Mitchell and Morgan (1987) found that food accounted for over two-fifths of the expenditure of a family on supplementary benefit. In a later local study in Tyne and Wear, Bradshaw and Holmes (1989) found that respondents spent 30 per cent of their budgets (excluding housing costs) on food. In that study they point to the importance of food expenditure as an indicator of poverty:

> The proportion of household expenditure going on food has for a century been taken by experts as a good indicator of relative levels of living – the higher the proportion spent on food, the lower the relative level.
>
> (Bradshaw and Holmes 1989, p. 67)

Despite its obvious importance, food is often regarded as a 'flexible' item in the family budget, to be cut back when money is short:

> Of all the basic necessities, spending on food is the one over which the housewife can exercise most control. Housing and, to a lesser extent, fuel, are fixed items on the household budget, offering little opportunity for economy. Families on low incomes, therefore, turn to their food budget in an attempt to make ends meet.
>
> (Graham 1984, p. 128)

In a study of 65 families with children conducted in 1980, Burghes (1980) found that four-fifths of the 65 families studied often missed meals because they could not afford them. She also found that the distribution of food within the family was not equal. Thus parents went without to feed their children, and women went without to feed their husbands (Burghes 1980; see also Graham 1984).

In the mid-1980s Edwina Currie, as Minister for Health, launched her own personal campaign to persuade families, especially low-income families, to eat a healthier diet. However, buying food which is higher in fibre and lower in fat and sugar is expensive. It has been estimated that the diet recommended by the National Advisory Committee on Nutrition Education (NACNE) costs 35 per cent more than the typical diet of a low-income family (Cole-Hamilton and Lang 1986). Fresh fruit and vegetables are expensive, particularly at certain times of the year, and the choice of expensive organic vegetables is not a realistic one for those on a low income. Jams and other products are much cheaper if they have a lower real food content and a greater number of artificial additives. One lone parent in the Leeds survey had been advised to make the switch from the latter to the former because one of her children was hyperactive, but she could not afford to do so. Data from the Family Expenditure Survey reveal that the quality of the diet of poor people is inferior to that of the affluent:

> High income families spend twice as much on fresh fruit and carcass meat as poor families, but less on the 'filler' foods of bread and potatoes.
>
> (Graham 1984, p. 124)

The families in Burghes's study (1980, p. 31) faced similar problems on the kind of food they could afford to buy:

> At least a third of the families said that they 'never' or only 'now and again' bought cheese, fresh vegetables, fresh fruit, fresh meat, butter and fresh fish. Similarly, about a third of families rarely or never bought biscuits and cereals, more than a half coffee and two-thirds jam and cakes.

As the food budget is cut back, cheaper, less healthy foods form a greater part of the diet. Poor families are more likely to have poorer diets and are therefore prone to obesity and illness. In her review of health inequalities, Whitehead found that, contrary to Edwina Currie's criticisms, poor families had tried to move towards a healthier diet:

> ... in terms of the foodstuffs listed the richest income group continues to have a healthier diet than the poorest group. However, there are signs that, within the limits of their income, the poorest group may have responded to nutritional advice to the same extent as other groups, for example wholemeal bread consumption.
>
> (Whitehead 1988, p. 293)

The choice of food is not only governed by nutritional and cost considerations. It is also subject to social conventions and pressures. Thus, fish fingers and sausages may not have the protein content of fresh fish and meat but they are projected as such in advertising and packaging and are often more acceptable to children. An eloquent answer to Edwina Currie's exhortations to poor families to eat more healthily was given by George Orwell in *The Road to Wigan Pier*. Talking of the miners, he commented:

> The basis of their diet is white bread and margarine, corned beef, sugared tea, and potatoes – an appalling diet. Would it not be better if they (the miners) spent more money on wholesome things like oranges and wholemeal bread... Yes, it would, but the point is that no human being is ever going to do such a thing. The ordinary human being would sooner starve than live on brown bread and raw carrots. And the peculiar evil is this, that the less money you have the less inclined you feel to spend it on wholesome food. A millionaire may enjoy breakfasting off orange juice

and Ryvita biscuits; an unemployed man doesn't... When you are unemployed, which is to say when you are underfed, harassed, bored and
miserable, you don't want to eat dull wholesome food. You want something a little bit 'tasty'... White bread-and-marg and sugared tea don't
nourish you to any extent, but they are *nicer* (at least most people think
so) than brown bread-and-dripping and cold water. Unemployment is an
endless misery that has got to be palliated and especially with tea, the
Englishman's opium. A cup of tea or even an aspirin is much better as a
temporary stimulant than a crust of brown bread.

> (quoted in Jones, Brown and Bradshaw 1978, p. 27)

In a study by Land of 86 large families, food was described as 'our only
luxury':

> Butter had a particular psychological significance, as did Sunday lunch.
> Most of the families made a major effort to provide a joint even though
> much more of a cheaper form of meat could be bought for the money.

> (Ashley 1983, p. 149)

In the Leeds study respondents frequently referred to aspects of their diet
when commenting on their standard of living. The most common complaints
were the lack of choice, the inability to share in that most fundamental of
British customs – the Sunday joint – and their inability to buy fresh fruit and
vegetables. Two-thirds of householders over retirement age and approximately three-quarters of those below said they did not have 'enough money
to buy food'. Meat was the first item on which respondents said they cut
down, followed by fresh fruit and vegetables and 'extras' like cake and
biscuits. The quality of diet described was often poor, and there was little
variety.

> Our basic diet is egg and chips at the moment. There's a lot we can't afford
> to buy ... butter, cheese, meat ... the kids always eat, but sometimes we
> don't.

> (unemployed man)

> Oh yes, there's always a lot (of food) in. It's just the necessities – no fruit
> cake.

> (lone parent)

The information on diet collected in this study would appear to be consistent
with later findings (Bradshaw and Holmes 1989, p. 78):

> We asked the families what they thought of their diets. Altogether 23 per
> cent thought they were adequate and interesting, 54 per cent thought they
> were adequate but boring, and ten per cent thought their diets were poor.

Only 13 per cent thought their diets were good. There certainly was a lack of variety in the food listed as bought by the families... Bread, biscuits and cereal (together making up 15 per cent of expenditure) provided, with potatoes, cheap background bulk.

The nutritional inadequacy of the diet of a family on supplementary benefit was shown in an examination of expenditure data collected for the Family Expenditure Survey (Bradshaw and Morgan 1987, p.78).

They found that a two child family had an overall deficiency in calories of 6,500 and all members of the family were consuming too much protein, the diets were low in fibre, high in fat and salt, and the children's diets were slightly deficient in iron and calcium.

To add insult to injury, poor families not only spend a higher proportion of their income on food and eat worse food than better-off families, they often pay more for it (Caplovitz 1963; Williams 1977). The cost of food is higher for poor families because they are unable to take advantage of the economies of buying in bulk. Their lack of transport precludes them from making regular use of the growing number of out-of-town hypermarkets which generally offer cheaper prices. Such retailers cater to the affluent shopper. For example, the price might fall not only with the size of the packet but often also with the number of a single product bought.

CLOTHING AND FOOTWEAR

Numerous studies from the mid-1970s on have shown that the purchase of clothing and footwear is another regular expense which claimants have difficulty meeting. In the Leeds survey, one-third of pensioners, over half the unemployed and sick and disabled respondents and two-thirds of the lone parents interviewed said that they did not have sufficient clothing to meet even the minimum standards laid down by the SBC. This finding was similar to that in a study of unemployed and sick and disabled claimants in 1969 (DHSS 1972). In their more recent study in Tyne and Wear, Bradshaw and Holmes (1989) found that three-quarters of the men and women lacked more than two items of basic clothing and were more likely to lack essential items the longer they had been on benefit. Children were better provided for but 60 per cent lacked more than two items.

... despite the debts that many families incurred with mail order catalogues and clothing clubs, nearly half the families in the sample said that they were 'short of clothes'. Shortage of clothes can be exacerbated by difficulty of access to a washing machine or launderette or the expense of doing a wash.

(Bradshaw and Holmes 1989, p. 65)

Many people on benefit are reliant on credit or second-hand sources for many of the clothes that they do have. In the Leeds survey approximately three-fifths of pensioners and people categorized as sick and disabled were able to buy new clothes for cash, while less than one-half of the unemployed and only two-fifths of lone parents could. The rest had to try to get hold of things second-hand – either passed on from friends or bought from second-hand shops or jumble sales. Between one-quarter and one-third of respondents in each group said they could not *normally* afford to buy their own or their family's clothes new. One-third of the respondents in the unemployed, sick and disabled and pensioners groups, and over one-half of lone parent respondents sometimes or always bought their clothes from second-hand shops or jumble sales.

The difficulties which claimants face in obtaining adequate clothing have been exacerbated by the various changes to social assistance which have occurred over the last ten years. Up until 1980, clothing and footwear accounted for the largest number of single payment grants. The 1980 reforms restricted payments for clothing to cases where the need had arisen for reasons other than through normal wear and tear. Under the social fund provisions, which were introduced in 1988, grants and loans for clothing are generally confined only to those who literally have none, such as people coming out of institutions, and then only subject to there being funds available. This is discussed in more detail in the next chapter.

CONCLUSION

Social assistance is now a mass scheme, dealing with the needs of millions of people with extremely diverse needs and demands. Any attempt to examine whether or not benefit rates are sufficient must take this into account, as must governments when they devise and administer schemes to alleviate poverty. National assistance and supplementary benefit endeavoured to cope with that diversity through a flexible system of payments. Income support does not recognize individual differences, only broad differences between some groups of people. In so doing any shortcomings of that structure fall on those who come low in the 'premium hierarchy'.

The evidence presented in this chapter shows that some people are worse off than others. In particular, pensioners have been shown to be in less difficulty than claimants below retirement age. This is because they receive the highest rates of benefit and because the absence of dependent children enables them to retain tighter control over their expenditure. Among claimants under retirement age, those with children, in particular lone parents and unemployed people, have been shown to be worst off according to a number of factors: they have less savings, more credit and more debts, and they have the greatest difficulty in managing on their weekly income. The main worries of claimants remain key areas of expenditure, such as the cost of fuel and, particularly for families with children, clothes. These are expenses which even subsistence benefits should cover. This pattern and level of hardship is very similar to that shown in studies in the 1960s and 1970s (eg DHSS 1972).

Such comparison between groups has to be treated with extreme caution. While evidence shows that some groups are worse off than others, it also shows that none is well off. Therefore, the strategy of 'rough justice', of diverting resources to one group at the expense of another, which began with the 1976 supplementary benefits review, is quite inappropriate. In both the 1980 and 1986 legislation, the reforms sought to make improvements for some groups, in particular families with children, at the expense of other groups – older people and childless couples in 1980 and young people in 1988. The evidence presented here shows that, while it is undoubtedly the case that people with children face the greatest hardship, *all* claimants find life on benefit difficult. The solution to the problems of the least well off should not be to reduce the living standards of other groups who are not quite so poor. Redistribution of resources among claimants leads to more poverty not less.

For the vast majority of people, social assistance offers an inferior standard of living to that experienced before claiming benefit. The main exceptions are, first, those people who were eligible for benefit but not claiming it previously – a problem which the system should address more forcefully than it has traditionally done. The second group are women whose partners have not shared the family income equitably. The social assistance scheme can do nothing to change this situation when the partner's income comes from employment; it is in their power to make different arrangements for couples on benefit. The preferred option would be individual assessment for benefit, though it is recognized in the current climate that the cost of this makes it unlikely even in the medium term. However, alternative administrative and payment methods could be considered which would guarantee both partners some security of income, regardless of the behaviour of the other.

It has been shown that people on benefit are not greedy. They have very modest aspirations. But do we as a society really want to argue that the poor should not enjoy themselves? Do we want to maintain the privations and stigma of the Poor Law and punish people for their poverty? Claimants generally aspire not to continental holidays, nor a car, but merely to be able to choose the kind of food they would like: meat, fresh fruit and vegetables; to be able to keep warm and pay their bills without worry; to give their children the same things that their friends have, and not to have to panic when they have to pay for the school trip or buy a packet of soap powder. Most of all, claimants want dignity and that means being full members of the society in which they live.

Far from solving the problem of poverty on an individual basis, social assistance can actually drive people into poverty. Can a scheme of last resort assistance said to be working when the majority of recipients run out of money each week and when they continually worry about how the next bill will be paid? Is a scheme effective when diet is controlled not by nutritional factors or even choice, but by what can be afforded, and when, in Britain in the 1990s, people have to dress themselves and their children from jumble sales, not out of choice but of necessity?

Critics argue that the problem is not the amount of money claimants have but what they do with it. They do not manage their budgets efficiently. This is the issue we turn to next.

5 Making ends meet

Although money has enormous significance and power at all income
levels, the handling of it becomes the more critical the less there is of it.

(Ashley 1983, p. viii)

It is true that it is particularly crucial for people on low fixed incomes to
manage their money efficiently; failure to do so can have dire results for their
living standards. It is equally true, especially for those dependent on state
support, that their expenditure habits are closely examined and any
'inefficient' or 'wasteful' expenditure is heavily criticized (see Moore 1989;
Golding and Middleton 1982). However, 'managing' on a low fixed income
requires great skill and it is inevitable that some do not succeed. Failure to
'manage' can be caused by a number of factors which, broadly, can be
divided into two types: poor budgeting or lack of money. The following
discussion considers how far claimants' ability or inability to make ends meet
can be attributed to these two sets of factors.

State benefits are normally paid weekly or fortnightly through the post
office. In recent years, some groups of benefit recipients, such as those in
receipt of child benefit and retirement pension, have been encouraged to have
their money paid monthly, direct into a bank account. As long as there are
no hiccups in payment – which, in fact, happen more often than is desirable –
recipients have a secure and reliable source of income. However, unlike wage
earners and salary earners who sometimes have pay rises, bonuses or perhaps
overtime payments which can provide a welcome boost, benefit claimants
have no prospect of any extra money. The annual uprating is rightly regarded
only as making good the erosion of the value of the benefit over the year.
Most claimants under retirement age are not even entitled to the £10 Christmas bonus, and since 1988 the minority of claimants who received single
payments lost this source of extra help. It is not surprising then that a frequent
complaint of people on benefit is of its relentlessness: the knowledge that
there will be no real improvement, next month or next year, or, for those

he was Secretary of State for Social Security, John Moore (1989, p. 5) remarked:

> ... it is hard to believe that poverty stalks the land when even the poorest fifth of families with children spend nearly a 10th of their income on alcohol and tobacco.

It is true that rates of smoking vary inversely according to socio-economic status, with those in social class I (professional) smoking least and those in social class V (unskilled manual) smoking most. Smoking habits also vary according to economic status: 'For example, in 1984 36 per cent of men in work were smokers, compared with 61 per cent of unemployed men. The corresponding figures for women were 34 per cent and 48 per cent' (Whitehead 1988, p. 291). Furthermore, there has been a much smaller decline in the rate of smoking among this latter group, especially by women. While many people would agree with Moore's implicit criticism of such behaviour, others have offered a quite different explanation. For example, research has shown that cigarette smoking is one of the few ways mothers can relieve their immediate tension (Graham 1976; Jacobson 1981):

> ... actions, which would be labelled irresponsible by some professionals, may be the only way in which mothers can stay sane and act responsibly towards their family.
>
> (Whitehead 1988, p. 302)

Whitehead also points to the psychological importance of people being able to indulge themselves or their children occasionally:

> ... (Coping) with the stress of caring for the family on a low income, ... often involves a juggling act of keeping within a very limited budget while at the same time seeing that the children are well and relatively contented... Sweets tend to be used as a quick and easy way of keeping children quiet on shopping trips and on other stressful occasions.
>
> (Charles and Kerr 1985, quoted in Whitehead 1988, p. 301)

Analysis of the lifestyles of people living on benefit described in this and the previous chapter reveals that there is very little scope for people to ill-use their money. Although, obviously, money spent on cigarettes cannot be used for other more 'essential' expenditure, Bradshaw and Holmes (1989, p. 80) concluded that despite the high incidence of smoking among their respondents which 'must have made at least a small difference to the money available to other things ... there (was) no evidence that heavy smoking by the adults affected the family diet'. Bradshaw and Holmes found 'little embarrassment' about money spent on smoking. The findings of the Leeds survey were rather different.

Many of the claimants in the Leeds survey held very puritan views on how their money should be spent. Many said that they thought they personally spent money unwisely. The majority of expenditures mentioned in response to this question were those that might give some 'pleasure', and were not essential for subsistence. By far the most frequently mentioned were cigarettes; other items were entertainment (including television), clothes and alcohol. Items mentioned less frequently were car expenses, telephone, sweets for children, magazines, birthday and wedding presents and food for pets. None of these expenditures might be considered wildly extravagant in today's society.

MAKING ENDS MEET

There are two strategies that can be adopted to make ends meet. The first is to reduce expenditure to fit the money available, which as the above discussion shows is an option often chosen or forced upon people. The second is to use extra resources to make the weekly benefit stretch. Those who are able to adopt the latter policy are fortunate, they are also in the minority.

As discussed earlier, social assistance offers little reprieve from the fixed weekly benefit. The £10 Christmas bonus helps some but, having never been increased, is widely regarded as inadequate and miserly. Social assistance claimants lost an important formal source of extra help when the single payments system was abolished in 1988. Such payments were extremely important in providing, at least for some claimants, extra resources in addition to the fixed weekly benefit. Informal sources of support, such as families and friends and sometimes charities, are the main ways in which extra help might be obtained. However, such extra help is not available to everyone.

Within a low, fixed budget, any extra help which might be received can have an importance beyond its financial significance. Marsden (1969) found, for example, that although gifts had only a small impact on living standards they had an important effect on morale. For some (fortunate) people on benefit, success in managing is made possible because they have extra resources available to them in the form of savings, earnings or help from relatives. The importance of extra resources is confirmed by Ritchie (1990, p. 33):

> Without exception the families had called on resources other than their benefit income during their period of unemployment ... some of the families who were 'managing' best had had, or found, more resources to call on. Some of the families explicitly said this was how they were able to manage. Regular help from family and friends, use of savings and the

sale of possessions, casual earnings and additional income from other household members were of particular significance in this context.

The extent to which claimants can enhance disposable income by income from other sources is strictly controlled through the means test. Some types of income, such as maintenance and national insurance benefits, are deducted in full from benefit. Others, like earnings, are deducted if they exceed a certain figure. Similarly, benefit will be reduced if savings exceed a certain level. Consequently, only a minority of claimants, 15.6 per cent in 1989 (the latest year for which stastistics are available), had any income in addition to their social assistance or other state benefit.

'PUTTING A BIT BY' – AND KEEPING IT

In the benefit year 1990/91, income support recipients were allowed to have up to £8,000 in savings. For each £250 or amounts up to £250 that a claimant has over £3,000, £1 is deducted from income support. In 1989, only 14 per cent of claimants had any savings and of those less than one per cent had amounts of £3,000 which affected their level of income support. This latter figure is half the number in the previous year, which might have been expected to be artificially low because it was the first year of the new capital rules. Clearly, income support claimants are using up their savings. The group most likely to have capital are retired people. In 1989, 29 per cent of IS claimants over 60 had capital. The proportions for people below retirement age were much smaller: 4 per cent of unemployed claimants, 7.6 per cent of claimants in receipt of disability premium and 2.2 per cent of lone parents.

Having savings undoubtedly eases the pressure for those claimants who are fortunate enough to have them. The OPCS study of unemployed people found that savings played an important role in sustaining levels of consumption well into the second year of unemployment (Heady and Smyth 1989, p. xvii). In the Leeds study a higher proportion of those with savings than those without reported that they were managing well, and fewer said they were getting into difficulty. This was because these claimants had used all or part of their savings to supplement essential expenditure. Most had used their savings to supplement current income and meet expenses supposed to be covered by the scale rates. Over one-third of those who had spent part or all of their savings had used them to pay fuel bills and the same number to buy food. Slightly fewer used their savings to buy furniture.

In some cases, savings were used when the claimant had just come on to benefit to ease adjustment to their lower income. One respondent had used her savings when she faced her first Christmas living on benefit.

Christmas obviously. It's pride as well. The kids have never done without. I more or less cleared it out at Christmas.

A couple who were in the 'honeymoon' period of their social assistance claim at the time of their interview were supplementing their income from their savings.

(We) live reasonably well – but at the end of the week there's nothing left out of what they allowed us ... have £1 left to do what we want with ... any emergency would have to come out of savings.

This couple had not fallen behind with any bills and they were 'just getting by' but only thanks to their savings. However, this situation could not continue very long as their savings had fallen very quickly to less than £300:

Not (worried) now because we've got that little bit you can draw on. But you keep nibbling at it, and worries will start then... We're quite happy only thing is we find is nibbling into our savings... I (will) try to get a bit more if we can; bit of savings you've got, don't want it dipped into ad lib until nothing to fall back on.

EARNINGS

A second way of increasing the weekly income is to work. Because of their means-tested basis, social assistance programmes usually have firm rules on the amount recipients are permitted to earn. Government statistics show that a tiny proportion of claimants or their wives have earnings from part-time work. In 1989, only 3 per cent of all claimants and only 6 per cent of claimants' wives reported part-time earnings (DSS 1989). The earnings disregards (the amount of money claimants are allowed to keep without their benefit being affected) were restructured twice during the 1980s. As part of the supplementary benefit changes introduced in 1980, the government brought in a tapered earnings disregard for lone parents. This allowed lone parents to keep, after expenses, the first £4 of their earnings and half of anything they earned between £4 and £20. Other claimants could earn only £4. The changes introduced in the income support scheme in 1988 represented an improvement for some people, but a reduction for others. The earnings disregards for the long-term unemployed and those in receipt of the disability and lone parent premium increased to £15. This represented a very considerable increase for the first two groups. Other claimants were entitled to keep the first £5. The sting in the tail of these increases was that under the supplementary benefit system claimants had been able to offset work expenses; under income support they could not. Thus, anyone with any work expenses, for example for travel or child care, would be likely to be worse off under the income support rules. While it is too soon to see whether the changing level of disregards introduced in 1988, which represented a three-fold increase for some claimants though a fall for others, has led to any increased participation in the labour force, there was little change during the 1980s. No adequate solution has been found to the question of how to encourage claimants to take part-time work without creating a disincentive effect on people's willingness to look for and accept full-time work.

In those families where the claimant or partner does work, part-time earnings can help to relieve pressure on the weekly budget. The Leeds survey was conducted while the tapered earnings disregard still applied. One in five of the lone parents interviewed, who had part-time work, said they could manage each week; that was twice as many as those who did not work. More generous earnings disregards could make a big difference to claimants' living standards.

In the Leeds survey, just one pensioner worked part-time, compared to one in ten of the unemployed, one in eight of the sick and disabled (including those working in sheltered workshops or at day centres for people with disabilities) and one in six lone parents. Getting a part-time job was discounted by many claimants. Some thought claimants were not allowed to work at all, others thought the disregard was too low and not worth the additional trouble, expense and administrative hassle involved (for fuller discussion see Walker with Dant 1984, p. 84). In a longitudinal study of 30 unemployed families conducted between 1983/84 and 1988, Ritchie (1990) found that few respondents thought it was worth getting regular part-time work as they would only be allowed to keep £4 of their earnings (£5 at 1990/91 rates).

> I know two or three part-time jobs I could get ... but I done it once and I told them down there that I earn £10 and they just took £10 off me so I thought well I've dug that bloke's garden for nothing – 'put your money in your pocket' you know and dig it for nothing. I mean the only person that gained out of that was the DHSS, wasn't it?
>
> (1990, p. 48)

The lack of financial reward, however, was not the only reason that claimants might be deterred from taking part-time work. Some respondents in Ritchie's study were deterred from taking casual work because of the difficulty of getting the benefit rate back to normal once it had been interrupted.

> The budgeting in many of the families was sufficiently fragile that the thought of having a reduced benefit income for a few weeks, even if there was back pay, was not something they wanted to risk.
>
> (Ritchie 1990, p. 48)

Other groups dependent on benefit are also discouraged from working part-time. There is evidence that there are additional pressures on the wives of unemployed men to give up work. The DHSS cohort study of unemployed men conducted in 1978/79 found that only 32 per cent of wives were in paid work, compared with 56 per cent of all married women. The women were also less likely to be in part-time work, 16 per cent versus 31 per cent nationally. Of those in receipt of social assistance, two-thirds of those who had been employed before their husbands registered as unemployed left employment, a figure three times higher than among the wives whose husbands received unemployment benefit only (DHSS 1984, p. 129). The study concluded that though there was a need for further exploration of this issue, there was 'prima facie evidence of a disincentive effect on the economic activity of wives of unemployed men created by the social security earnings rules' and particularly the supplementary benefits rules (Moylan *et al.* 1984, p. 129). A similar disincentive effect was found in a study by Dilnot and Kay for the Institute for Fiscal Studies. They concluded that receipt of supplementary benefit was 'fundamentally incompatible with women's work' (quoted in Brown 1989, p. 76).

An OPCS study of unemployed people and their families again found changes in work patterns of wives 'consistent with the idea that the benefit system provided a disincentive for wives to work' but the numbers leaving the workforce was smaller and in part might be attributed to other labour market factors. They found, contrary to other studies, that 'even if wives' willingness to do paid work is affected by the benefit system, only a limited proportion appear to be deterred' (Heady and Smyth 1989, pp. 42–43).

During the 1980s, the part played by the earnings disregard in encouraging lone parents to work, or discouraging them from working, underwent considerable investigation. In their study of the tapered earnings disregard which applied to lone parents between April 1980 and April 1988, Weale and his colleagues concluded that it was only one of many factors which lone parents took into account when deciding whether or not to work:

> for lone mothers the decision to take paid work depends upon a complex interaction of preferences, child care constraints, job opportunities and financial returns... Our analysis suggests that the proportion of persons who will be influenced positively to participate in the labour market is quite small if policy is restricted solely to the manipulation of economic incentives.
>
> (Weale *et al.* 1984, p. 190)

A later review conducted for the Social Security Advisory Committee concluded that:

The key to increasing the participation of lone mothers in the labour market is not to be found only in relatively modest adjustments to social security rules, but in a package of measures directed to the daily realities of living as a one parent family.

(Brown 1989, p. 96)

HELP FROM RELATIVES AND FRIENDS

Many studies have shown the importance of the help provided to people on benefit by families and friends (see, for example, Marsden 1969; Bradshaw and Holmes 1989; Ritchie 1990). In the Leeds study too some respondents were fortunate in having contact with relatives who could offer help. Most commonly this took the form of practical domestic help, but many also were able to help with short or long-term loans. Friends and relatives were particularly important in helping people get through to the next pay-day if their money ran out. Others were in touch with relatives who could give no financial or practical assistance but could provide emotional support and company. Undoubtedly the existence of close family or friends can make a substantial difference to many claimants' emotional well-being as well as ease financial pressures. However, relying on help from family can also have costs. For young people, especially, it can mean a loss of independence and be a cause of friction with parents regardless of whether or not the parents are helping financially. Thus, where young people live in the family home they often have very little independence. The changes in benefit for 16/17 year olds and for single people under 25 introduced in 1988 have meant that in its eagerness to remove young people from dependence on the state, the Conservative government increased dependency within the family.

Of course, not all young people have a family who are willing and/or able to step in when state help is withdrawn. Neither do many other claimants. Some claimants lose touch with friends and relatives once on benefit either because of a loss of self-esteem or because they cannot afford to enter into reciprocal social relationships. As one of the lone parents in the Leeds survey said:

What I don't like about being on social is that I can't have friends to a meal, can't do that, can't make what you have got go round. Lost lots of friends through that ... cousins with kids, they used to visit us, but I can't do it because I haven't got it.

Overall one-third of the respondents in the Leeds survey said they had no one to whom they could turn for help. The group most likely to report this was, ironically, given developments in community care policy, the group recorded as sick and disabled. Policies intended to encourage or force families to help more, either financially or with other kinds of support, are inappropriate and inadequate because this is clearly not an option open to many claimants.

One group of relatives that have received particular attention in recent years are absent parents. The Conservative government showed particular concern at the growing numbers of lone parents on social assistance. Between 1979 and 1989, they doubled in number to 750,000 (DSS 1989; Cm 1264 1990). In 1988/89 the cost in real terms of means-tested benefits for lone parents (income support, housing benefit and family credit) was £3.2 billion compared to £1.4 billion in 1981/82 (Cm 1264 1990). A further concern was that only a minority of lone parents (30 per cent of lone mothers and 3 per cent of lone fathers) received regular child maintenance payments. Only 23 per cent of lone parents receiving income support did so in 1989 (HMSO 1990). In October 1990 the government published a White Paper, *Children Come First*, setting out its proposals on maintenance payments for children. The main thrust of the proposals was to increase the contribution from absent parents towards the costs of their children. This would be facilitated by the setting of fixed levels of maintenance payments and also by the creation of an independent agency to ensure court orders were honoured. Overall less than one in ten lone parents will benefit financially from this legislation. The changes do nothing to improve the financial position of women on social assistance as maintenance payments will continue to be deducted in full from benefit. However, it is feared that such a scheme will give rise to a new problem. Where a maintenance order is made against an absent partner the partner might then, with some justification, demand access to the children. Where there is a history of violence, some lone parents would be frightened or reluctant to grant this (Brown 1989). Any lone parent on income support who refuses to provide information about the father of her children may have her benefit reduced by 20 per cent for the first six months and 10 per cent for the following 12 months. In one study, 67 per cent of lone parents interviewed indicated that they would not want to comply with such a rule (*Guardian*, 6 August 1991).

WHEN ENDS DON'T MEET

From the earlier discussion, it is not surprising that there are many occasions when claimants do not manage to make ends meet. When people do run out of money there are a limited range of options available: they can sell something, borrow or get into debt. In the Leeds survey the most common option reported was the former. One in three people below retirement age and one in eight of those over retirement age had tried to raise money by selling belongings or by cashing in insurance policies prematurely. Most frequently, the money raised was used for essential expenditure: food (29 per cent), fuel bills (25 per cent), clothes and shoes (24 per cent), furniture (9 per cent), and rent, including arrears (6 per cent). Raising money by selling belongings was also common in Ritchie's study of 30 unemployed families. Two-thirds of the car owners had sold their vehicles and just under one-half of the families had 'sold other items of transport, household items, or personal effects' (Ritchie 1990, p. 50).

There is a limit to what poor people have to sell, so many people have to resort to borrowing. The use of credit has increased generally in Britain during the 1980s. Between 1980 and 1988 outstanding consumer credit grew by 220 per cent (Ford 1991). Low-income families are less likely to use credit than more affluent households, partly because it is more difficult to obtain and partly because they are unable to afford to take on such extra commitments. The main sources of credit for benefit claimants and other poor people tend to be informal, such as borrowing from friends or relatives (Berthoud and Kempson 1990; Walker with Dant 1984; Bradshaw and Holmes 1989). Despite the convenience and necessity for such arrangements, borrowing from friends or relatives is fraught with tension. Studies of people in debt have shown that recipients are embarrassed to reveal their inability to manage, and they fear they might be criticized for the position they find themselves in. Most importantly, accepting such help conflicts with their desire to remain independent.

> I am an independent person and I like to provide for my own child, but I can't. I will always feel a debt to other people.

> I feel like the poor relation having to rely on my family to buy my son a present.

> (Oppenheim and McEvaddy 1987,
> quoted in Ford 1991, p. 68)

Growing numbers of poor people are turning to formal sources of credit. Between 1980 and 1988 the number of low-income households using credit increased from approximately one in five to seven out of ten (Ford 1991, p. 23). However, the type of credit available to the poor is restricted and expensive. There is less reliance on bank loans, overdrafts and credit cards and more on catalogue clubs, tallymen and loan sharks.

For the poor, unlike the affluent, credit 'tends to be associated with necessity rather than choice' (Ford 1991). It is a device used to help them manage their poverty. In the PSI study of supplementary benefits claimants, nearly one-quarter of all claimants in the study, and over one-half of families with children, had borrowed to meet a large expense; one-third of the whole sample and nearly three-quarters of families with children had borrowed money just to help them make ends meet (Berthoud 1984, table A25). In the

Leeds study, similarly high proportions of people had had to borrow at some stage. Three-quarters of the unemployed and lone parent respondents had borrowed money in the twelve months prior to the interview. The pattern of borrowing reflected how well each group said they managed. Those who were able to manage least well were most likely to borrow. Respondents borrowed on a regular basis both to see them through to the next pay-day and to meet specific large expenses. The money was usually used for essential expenditure supposed to be covered by the scale rates. Over one-half of those who borrowed said they did so in order to buy food; approximately one-third bought clothes and shoes, and a similar proportion used the money to pay their fuel bills.

Although some respondents in these studies found it difficult to negotiate hire purchase or credit sale agreements, nearly one in six of the unemployed respondents and one in seven of the lone parents had either hire purchase or credit sale agreements, and about half that proportion of sick and disabled and pensioner respondents did so. Those respondents with bank loans or other credit agreements had usually negotiated them before they came on to benefit, and it was then usually a struggle to keep up with the payments on their reduced income. Under the supplementary benefits scheme, it was possible to get weekly additions to benefit or lump sum payments to clear hire purchase agreements for 'essential items'. However, none of the respondents in the Leeds study received such help. Under the new income support scheme no such help is available and all claimants have to cover any repayments regardless of the cost or the kind of item purchased. The difficulty that people have in managing credit payments has an important implication for the effectiveness and usefulness of social fund loans for people on benefit (see Chapter 7).

The weekly catalogue club is one of the most common forms of credit used by poor people as it is usually easily obtained. Well over half the respondents in the Leeds study in the lone parent group, nearly one-third of the unemployed and about one-sixth of the sick and disabled and pensioners used this form of credit. Catalogues provide people with an acceptable, though often limited and expensive, way of buying clothes and household goods. Catalogues were mentioned as the second most frequent way respondents bought clothes. It was most popular among lone parents, one-fifth of whom bought clothes in this way. Approximately one in eight of the respondents in the unemployed and sick and disabled groups and only five people in the pensioner group did so. Despite this widespread use of credit and of second-hand sources, studies of the standard of living of claimants over the last 15 years have shown that many do not possess essential clothing (DHSS/SBC 1977; Walker with Dant 1984; Berthoud 1984; Bradshaw and Holmes 1989).

FROM CREDIT TO DEBT

Despite adopting various ways of budgeting by cutting down or raising money, debt is a common experience for people on benefit as it is for other poor people. Incomes are so tight that a carefully managed budget can easily be tipped into debt. As Table 5.1 shows, debt becomes much more likely once on benefit. For example, in the Leeds survey, many people fell into debt only *after* they came on to benefit. A substantial number of the householders interviewed said they had never been in debt before. While they had always been able to manage before, albeit often on low incomes, they were unable to manage once relying on the state safety net.

Table 5.1 Proportion of respondents who reported arrears

Debt incurred	Unemployed			Sick & disabled			Lone parent			Pensioner		
	Rent	Gas	Elec	Rent	Gas	Elec	Rent	Gas	Elec	Rent	Gas	Elec
	%	%	%	%	%	%	%	%	%	%	%	%
Before coming on to benefit	3	7	1	5	5	3	2	5	2	0	0	0
After coming on to benefit	47	16	29	36	12	18	50	22	37	12	10	13
Total no. reporting arrears	73			67			111			94		

Falling behind with bills and getting into debt can cause great distress to anyone but particularly to those who have never been in debt. In general, people take great pride in being up to date with commitments. Not managing to do so produces a sense of failure, in addition to the natural anxiety of how the bill is to be paid. The most common reason given in the Leeds survey for incurring arrears was simply that the claimant ran out of money. This was inevitable when so few were able to put money aside for their bills regularly. A related cause of debt was that respondents used money put aside for one bill to pay another.

Debt provides claimants with another device for managing their poverty when the rest of their limited set of options have run out. 'Robbing Peter to pay Paul' buys them short-term relief from pressing commitments. In the Leeds survey, this was particularly so with rent (the interviews were conducted before the introduction of housing benefit). Some local authority tenants, who were normally prompt payers, would miss paying the fortnightly rent if another more pressing expense came up. An unemployed couple with three children said they owed £64 in rent because:

For some weeks we needed things for the kids, so it was a matter of priorities ... because we're usually good payers they've given us time.

The introduction of housing benefit means that claimants have lost this flexibility, because any benefit to local authority tenants is paid direct from the benefits section to the rent section. A small but significant number of respondents in the Leeds study had fallen into arrears when they went into hospital. Given other pressures and anxieties, claimants did not always inform the local office of their changed circumstances. This could lead to complications and financial difficulties later.

CONCLUSION

The evidence revealed in this and the previous chapter shows that social assistance provides for a very meagre existence. Yet claimants have few strategies at their disposal to ease the problem. Social security offers a regular, usually secure, income but it offers little hope. Claimants can see no likelihood of improvement in their living standards. The break in the link with benefit upratings and earnings ensures that this will remain the case and that those on benefit will fall further behind the rest of community.

Given that certainty, claimants have to try to find strategies for managing their poverty but the options available are limited. The first option claimants choose is to cut down or do without. Often the difference between the 'good' manager and the 'bad' manager is the level to which each is successful in doing this. While most people would expect to have to cut down once they are living on state benefits, the extent to which claimants are forced to do this is unacceptable. Many claimants are ill-fed, ill-clothed and go cold. Those who on the outside appear to be managing well because, for example, they are up to date with all their bills, do so at the cost of great deprivation and hardship. Those people who are seen to be managing are often presented as proof that benefits are adequate and that it is only inefficient managers who get into difficulty. The evidence collected over three decades shows that it is those who *cannot* manage who are really the norm. And it is the managers who are the exceptions proving the rule.

The second strategy which can be used to help claimants manage their poverty is to increase the weekly income. Unfortunately, the means test ensures that this option is not available in many circumstances, and where it is, it only allows modest improvements in disposable income. Social assistance rates represent not only the minimum on which a family should normally live, they also represent, through the means test, the maximum. Only a very small minority of claimants have regular weekly income apart from benefits. Only a minority of those benefit from it.

Part-time work, even if available, is deemed unattractive mainly because of the small amount of earnings which a claimant can keep. Other family pressures, for example those on the wives of unemployed men and lone parents, mean that part-time work may create more problems than it solves. Few claimants have savings, and where they do the savings are eaten into very quickly as they are used to subsidize the inadequate weekly income. It is ironic that the security offered by having some money in the bank is soon lost as savings inevitably go down.

Government action in the early 1990s on maintenance payments to lone parents has been concerned only to reduce the cost to the social security system. There has been no attempt to increase the standard of living of a group known to be among the poorest or to improve their access to the labour market. Despite pressure, the Conservative government refused to allow lone parents on income support to retain any part of their maintenance payment. As there is consequently no carrot which can be used to encourage lone parents to divulge the names and whereabouts of absent fathers, a new stick was introduced in 1991, whereby if they refuse to do so, benefit is reduced. The main victims of such a policy are the children.

Changes in social assistance policy and community care policy during the 1980s aimed to force families to take more responsibility for their members. However, in many cases there is no one available to help. Where there are relatives willing and able to help, they provide great emotional support, as well as financial or practical help. However, if families are *forced* to provide financial support and people are forced to seek it, then not only is the principle of a national social security system for all shattered, those very relationships are also threatened. Social relationships are based on reciprocity. If that cannot be maintained then the relationship is at risk of breaking down.

Finally, credit and debt are playing an increasingly important part in claimants' budgeting strategies. Credit is used not, in the words of one credit card advertisement, 'to take the waiting out of wanting' but as a means of obtaining necessities which cannot be met from weekly benefit. On a finely balanced budget, the divide between credit and debt is very narrow. The state safety net provides no safety net. If an unexpected expense comes up, or a predictable but unavoidable expense like Christmas occurs, the slide into debt is often inevitable. It is an indictment of British social assistance that many people experience debt only *after* claiming benefit.

For three decades research has shown that social assistance rates are insufficient to meet basic needs. Three major reforms have failed to tackle that fundamental weakness effectively. Reform has concentrated on trying to alleviate the consequences of that inadequacy for benefits administration, not on trying to solve the underlying problem for claimants. The perennial debate on the role and efficacy of payments made in addition to basic weekly benefit is a testimony to that omission. That debate is the subject of the next chapter.

6 Meeting need
A safety net for the safety net?

A range of evidence has been presented in the previous two chapters to illustrate the standard of living which dependence on social assistance affords. All the empirical evidence shows that the standard of living is meagre and devoid of choice. The level of income on which claimants are expected to live leaves them with very little room for flexibility in their expenditure. Furthermore, a significant number cannot manage on their benefit. Even where it might appear from the outside that someone is 'managing', closer examination reveals that this is achieved only by making great sacrifices: by maintaining an inadequate diet, going cold in the winter and withdrawing from social contacts.

The various social assistance schemes which have operated in Britain have aimed to provide an income at subsistence level. Thus benefit levels were intended to cover basic necessities but no more. As the discussion in Chapters 4 and 5 illustrate, how far this modest goal has been achieved is extremely doubtful. In trying to maintain the subsistence principle, even if more in theory than in fact, governments faced the difficulty of how to deal with the essential, special expenses some claimants have. Subsistence level benefits provide no slack which can be used to cover any extra expenses which might arise because of ill health or for some other reason. Therefore, ever since the full implementation of unemployment assistance in 1936, social assistance provision has included a system of additional payments designed to meet special needs (Walker 1983, p. 12).

THE DEVELOPMENT OF A SAFETY NET FOR THE SAFETY NET

The additional help provided within British social assistance has taken two forms: first, occasional lump sum payments known after 1966 as exceptional needs payments and then, from 1980, as single payments; and, secondly, weekly additions to benefit, first called exceptional circumstances additions and then, from 1980, additional requirements. Until 1980 such payments were covered by the discretionary powers of the National Assistance Board (NAB) and later the Supplementary Benefits Commission (SBC). The Social Security Act 1980 replaced these wide ranging discretionary powers with a system of regulations which laid down eligibility criteria and often the level of payments that could be made.

Many criticisms have been made of this part of social assistance provision. Both the National Assistance Board and the Supplementary Benefits Commission expressed concern at the extent to which extra payments were made. Both saw a growth in the number of weekly and occasional payments claimed and awarded, causing severe administrative problems. Between 1948 and 1965, the proportion of claimants receiving a discretionary weekly addition to benefit doubled from 26.2 per cent (265,000 claimants) to 57.9 per cent (1,157,000). Weekly additions to benefit were paid for a wide variety of expenses including nightcaps and window cleaning, but four types of expenditure predominated: laundry costs, domestic assistance, special diets and fuel. The total number of weekly additions rose from 319,000 to 2,210,000, each of which had to be individually assessed and administered. During the same period, the number of claims for lump sum payments trebled from more than 100,000 in 1948 to 345,000 in 1965 (see Walker 1983, p. 14). This increasing reliance on extra payments between 1948 and 1965 led the NAB, in what was to be its final Annual Report, to argue for reconsideration of the system:

> There is now a strong case for compounding, in appropriate categories, the smaller and commoner special needs with the basic scale rates and providing a scale rate which they will all receive and which is sufficient for all normal needs, including small expenses for which special discretionary additions have up to now been made.
>
> (NAB 1966, p. xii)

When supplementary benefit replaced national assistance in 1966 another attempt was made to bring the number of weekly additions under control. The new supplementary benefit scheme included a long-term addition to the scale rates for pensioners and, after two years' receipt of benefit, for all other beneficiaries except unemployed people. At first the introduction of this addition was successful in reducing the number of discretionary additions. The number of exceptional circumstances additions (ECAs) almost halved despite an increase in the number of claimants when the new scheme took effect. The downward trend continued until 1971 after which it began to climb once again. By 1975, 39 per cent of all claimants were again in receipt of a weekly addition to benefit. In the year up to November 1980, when additional requirement payments replaced ECAs, 61 per cent of claimants were getting such payments.

A similar pattern developed with regard to lump sum payments. Berthoud refers to an 'explosion' (1984, p. F16) between 1968 and 1976 as the number of exceptional needs payments doubled. There were two reasons for this growth. First, the structure of the claimant population changed over this period. For the first time, the number of claimants below pension age began to overtake the number over retirement age. Such claimants made greater demands on these special payments. Secondly, it was due to a 'real change in policy and practice' (Berthoud 1984, p. F16). The SBC used its discretionary powers increasingly flexibly in favour of broad groups of claimants. Guidelines were laid down for staff, according to which some payments became almost automatic. Certain customs and practices arose in the case of lump sum payments. For example, in deciding whether to make payment for clothing, officers were instructed to pay special attention if the claimant had been on benefit for some time (in practice a benchmark of two years was used), if there were dependent children, if there was a serious illness or if hardship would result were a payment not made (Lister 1976, p. 23). Similar guidelines were laid down for household necessities.

> Exceptional needs payments are made for essential items of bedding and, in some circumstances, furniture and household equipment... The items normally regarded as essential are sheets, blankets and pillows; curtains and floor coverings ... ; tables and chairs; beds and mattresses; household appliances such as cookers and gas fires where appropriate. This list is regarded as the normal minimum standard but is not exhaustive. For example, cupboards, wardrobes and kitchen cabinets may be provided if there is no adequate storage space.
>
> (DHSS/SBC 1977, para. 88)

WHO CARRIES THE CAN? RIGHTS VERSUS DISCRETION

Until November 1980, the availability of extra financial help had been determined at the discretion of the NAB and then the SBC. This widespread use of and dependence on discretionary powers provoked a lively debate during the 1960s and 1970s. In 1970, Richard Titmuss, deputy chairman of the SBC, wrote an influential article in favour of some 'element of flexible, individualized justice' (Titmuss 1987, chap. 14). A subsequent chairman, David Donnison, did not share Titmuss's view and, as he revealed in his reminiscences of his time at the SBC, precipitated a reopening of the debate in the 1970s:

> ... to arrest the continuing spread of discretionary benefits and compel everyone to think again, we had to take rather belligerent initiatives: no-one else was going to do it. For a couple of years, with the full support

of the Commission and our senior officials, I wrote articles 'Against Discretion', made speeches about it at every professional conference, and posed these problems pretty starkly in our Annual Report. The angry response of some of the welfare rights people and social workers and my own ripostes to them threatened for a while to focus the whole debate about SB upon a central dilemma. Do you want administrative flexibility, policies shaped by the Commission and its civil servants, and 'creative justice' attuned to the infinite variety of human needs? Or do you want legal precision, policies shaped by Parliament and the lawyers in tribunals and courts, and 'proportional justice' treating broad categories of people in predictable and reasonably consistent ways? Do you want discretion or rights?

(Donnison 1982, p. 93)

Donnison recognized that a degree of administrative discretion did have some advantages in being able to push the system to provide assistance with emerging needs:

Discretion is needed ... to adapt the service promptly to new and unforeseeable developments. Anything important which happens in Britain hits the poor sooner or later... This is discretion used as the flexible leading edge of a public service voyaging through an unpredictable and constantly changing environment... If every link in this chain works well, then discretion becomes not an alternative to rights but the route to a constantly developing pattern of more clearly understood rights.

(Donnison 1982, pp. 94–96)

It was precisely this 'leading edge' which the SBC had used as a lever to meet emerging needs, such as higher fuel costs in the late 1970s.

The SBC put forward a number of arguments to justify this assault by the scheme's administrators on the widespread use of discretion. First, it led to inconsistent decision-making and inequitable treatment of claimants. This could happen most obviously as thousands of officers made individual decisions in response to thousands of individual claims. The result was difference in the treatment of and outcome for different individuals and groups of claimants. The SBC also revealed considerable disparity in the number of payments made by the twelve DHSS regions. For example, in 1977 the number of ENPs as a proportion of the workload ranged between 14.7 per cent and 22.6 per cent. The variations between local offices within regions was even greater. 'The highest local office ratio ... (could) ... be as much as 10 or 11 times that of the office with the lowest ratio' (SBC 1977, p. 111). For example, in Glasgow, local offices awarded clothing grants almost as a matter of course every six months. In other parts of the country, it could be virtually impossible to get such help. The SBC's attempts to standardize the exercise of discretion by its staff at the local level led to another persistent problem facing the scheme, complexity, which arose from the voluminous and detailed guidelines issued by the SBC to its staff. In 1975, about 10,000 pages of new or revised instructions were issued to local offices (Expenditure Committee 1977, vol. II, p. 399).

This disparity of treatment gave rise to the Commission's second objection that a discretionary system led to conflict: between claimants and between claimants and staff. Between claimants because they were aware of real disparities of treatment, and feared many more, and between staff and claimants because staff were seen to be personally responsible for turning down a claim.

The SBC's third objection was that the administration of discretion was 'on the basis that the initiative generally lies with the claimant' (DHSS/SBC 1975, para. 60), with the result that it was those with the greatest knowledge who demanded and benefited most, not those in greatest need. For example, unemployed claimants with children tended to receive fewer lump sum payments than other groups of supplementary allowance recipients, despite sustained evidence to show that they were among the poorest claimants (see DHSS/SBC 1977a).

Fourthly, the SBC argued that the system of extra payments was intended 'to help those who would otherwise fall below the standard of living provided by the supplementary benefit scheme; it is not designed to raise people above it' (DHSS/SBC 1977a, para. 81). However, it was recognized that in using discretionary powers so widely, the real problem – the low level of benefits – was obscured:

> to extend endlessly the range of discretionary benefits ... is ultimately a destructive process because it distracts attention from the adequacy of the basic scale rates and provides justification for keeping them lower than they should be.
>
> (SBC 1977, para. 7.50)

Claimants and many pressure groups also felt strongly about this issue. It was argued that the widespread use of additional payments was a cheap, inequitable and inefficient way of subsidizing inadequate basic benefit levels. Evidence to support this case came from the kind of needs that were being met. Thus, so-called *exceptional* needs payments were made primarily for wholly unexceptional needs such as clothing and footwear; *exceptional* circumstances additions were given most frequently to help with the quite predictable cost of heating.

A further impetus to the SBC's arguments against discretion stemmed from the independent appeals system which was linked to the rapid growth of a welfare rights movement. The appeals system was faced with a growing number of challenges to discretionary decisions. In a discretionary system, that minority of claimants who appealed effectively had another bite of the cherry, with an independent tribunal re-examining their case, quite unfettered by any guidelines or constraints issued by the SBC. This made a mockery of the SBC's attempt to standardize the decision-making process within its offices or to control the amount of money spent. The recommendations of a Committee set up to examine the appeals process threatened to reduce further the SBC's control over the system by moving towards a judicialized system which would set precedents to bind future tribunal decisions (Bell 1975).

The development of the welfare rights movement in the 1970s had an impact on the number of appeals submitted, and also on the demand for extra payments. Donnison recognized the enormous implications of a zealous welfare rights lobby which could increase the demand for additional payments with serious ramifications for both cost and staff workload. In a critical assessment of one of the first take-up campaigns, David Donnison warned that the system simply could not cope with such activity on a wide scale (SBC 1977, p. 115).

> There is a basic contradiction between the concept of entitlement to benefit and the widely ranging use of discretionary powers. Nevertheless, the system was viable for so long as additional payments were exceptional... It must be highly doubtful, however, whether it could continue to be so if pressures for welfare rights on the scale experienced in the Batley ENP campaign were to develop in other areas and on a continuing basis. The administration of the supplementary benefit scheme could not cope with similar pressures throughout the country.

The campaign led by the Batley Community Development Project (CDP), to which Donnison referred, led to half of those seen applying for an ENP, all but one of whom received a payment. That was sufficient justification for the workers involved. However, rightly sensing that the success of such campaigns threatened its attempt to exercise some control and restraint over the system and recognizing the heavy burden which they placed on local offices, the SBC expressed scepticism about the impact of such coordinated activity. It was argued that such campaigns did not necessarily help those most in need of help. Applications were made on the basis of the checklist of items for which a payment could be made. Although payments could only be made where a need was proved to the satisfaction of the SBC guidelines, the SBC was still dubious about the validity of payments being made for items for which claimants had not originally sought help. The SBC argued 'that many staff were rarely confident that they had made the most appropriate decision to suit the circumstances of the case' (SBC 1977,

p. 115). This view, that claims were being made to fit the regulations rather than to meet the individual's actual needs, was to be reiterated when the Conservative government cut back single payment provision in 1986.

STEMMING THE TIDE

The introduction of both supplementary benefit in 1966 and the long-term rate of benefit had been intended, at least in part, to reduce the number of additional payments being made. As the earlier discussion shows, both attempts failed. Bringing and keeping the discretionary system under control was also one of the major concerns of the supplementary benefits review, which was set up by the Labour government in 1975. The review team did not underestimate the difficulty of achieving this goal and were mindful of earlier unsuccessful attempts to find permanent solutions:

> ... (which) offer the best prospect of laying down broad and simple rules centrally in legislation to ensure fair treatment for all, ... without leaving the door open to further pressures for complication and extension of the scheme which would quickly get it back to its present unsatisfactory state.
>
> (DHSS 1978, p. 5)

The review team's recommendations and the subsequent reforms introduced by the incoming Conservative administration in 1980 replaced 'creative' justice with 'proportional' justice. Under the provisions of the Social Security Act 1980, all decisions relating to additional payments were governed by regulations approved by Parliament. This new legal framework inevitably led to a loss of flexibility in the scheme; instead of being geared to the individual circumstances of individual claimants, provision applied to the needs of broad groups of people. As the later discussion shows, such a development inevitably led to an improvement for some, but a loss for others.

Unlike the 1966 reforms, the 1980 changes did not attempt to cut back on the number of weekly payments. The regulations set out the conditions of eligibility and, in many cases, the actual level of payment. Weekly payments were paid automatically to certain groups of people; for example, all claimants with a child under five in the household, and all claimants aged over 75 (reduced in two stages to age 65), received a heating addition. This led to an increase in the number of heating additions, but overall little change in the total number of weekly additions.

The 1980 changes had a significantly greater impact on the system of lump sum payments. Following the introduction of the Social Security Act 1980 the number of single payments fell by one-quarter, from 1,130,000 to 830,000. However, as Berthoud has pointed out, this change was more 'strongly influenced by the substance of the rules than by their legal basis'

(1984, p. F16). The drop in payments was caused not by the change from discretion to regulations but because the regulations were far more restricted than the SBC policy they replaced. The most common expenses for which lump sum payments had been made prior to 1980 were excluded in the new regulations. Most importantly, payments for clothing and footwear, which had accounted for over half the single payments made by the SBC, could only be made in exceptional circumstances and not if the need had arisen, as it did in most cases, through normal 'wear and tear'. The regulations were more significant for the help they did *not* give than the help they did give. The 1980 Act extended claimants' rights, but it offered them less help. This cutback in help with the most common needs led to dissatisfaction among staff. In his study of officers working in the post-1980 SB scheme, Beltram (1984) found that staff disliked the regulated scheme because the needs which could be met under the regulations were not necessarily the most urgent needs faced by claimants.

> There was widespread feeling among DHSS staff and claimants' representatives about the illogicalities in the law on SPs (single payments). They saw little rationality in refusing a payment for a winter coat but giving one for a pair of sheets.
>
> (Beltram 1984, p. 46)

Despite such frustrating, and not infrequent, anomalies, Beltram's study revealed that most staff welcomed the shift from discretion to regulations:

> The fact that a decision can be explained by reference to legal rules, when in the past it would have rested on Commission policy and perhaps on 'officer discretion', should make the claimant more confident that the payment, or refusal of payment, is in accordance with the law and therefore not arbitrary or discriminatory.
>
> (1984, p. 43)

The new regulation-based system met one of the SBC's criticisms of the old scheme, namely that discretion led to conflict between staff and claimants. Under the new system, staff could disassociate themselves from any personal responsibility for their decisions, passing the blame for negative ones on to the regulations. Hence, the appropriateness of the title of CPAG's review of the first year of the reformed SB scheme (based on a commonly held but incorrect interpretation of the rules): *We don't give clothing grants any more* (Allbeson and Smith 1984).

The introduction of regulations did not, as anticipated by the review team and commentators, simplify the system. Indeed, even before the reformed scheme was introduced in 1980, civil servants were saying publicly that, while regulations had many advantages, simplicity was not among them. The goal of simplification was therefore soon seen as being doomed. The new scheme was not easy for either staff or claimants to understand, but it took a High Court Judge to point out that such an outcome had been inevitable.

A high price has to be paid for converting discretion into legal rules: it is the price of complexity. No claimant can hope, unaided, to understand the Regulations.

(Lord Scarman, in Lynes 1981, p. 15)

The Conservative government later used this complexity as one justification for getting rid of extra payments almost entirely.

There are over 500 pages of law of the scheme. The rules on single payments alone run to over 1,000 lines of law: one regulation alone contains 20 separate categories of essential furniture and household equipment even before rules are set on which claimants are eligible for them.

(Cmnd 9518 1985, p. 18)

Despite the complexity, a rule-based system did offer an important advantage to claimants. Even if they found it difficult to get hold of or understand the regulations, gradually the DHSS and advice workers did. It was possible, in many circumstances, to set out clearly who would be eligible for a payment and in what circumstances a payment might be made. For the first time the DHSS was able to publish a leaflet giving information on the availability of single payments. Numerous advice centres produced brief leaflets and application forms for different types of payments. With the assistance of expert advisers, the government's claim that regulations would offer claimants a clearer understanding of their entitlement became a reality.

As the previous discussion and the empirical material presented later in this chapter shows, the introduction of the 1980 scheme was clearly a mixed blessing for claimants. For the Conservative government, the 1980 reforms failed in their central objective of holding down the number of claims. Despite the switch to regulations and the cuts in provision which were made, the number of single payments soon began to rise after the initial sharp fall in the first year. The number of single payments rose from 1.1 million in 1980 to 4.1 million in 1985; this was equal to an increase in the rate per thousand claimants of nearly 2½ times (see Table 6.1).

The initial fall in the number of grants was almost entirely due to the tighter rules governing clothing grants; as Berthoud's analysis of the official statistics over the first year of the scheme showed, the claims for other expenses remained constant. Between 1979 and 1981 clothing grants fell from 11.2 per cent of all payments to 1.5 per cent; grants for bedding and

Table 6.1   Single payments to meet exceptional needs: average amount

	All payments		Payments to		
	Thousands	Average amount £	Pensioners	Unemployed Thousands	Others
1970	560	6.86	181	101	273
1976	1110	21.56	288	362	465
1980	1130	42.90	243	402	483
1981[1]	830	53.83	129	355	345
1982	1150	54.30	300	680	580
1986	4730	78.28	717	2072	1941
1987[2]	2650	77.46	393	1088	1164

1 Following Social Security Act 1980
2 Following changes in regulations 1986

Source: DSS 1989, table 34.97

furniture rose from 3.8 per cent to 4.4 per cent and 6.7 per cent respectively (Berthoud 1984, table F13).

A remarkable feature of the (official) statistics on lump sum grants is the stability of the *pattern* of grants over time and between places, while the total *number* has varied. Apart from the cut in clothes payments between 1980 and 1981, the number of grants going to meet different needs has risen and fallen in parallel with the grand total. And the types of people most and least likely to obtain payments ... also have stayed the same.

(Berthoud 1984, p. H19)

In 1987, the last year of the single payments scheme, unemployed people were nearly twice as likely as pensioners to get a payment. Other claimants (two-thirds of whom are lone parents and one-third sick or disabled) were four times as likely to get one. This was despite the severe cutbacks made in 1986 which concentrated help on people over retirement age and people with disabilities (DSS 1989).

Berthoud also found that the new regulation-based system had not overcome the regional or other inconsistencies in the level of awards made. The PSI study revealed that the disparity in the number of payments made by different offices had reduced only slightly following the reforms and remained wide. It would appear that custom and practice still had a role to play even in a regulation based system. After all, officers still had to exercise judgement and this too can lead to different treatment. Striking differences were found in the payments made in different countries. In Scotland grants were on average £10 higher and in Northern Ireland £25 higher than in England and Wales:

It cannot be shown for certain that an identical request would obtain more generous treatment in one country of the UK than in another, but the evidence is certainly consistent with such a possibility.

(Berthoud 1984, p. E9)

But it was the increase in the overall number of payments which was of greatest concern to the Conservative government. They did not welcome the rise as a victory for the claim set out in the 1979 White Paper, *Reform of the Supplementary Benefits Scheme*, that 'all claimants will reap the benefits of the emphasis on legal entitlement and published rules, and on simplification' (Cmnd 7773 1979, para. 8). In 1985, Tony Newton, then Minister for Social Security, told the House of Commons that the increase was a result of 'misuse and abuse' of the system (SSAC 1987, p. 23). Claimants had not claimed for items such as furniture and household equipment in such large numbers before 1980 and therefore, it was implied, these needs could not be genuine now. It was argued that people were claiming because the grants were there, not necessarily because the need was there. This somewhat more cynical explanation for the growth led, in 1986, to new regulations which were intended both to tighten the conditions for the receipt of single payments and to limit the items for which single payments were allowed (SSAC 1987, p. 23).

In their Annual Report which was published after the 1986 changes, the Social Security Advisory Committee (SSAC) protested that a distinction should be drawn between 'increased use of the system which, whether or not it had been intended by the Government, was perfectly legal, and fraud and abuse of the scheme' (1987, p. 23) and offered a rather different explanation for the increase, which the discussion later in this chapter substantiates.

What information was available to us prompted further questions which we felt required answers. For example, why should the incidence of single payment claims per thousand claimants in one area of Glasgow be four times the rate of some inner city London offices? One possibility which we felt worthy of examination was the suggestion that the regulated scheme had uncovered a reservoir of need which had not been met under the old discretionary scheme.

(SSAC 1987, p. 23)

The August 1986 changes, which led to a sharp reduction in the range of grants available, concentrated help on elderly people or those with a disability and cut back on help for lone parents and unemployed people. These new regulations led to the second largest volume of representations to SSAC on any set of proposals, almost all of which were critical of the government's plans (SSAC 1987). Expenditure on single payments fell from £360 million in the last full year of operation of the single payments system (to April 1986) to £200 million in the year to April 1988 when these payments were abolished. It was this much reduced figure which was later used as a basis for determining the level of expenditure in the government's next phase of its war against extra payments in British social assistance policy: the social fund.

THE SAFETY NET FOR THE SAFETY NET: THE REALITY

The problem of how best to meet claimants' additional needs within a subsistence benefits system has repeatedly reared its head in the policy debate on social assistance. The high profile of this issue has persisted not because of the level of expenditure involved (it is a tiny proportion of even social assistance spending, let alone social security spending, amounting for example to less than one per cent even before the 1986 cuts) but primarily because the administration of such schemes has been judged by officials and government to be out of proportion to the amount of money actually dispensed. The changes to a regulation-based system following the Social Security Act 1980 and introduced in November the same year were the first radical attempt to provide a permanent solution to the problem. The Social Security Act 1986 was still more radical, leaving only the vestiges of a system of extra support to run alongside and in addition to the weekly subsistence benefit.

In examining past provision, there is a danger that the passage of time disguises many of its inadequacies and highlights only its advantages over subsequent schemes. This is particularly true of policy changes in the 1980s when the pressure was to cut public expenditure, including social security spending. As Lister has pointed out: '... there has always been a danger that defence against attack might be interpreted as defence of the status quo as a good thing in itself' (1989a, p. 212). In such circumstances previous provision looks better merely because it was more generous, regardless of any concomitant problems of inequity, complexity and so on. The purpose of this discussion is not to eulogize about the past – it is important not to forget that the early development of the welfare rights movement occurred because of dissatisfaction with earlier provision. Each system has its own set of issues and problems. The purpose of the rest of this chapter is to examine, primarily from the claimants' perspective, whether the various reforms have tackled the problems of their predecessors and, most importantly, made effective provision for the additional, special needs of claimants.

Occasional needs

The first test of whether provision for special needs is adequate is to see how far that provision meets the needs which are being presented by claimants. As the earlier discussion showed, at the same time as the government moved from a discretionary to a regulation-based scheme in 1980, they made significant cuts in the level of provision. It is not surprising then that the studies monitoring the 1980–88 scheme (see Berthoud 1984, Walker 1984) showed that there was a large gap between the declared needs of claimants and the help available from the SB scheme. The gap was particularly evident when comparing those expenses which were supposed to be met by the weekly scale rates (most obviously clothes and fuel) and those which were not. Prior to 1980, the SBC had frequently helped with items supposedly covered by the scale rates, especially clothing and shoes. However, the 1980 regulations precluded giving help for these expenses if, as was usually the case, the need had arisen merely through normal wear and tear. Payments for clothing could only be made in special circumstances, for example, where there had been exceptional weight gain or loss or if an item had been exceptionally damaged. Thus, if a child tore her trousers climbing a tree a payment would not be made; if she tore them falling out of the tree then a payment could be made.

Removing some of the most common needs from the scope of the regulations does not, of course, make the need disappear. Thus, the Leeds study of claimants found that requests for help with adults' clothes and children's clothes featured second and third in the frequency of single payment requests (Walker with Dant 1984). However, payments were made only in one in five cases for the former and in only one case was a grant for children's clothing made. The success rate for other items was much higher: 87 per cent of requests for furniture, which topped the list of requests, were successful; 83 per cent for household furnishings; 78 per cent for essential domestic electrical appliances and baby equipment were successful; and 65 per cent of requests for help with sheets and bedding. The PSI study revealed a similar pattern of refusals: three-quarters of all applications for clothing were turned down, and five out of six requests for children's clothing. This was much higher than for any other single payment request (Berthoud 1984, p. E8). In the light of such results it is not surprising that the pattern of applications began to change and that, as was discussed earlier, officers should feel that the new regulations were not addressing claimants' most pressing needs.

Fuel and clothing were the two items which respondents said gave rise to greatest anxiety and for which little help was available. The exclusion of replacement clothing in all but exceptional circumstances under the 1980 regulations meant that this key area of need could not be met by the single payments regulations. Because of this it was in the area of clothing for children and adults that the greatest disparity was reported between requests for single payments and the help awarded. This only partly reflects the extent to which claimants are actually in need of clothing. Respondents were asked whether they had 'sufficient' clothing. (The definition of 'sufficient' was based on form B0/40, a list of standard items drawn up by the SBC and used as a guide to officers in making discretionary payments under the pre-1980 system.) Among adults, one-third of pensioners, over half the unemployed and sick and disabled respondents, and two-thirds of lone parents, did not have sufficient clothing to meet this minimum standard. This finding is comparable to that of studies of unemployed and sick and disabled claimants conducted in 1974 and 1972 respectively and, therefore, reflects little improvement over the decade (see DHSS/SBC 1977). In addition almost two-thirds of the unemployed respondents with children lacked basic items on the list. One-fifth of the pensioner group, one-third of the sick and disabled, half the unemployed and two-thirds of lone parents said that they, or a member of their family, owned only one pair of shoes. Two-thirds of supplementary allowance respondents and one-third of pensioners said they faced problems because they did not have sufficient clothes. In addition, a significant proportion of respondents said they relied on credit or getting things second-hand for what clothing they did have. Some examples of the kind of claimants' needs reported are listed below:

> Claimant refused clothing after he had come out of hospital. His existing clothing stock had become mildewed while he was in hospital. He eventually got replacements at a jumble sale.

> I need corsets. I get pain in my stomach and it would help give me support ... (I need new clothes). It embarrasses me, my social life suffers, I don't like to go out.

> They told us that the clothing grants were now finished and that we couldn't have them anymore ... we really needed some jumpers and trousers for (son). We had to borrow the money from my father.

The cost of fuel was also a major worry for claimants (see Chapter 4) and yet single payments could not normally be made to help with the cost. Help was provided after a very severe winter but even that proved to be woefully inadequate. Few people actually claimed it, and the amount of help given to the few people who received these grants was regarded as totally inadequate: £10 towards an electricity bill of £90, £19 towards total fuel bills of £170.

It was a pittance they gave me. I don't know how they expect you to find the money for such a large bill.

(lone parent)

In 1987 the government relaxed the regulations when it was found that even the coldest temperatures for 25 years were not sufficient to trigger the system of cold weather payments. A similar situation occurred in the winter of 1990/91, when again the level of help provided for heating was increased following criticism of the plight of many older people and families during the exceptionally cold weather. Severe weather payments are a good example of how provision does not meet need. On both these occasions, more generous payments were made only after extensive press criticism. It is harder to mobilize such pressure to seek improvements in other aspects of inadequate provision, such as clothing, where the impact is less sensational or less seasonal and therefore less newsworthy.

The number of requests which were made for help with fuel bills in the Leeds study did not reflect the difficulty which many people faced. Fifteen per cent of householder respondents had fallen behind with their gas bills since coming on to benefit and 25 per cent had fallen behind with their electricity bills. This had happened even though, as discussed in Chapter 4, many people had tried to avoid the problem of high bills by cutting down on their heating.

This disparity between the level of need and the pattern of claiming disproves the government's justification for cutting back on single payments in 1986 and supports SSAC's supposition that the increase might have been due to the discovery of a reservoir of untapped need (1987). The increase in the number of claims could well have happened because people were becoming aware of, and claiming, their rights.

A second test of whether the system of support for extra need is working is to examine how far people get help with expenses covered by the system. A substantial proportion of respondents in the Leeds survey had bought essential household furniture or furnishings in the twelve months prior to the interview. Approximately, one-quarter had bought a bed, one-third had bought curtains, floor covering, or sheets and bedding, and over half had bought decorating materials. Only a minority of those claimants who had incurred this expenditure had received a single payment to help with the cost. Two-fifths received help with the cost of a bed; roughly one-quarter did so with floor covering and sheets and bedding; just one-tenth got help with curtains and only one-twentieth received help with the cost of decorating materials. People like these, who learnt of their entitlement after 1980, might find themselves among those accused by the Minister of Social Security in

1986 of misusing the system because they were seeking help where they had not sought it before.

It is difficult to be precise on whether those who did not get a single payment were actually entitled to one even under the regulatory system. A small proportion would have been ineligible because they had savings. For the rest, there is a difficulty in assessing whether a 'need' existed in terms of the regulations. In some cases this is obvious, such as for those who had themselves paid for beds and bedding even though they had less than the minimum level set down in the SB regulations. In other cases it is a matter of judgement. All but 6 per cent of those respondents who had purchased floor covering had done so because they did not have any or because they believed what they had was damaged and unsafe. Three out of ten respondents who had bought curtains had done so because they did not have any, a further three out of ten said what they owned were 'shabby'. At what point does badly worn lino become 'unsafe'? At what point are curtains 'shabby' enough to warrant replacement?

The problem of assessing 'need' is illustrated best when considering the state of decoration of claimants' houses. Under the 1980 regulations, the cost of redecoration would only be met if it was 'essential'. In the Leeds study only ten respondents had asked for a single payment to help with decorating costs, even though half the householder respondents said their accommodation was in need of redecoration and almost three-fifths had decorated rooms since the 1980 reforms and while receiving supplementary benefit. This is partly explained by the fact that many respondents were unaware that such help was available. In addition, many respondents said that they did not think they would qualify for help because they would never let their property deteriorate to the point at which a single payment might be made:

> It has to be *really* bad, water pouring in the house; nothing like that here.
>
> (pensioner)

This caused some resentment towards those who did get such help. It was once more a case of those who chose to manage alone, regardless of the sacrifice involved, feeling it was those less thrifty and less independent (and, by implication, less deserving) than themselves who got the most help:

> When you are a good manager you don't get help. It's only when you're a bad manager they help you. Look at my house (clean and tidy), they won't help me ... because I manage I don't get help; because others let their houses get in a state, they get help.
>
> (lone parent)

In the case of items such as decorating expenses, the use of objective criteria alone is not sufficient to establish need. Claimants are likely to spend much more time in their own homes than those who work, or those who can afford to go out more often. The condition of their homes becomes very important to them. Several respondents were almost totally preoccupied with the state of decoration of their homes. One example which stands out most clearly is of the pensioner who had always managed to decorate her living room every year. She was extremely depressed and anxious because she could no longer afford to do so. To an outsider, the room looked presentable but, to her, it was a cause of great distress and embarrassment.

Respondents in the Leeds survey had several complaints. The most obvious was the lack of generosity of the system; the fact that they often could not get help with what they regarded as legitimate expenses. Berthoud found that in most cases refusals were due to a mismatch between what the claimant and what the officer believed was needed.

> The great majority of the refusals appeared to be on the grounds that the article was not needed, one way or another, rather than because the claimant was excluded by the conditions of entitlement in the regulations.
>
> (Berthoud 1984, p. E15)

Among the Leeds respondents, even where grants were made, there were many complaints that they were too small.

> Got £54 for clothes. Not enough. I had to shop around, you couldn't buy them at the price they quoted.

> (Got £50) to buy two skirts, shoes, coat, jumpers ... not enough.

> We didn't buy the curtains. They only gave us £4.80 for the curtains and we couldn't get any for that amount.

Regular expenses

The second type of extra help which was an intrinsic part of social assistance policy until April 1988 was in the form of regular weekly additions. Like lump sum payments, weekly additions were not without problems, but the move from discretion to regulations in 1980 gave some important clues to how such a scheme could be made to work. The regulation-based system did lead to more equitable treatment and ensured that take-up of certain types of additions was high. Those payments which were paid automatically on the basis of clear objective criteria, such as age-related heating additions, appear to have reached most of those eligible (Berthoud 1984; Walker with Dant 1984). However, payments based on an individual assessment of need remained problematic. Thus, in the Leeds study, age-related heating additions went to most (though not all) of those eligible whereas few respondents received an addition on ill-health grounds alone, even though many reported ill health; none seemed to be getting heating additions because their accommodation was hard to heat, even though this was one of the qualifying criteria.

Whether or not a heating addition was being made seemed to make little difference to claimants' use of fuel, or whether they were able to heat all the rooms they used. Over half the respondents in receipt of a heating addition said they sometimes or often went cold in the winter compared to two-thirds of those who did not get this help. Furthermore, supplementary allowance respondents who spent a higher proportion of their weekly income on fuel than pensioners (25 per cent unemployed, 23 per cent sick and disabled, 21 per cent lone parents, 17 per cent pensioners) were less likely to be receiving help with their heating costs.

The relationship between fuel consumption and receipt of a heating addition is weak because, as shown in Chapter 4, the cost of fuel is one of the main financial problems faced by *all* claimants. The majority closely controlled their fuel consumption, and would go cold rather than risk a high bill, regardless of the level of benefit. Receipt of a heating addition was not sufficient to alleviate concern about fuel bills, let alone to induce the confidence necessary to increase consumption. Following the finding of the PSI study (Berthoud 1984) that central heating bills did not necessarily lead to higher fuel bills than other forms of heating, the government abolished central heating additions in August 1986. This was an example of increasing equity between claimants at the expense of justice: more people needed help with the cost of fuel, not less.

Additions to help with the cost of special diets were not free from difficulty and seeming iniquity either. First, in the Leeds study, even those who were receiving an addition found that it did not cover the actual cost of the diet. For example, over one-quarter of those in the sick and disabled category said the cost of their diet was more than the level of the diet addition. There were many people who said that they needed a special diet but who did not get extra financial help. Among these, some had failed to receive an addition even though they had illnesses prescribed in the regulations. Others had been advised to follow special diets by their doctors, but for reasons which were not covered by the regulations. For example, some claimants needed to lose weight, on health grounds, and complained of the expense of fresh fruit and vegetables. Several members of one family suffered from allergies and had to avoid certain foods. A single parent with a hyperactive child had been advised to avoid foods with preservatives and colourings but she could not afford to do so.

Examination of the payment and non-payment of the other twelve additional requirements would no doubt have revealed similar problems. Any system of extra payments is only as good as the level of provision it makes. No system of regulations can cover all circumstances; some needs are bound to be left out no matter how detailed or complex they are. The problems which are experienced arise, first, because even those additions which are made are not given to all those who need them and, secondly, because the pressure on people's incomes is such that even with additions they have difficulty in managing their money. Finally, some needs are excluded by the regulations altogether. These are considered in the next section.

Proscribed needs

Apart from the general tightening of provision with regard to items such as clothing and fuel, the regulations enacted previous SBC policy to exclude certain types of expenses from both the additional requirements and single payments provisions. These exclusions were primarily applied to expenses which local authorities were empowered to meet, regardless of whether or not local provision was actually made. This 'firming of the frontiers' between social assistance and other parts of welfare state provision was begun in the mid-1970s under the chairmanship of David Donnison (SBC 1976). In the first SBC Annual Report, he argued that the SB scheme should not be the catch-all for the failures of other areas of policy.

The Leeds survey found that this policy led to considerable difficulties for many families as they could not get any help, for example with school-related expenses. Half the respondents with children at school said that they incurred regular expenses in connection with their children's schooling. One in ten families paid for their children's school dinners, and in one in twenty families the child took sandwiches or came home for lunch. The main reason for families failing to take up their free meal entitlement was that many schools operated the meals system in such a way that free school dinner children could be easily identified, and the parents did not wish their children to be singled out in this way. This problem has been exacerbated in the 1980s as more schools have gone over to a cafeteria style meal system where free school meals children are given a voucher which enables them to spend up to a specified limit. There is also a growing number of local authorities who offer a meals service only to those entitled to free meals. Both trends mean that poor children are easily identified by their peers.

One-quarter of families with children at school said they paid out for bus fares each week. Free bus passes were issued to some who lived more than three miles away from school. However, bus fares for journeys up to that distance had a considerable impact on the weekly budget, especially where the parent felt the child was too young to travel alone, and therefore had to pay an adult fare as well. Families who wanted their children to go to a school outside their catchment area, perhaps for religious reasons, received no assistance with travel costs. This prevented one family from sending their children to a Roman Catholic school which was some distance from their home. The freedom of poor families to choose a school can, therefore, be limited by the financial implications of that choice. Other smaller expenses included those for cookery or craft lessons, swimming, school trips, school photographs and 'voluntary' donations for charity. For some families the amount of money spent on regular school expenses could be considerable.

SBC practice and the subsequent SB regulations did not allow single payments to be made for school uniform. However, many local authorities do not give school uniform grants either because they do not wish to make this welfare payment or, as in the Leeds case, because school uniforms were not compulsory in their schools. In practice, however, at the time of the survey several secondary schools required dress in a certain colour and some had a full school uniform. This caused both parents and pupils considerable difficulty. One lone parent had found herself in the following predicament after her son had been sent home for not having the correct uniform:

> I rang the council and they said there's no law in the land that can make you wear school uniform. But the teacher sends him home. What am I supposed to do?

Altogether, three-quarters of families with children at school said they were required to provide a regulation uniform or clothes in a set colour. Of these, half had been unable to provide all the items required. In addition to school uniform, four-fifths of parents with children at school said they were expected to provide special clothing or equipment for certain school activities. Less than half managed to do so. Again this trend is exacerbated by the Education Act 1988. Those schools who opt out from local authority control may well decide to adopt school uniform, making it difficult for poor families to send their children there.

RIGHTS ARE GOOD IN PRINCIPLE, BUT IT'S MONEY THAT PAYS THE BILLS

A system of extra payments was an integral part of British social assistance up to 1988. Such payments were seen to be essential alongside the main subsistence-based income maintenance provision, even if, as was shown in Chapter 3, the adherence to subsistence has been pursued more in principle than practice. Extra payments allowed governments and the social assistance administering authorities, the NAB and the SBC, to be seen to be responding to the specific needs of any individual or a group of claimants without incurring the larger cost of increasing the scale rates.

However, this approach was fraught with difficulty. Both the discretionary system which operated up to 1980 and the subsequent regulation-based scheme had to assist so many people that this aspect of administration threatened to undermine the effective administration of the weekly payments system, and the ability to control costs began to wane. In addition, neither system helped *all* those who needed help. The pre-1980 system failed to do so because of the inherent vagaries of a discretionary system discussed earlier. The regulated scheme had several flaws which meant that it did not tackle some of the problems it inherited and introduced some new ones of its own.

There was an obvious gap between the areas of need identified by claimants and those set out in the regulations. Many respondents were caught out by the rule that the SB scheme would not help with any expenses with which local authorities were empowered to assist. In practice, the result was that no one helped. The disjuncture was greatest for those expenses supposed to be covered by the scale rates. The regulations precluded help being given for some obviously essential needs (such as fuel and, in most circumstances, clothes and shoes) while allowing help to be given for less essential items, such as gardening equipment. The absurdity of this situation was not lost either on staff (see Beltram 1984) or claimants. Much as supplementary benefit claimants might like to take a pride in their gardens, and should be enabled to do so, most would no doubt prefer to see their children adequately clothed.

This was an absurdity which was to be turned later to claimants' disadvantage. As claimants and their advisers began to fathom their way around the regulations and applications became more geared to the payments which were available, the number of applications and payments rose. It had been anticipated that the introduction of regulations would finally halt the growth in the number of *ad hoc* and weekly payments which had been a feature of all the pre-1980 social assistance schemes. This did not happen and this perceived 'failure' led the government to repeat the action it had taken in 1980. The area of greatest demand, which up to November 1980 had been clothing and footwear and which by 1986 was furniture and furnishings, was drastically cut back.

The government justified this action on the basis that, despite payments only being made in accordance with discretionary guidance or legal regulations, many of the needs being met should not have been. This argument could only be made because some of the most urgent needs (for example for clothing) were not provided for within the rules (whether legal or discretionary), while some apparently less urgent needs (for example for gardening equipment) were. And yet this situation arose precisely because over the years assistance with the most common and most urgent needs was gradually eliminated. Claimants were in a catch-22 situation. They could not get help with their most urgent needs because those needs were not provided for within the provisions of the social assistance framework; they were criticized for getting help with other 'less urgent' needs precisely because they were 'less urgent' than those for which they could not get help!

The second problem unresolved by the 1980 changes was that many people still did not get the help which was available. Despite improved publicity, many people were unaware that help could be given; others might have been reluctant to apply. The Leeds study showed that many people had bought and paid for items for which a grant might have been available. Given the tightness of individual budgets, claimants could only do this by going without some other essential expenditure.

Payments for both additional requirements and single payments were most likely to be made where there were clear-cut criteria. Thus, most people eligible for heating additions on age grounds received them. It was relatively straightforward to obtain certain single payments, for example for essential furniture. However, payments were least likely to be made where officers were asked to exercise judgement and where individual discretion still had a role to play: for example, in deciding whether a room needs decorating or a room is difficult to heat.

A benefits assessment exercise conducted as part of the PSI study found that nine out of ten claimants who were interviewed by welfare rights advisers were found to have an 'arguable' claim for more benefit (Berthoud 1984, p. D4). (The use of the adjective 'arguable' is interesting. Despite detailed and complex regulations, many decisions still rested on the assessment of need determined by the SB adjudication officer.) A fifth or more of the sample were thought to qualify for more money for laundry expenses, heating, extra baths, regular wear and tear on clothing due to ill health, and a special diet. Among 166 claimants, the welfare rights officers uncovered over 450 potential claims for single payments. Unusually, most of the people who took part in this exercise were awarded more money as a result of the advisers' audit of their benefit (if only social research could always be so financially rewarding for respondents!).

> More than a third had unmet entitlement of weekly allowances. Two-thirds had unmet entitlement to single payments. If these two types of benefit were combined by adding a year's worth of allowances to the value of lump sums, then a quarter of all claimants gained more than £200 from their participation. The total amount actually gained, including back pay on weekly allowances, was well over £28,000 ... £170 each.
>
> (Berthoud 1984, p. D29)

CONCLUSION

As the evidence presented shows, the 1980 changes to the additional payments available in the SB scheme did not solve the problems that had been identified – either by claimants and their representatives or by the government and administration. Many claimants were not getting the help that was available. There was no help for many in need. For the government, the reforms failed to reduce the pressure on the scheme. The failure of these reforms to stem the tide of demand for extra help was inevitable because they failed to address the main problem: that claimants could not manage on basic weekly benefit. Instead the reforms were a first step at 'targeting' though in a rather less structured way than was to come. The introduction of regulations without any increase in weekly benefit meant that they were bound to fail. There was still inequity of treatment between claimants, with wide variation in the rate of payments between offices. The changes did not lead to any simplification of the system and indeed led to a whole new set of complexities and anomalies (see Chapter 1).

Those complexities arose, however, because the government was still committed to providing a back-up to the mainstream social assistance scheme. That commitment was soon to evaporate. The regulation-based system was only five years old when the government announced its plans for still more radical surgery. The Social Security Act 1986 was to offer even less protection for claimants than its predecessor.

7 Another twist of the screw
1988 and beyond

When the Conservative government came to power in 1979 there was no reason to assume that social security would feature high on their political agenda. Only brief mention of social security policy had been made in the 1979 election manifesto and there had been no commitment to radical change. In fact, thanks to the review of supplementary benefits set up by the Labour government in 1975, their first social security legislation was passed within seven months of coming to office. The Social Security Act 1980 made important changes to the structure of supplementary benefit which were broadly in line with the proposals set out in the final report of the review team set up by the Labour government (DHSS 1976). This legislation also contained one of the most significant changes in social security provision to be made in their three terms of office. The first clause of the Act broke the link between the uprating of long-term benefits and the rise in earnings. Since November 1980 benefits have risen only in line with prices and have consequently fallen further behind average incomes (see Chapter 3).

A second Social Security Act was also passed in 1980. This allowed some short-term benefits to be increased by 5 per cent less than the rate of inflation, abolished the Earnings Related Supplement (ERS) and paid lower social assistance rates to the families of strikers. Next came the Social Security Contributions Act 1981 which led to increases in national insurance contributions, and reduced the Treasury supplement to the National Insurance Fund. The Social Security and Housing Benefits Act 1982 established housing benefit. This new scheme gave local authorities the responsibility for paying rent and rates (later poll tax) rebates to SB recipients as well as paying these benefits to other low-income families. The same legislation provided for the creation of the Statutory Sick Pay scheme, which replaced sickness benefit for most people, and transferred administration of benefits to most people off sick from the DHSS to employers. There were many other smaller changes to various aspects of the social security scheme during this first term of office, as well as a number of changes in other policy areas which affected poor people. These included cuts in the availability of free school meals and numerous increases in prescription charges.

Despite what might be regarded with hindsight as almost frenetic activity in this first term of office, Norman Fowler, then Secretary of State for Social Services, announced in 1983 what he later described as 'the most fundamental examination of our social security system since the Second World War' (Cmnd 9517 1985). The Fowler reviews looked at four aspects of social security provision (see Chapter 2), one of which was supplementary benefit. The principles behind the package of reform measures are discussed at greater length in Chapter 1. This chapter looks at how adequately the social assistance changes which were made addressed the problems facing claimants which have been highlighted in this book so far, and the impact they have had on claimants.

THE NEED FOR CHANGE

The proposals emanating from the four reviews were published in June 1985 in a Green Paper, *Reform of Social Security* (Cmnd 9517 1985) and survived virtually intact to be enacted in the Social Security Act 1986. Most of the major changes concerning social assistance came into force in April 1988. The Green Paper set out the three main objectives which underlay the reforms (Cmnd 9517 1985, p. 2). First, 'the social security system must be capable of meeting genuine need'. This was the justification for a greater concentration on means-testing which was referred to as 'targeting resources on those in greatest need'. Any such objective inevitably had serious implications for social assistance policy. The second objective was a 'social security system ... consistent with the Government's overall objectives for the economy'. This led to cuts in the State Earnings Related Pensions Scheme (SERPS) on grounds of cost. Under this heading the Green Paper also echoed an old, if largely disproved concern (see Chapter 2): that the social security system should not 'create barriers to the creation of jobs, to job mobility or to people rejoining the labour force. Clearly such obstacles exist if people believe themselves better off out of work than in work...'. The final objective was a 'social security system (which) must be simpler to understand and easier to administer', an objective sought but not achieved by previous governments or indeed the then government in previous legislation. All these objectives, but especially the first and third, had implications for the role and structure of social assistance.

Despite its claims to be a wide-ranging review of the whole social security system, with the exception of the severe cutback in SERPS and changes in widows' benefits, most of the changes affected the three main means-tested benefits. Housing benefit was cut once again, having already been the subject of several cuts in its short life; family income supplement, the benefit paid to low-income families in work who have children, was replaced by family credit, a new scheme structured slightly differently but fulfilling essentially the same role; and changes were made to social assistance provision. In the Social Security Act 1986 a distinction was made between the two main functions performed by social assistance: the payment of weekly benefit and assistance to help with special, extra need. Income support was introduced in the place of supplementary benefit to undertake the first task; the social fund was created to do the latter. By making this division, the legislation was tackling one of the fears expressed in the past by both the National Assistance Board (NAB) and the Supplementary Benefits Commission (SBC) as well as government ministers: that the pressure created by the demand for *extra* help was jeopardizing the effective operation of the payment of weekly benefit.

INCOME SUPPORT

When the plans to introduce income support were announced, the government did not provide any illustrative figures to show how much money claimants would actually receive. They justified this omission by stressing that their main purpose at the debate stage was to ensure that they had got the structure right. The structure of income support was quite different to that of either supplementary benefit or national assistance.

A means-test calculation has two elements: first a needs assessment and secondly an income assessment. If the former is greater than the latter, then the means-tested benefit is paid; if it is less then the claimant is not eligible. Income support retained the same structure of disregards on the income side of the calculation as had operated under SB, though some of the levels changed. Most importantly, the earnings disregards were increased: people in receipt of the lone parent premium, the disability premium and those who had been receiving benefit continuously for two years were allowed to earn £15; the disregard for other claimants and their partners was increased from £4 to £5. While for many people these disregards were more generous, many lost out because income support does not allow work expenses to be offset against income. Any claimant who incurred work expenses, for example for travel to work or for child care, would be worse off.

Most of the changes in structure were in the needs assessment. The needs element in the supplementary benefit calculation had comprised three elements. First and most important were the various different weekly scale rates set down by Parliament each year: the adult rates differed according to household status and the length of time on benefit (except for unemployed people); the children's rates varied according to age. The second element was to meet housing costs which, after the transfer of responsibility of rent and rates to the housing benefit scheme in 1982, covered mainly mortgage interest payments and water rates. The third element was the fourteen additional requirement payments for special needs, ten of which were related to health needs (see Chapter 6).

The needs assessment for income support (called the applicable amount) also has three component parts but they look quite different. The scale rates were replaced by personal allowances. The children's allowances are still age-related though a change in the age-band structure led to a once and for all increase for some families. The adult allowances for householders and non-householders are the same, despite research evidence discussed earlier in this book which shows that the former face more financial difficulty. The income support personal allowances finally ended the most overt discrimination against unemployed claimants who were ineligible for the higher long-term rate of benefit, regardless of how long they had been claiming. However, they are treated less favourably in other ways. The income support personal allowances vary according to the age of the claimant, and whether the person is part of a couple, a single parent or a single person. The payment of different allowances for single people above or below 25 introduced a new inequity, which affects mainly young, single, unemployed people. The personal allowance for a single claimant over 25 is approximately 25 per cent more than that paid to someone in identical circumstances aged under 25. The government's justification for this discrepancy was not that appetites suddenly increase on the 25th birthday, but that most single people under 25 are living with their families. The Social Security Advisory Committee (SSAC) argued that this proposal did not take 'account of social realities', given the steady trend towards the formation of independent households at younger ages (SSAC 1985, p. 21). Young unemployed people are more likely to be living in a poor household where their parents are able to offer them little financial support, even if they are prepared to do so. In addition, there are many young people under 25 who would wish, or because of family circumstances are forced, to leave the family home. For them the consequences of inadequate benefit can be very severe:

> ... for 16 and 17 year olds, the threat of absolute destitution is now a real one. Any single, childless person under 25 who cannot be entirely self-supporting is likely to find it difficult to manage to live independently because of the 'junior' benefit rate, which applies to both Income Support, and Housing Benefit.
>
> (Roll 1990, p. 63, quoted in Kirk *et al*. 1991)

The introduction of the 'junior' rate of benefit is in addition to a further provision of the 1986 Act which removed the right of 16 and 17 year olds to income support. For those young people for whom, despite government commitments, there is no appropriate Youth Training Scheme (YTS) place, the result is poverty and increasing homelessness (Kirk *et al*. 1991).

Like its predecessor, the income support scheme meets housing costs, primarily mortgage interest relief. During the 1980s the government sought ways of curbing this expenditure as more owner-occupiers came on to benefit. Since January 1987 only half the mortgage interest payment has been paid for people under 60 for the first 16 weeks of a claim. Thereafter it is paid in full for as long as the claimant is receiving benefit. Income support, unlike the supplementary benefits scheme, does not include the actual cost of water rates. Instead the April 1988 personal allowances included an extra £1 per week in compensation. As a result those claimants whose water rates bills were less than £1 were better off; the many more whose bills were more than £1 per week were worse off. The House of Commons Select Committee on Social Services (1989) argued that even those claimants who were entitled to more under the income support rules than under the supplementary benefit rules were often worse off overall because they no longer received the full cost of their water rates and they had to pay 20 per cent towards the cost of their poll tax (previously rates).

The third element in the income support needs calculation is premiums. The fourteen different SB additional requirements payments were replaced by seven premiums: family premium, disabled child premium, lone parent premium, disability and severe disability premium, pensioner and higher pensioner premium. Two further premiums were later added: the enhanced pensioner premium in October 1989 and the carer's premium in October 1990.

The introduction of premiums was the first part of the government's response to the problems concerning the extra payments which had been a constant feature of social assistance provision. Additional requirements allowed individual benefit to be increased in line with special, extra needs. Before 1980, this was done on a strictly individual basis, with the SB officer deciding whether an individual should receive a weekly extra payment or not. After 1980, payments were made on the basis of the broad categories of need laid down in the regulations. Both systems were accused of being too complicated.

Premiums are simple to understand and simple to administer. The qualifying criteria are clearly laid down in the legislation so most claimants are likely to receive the premiums to which they are entitled. (The only premium which has given rise to argument is the severe disability premium. Since its introduction, the qualifying criteria for this premium have been extended to include a wider range of people with severe disabilities.) The replacement of weekly additions by premiums does provide equal treatment within groups of claimants but that does not necessarily mean that these payments provide equitable treatment. The disadvantage of premiums is that they are geared to the average; everyone within a category receives the same regardless of the level of need. This point was made by SSAC in its evidence to the Fowler Supplementary Benefits Review Team (see SSAC 1985, p. 23). Those with fewest needs would have received least under the old system of weekly additions and gained most from a fixed premium. Those with greatest needs would have gained least, and in many cases lost out. Thus, the group that lost most from the shift to a premium-based system were people with severe disabilities with a high level of need who had received high weekly payments for additional requirements. The recipients of other premiums such as the family or lone parent premiums might be expected to have more similar needs but in reality their circumstances can vary widely (see Chapters 4 and 5).

Any payment based on an average will disadvantage some recipients. However, the number of losers will diminish and the number better off will increase if the premiums are set at an adequate level. Commenting on the 1986 Green Paper, SSAC argued that premiums would only be effective if they were set at a high enough level:

> As a general point, the premium system as a whole will need to be seen to be adequate to compensate claimants not merely for the loss of specific additional requirements ..., but also for the harmonization of the long and short-term scale rates. To command acceptability at all, the *relative* premium levels for the different groups will certainly need to be securely founded on evidence about the differential needs of different types of claimant, rather than be seen as an arbitrary award system. In terms of *absolute* levels, if the premiums are too small, the problems of those with high needs currently met individually will dominate and there will be pressures on the Social Fund.
>
> (SSAC 1985, p. 23)

The government did not heed SSAC's warning. Berthoud calculated that the level of family premium introduced in 1986 was insufficient to compensate families with children for the changes in the calculation of income support and the loss of single payments and needed to be twice or even three times higher (Berthoud 1986). Five years later, in 1991, the family premium was still worth only £7.95. In April 1990, the disabled child premium was doubled, reflecting, two years after its introduction, the inadequacy of the original figure.

The introduction of premiums meant that social assistance would be even less flexible to individual need than the regulation-based SB scheme had been. The rules for inclusion within a premium category are inflexible. This is particularly so of the qualifying criteria for the disability premium which, as SSAC pointed out from the outset, 'appear to equate disablement and its needs principally with incapacity for work' (SSAC 1985, para. 3.18). The disability premium is confined to people in receipt of certain benefits, those registered blind, and those who have been incapable of work for over six months. This premium, according to evidence provided to the House of Commons Social Services Committee by the Disability Alliance, misses out 'thousands of people', who might have been receiving any of the ten out of the fourteen additional requirement payments which were available for health-related expenses up to 1988 (Social Services Committee 1989). Thus, people who are seriously ill for up to six months or who need a special diet, no longer get any help. The regulated SB system was criticized because some people could not get help with the cost of certain types of special diet if the medical need did not fall within the rules. This anomaly has now gone but only by ensuring that no one gets any help unless they are sufficiently ill or disabled to get a disability premium. Because such people with health needs would not benefit from the disability premium, Berthoud concluded that, despite the government's stated priority of directing help to those in greatest need, the new system would be no more accurately targeted than the old one (Berthoud 1986, p. 13).

In its review of the operation of the changes implemented in April 1988, the Social Services Committee (1989) concluded that the government was trying to do two contradictory things with income support: target resources more narrowly on those groups identified by the government as being in greatest need, while trying to simplify the range of options for help available. The Committee concluded that 'income support is in many ways too blunt an instrument to do the job that the Government say it is intended to do' (1989, para. 24).

Most importantly, the premium system perpetuates the distinction between the 'deserving' and 'undeserving' poor. The 'deserving', those over retirement age and those with disabilities, receive the highest level of premium, and the 'undeserving', lone parents and the unemployed (for whom there is no premium but who predominate among those receiving the family premium), get the least. For some people, especially young people and childless couples, the premium system offers no compensation for the loss of the higher householder scale rate, making it very difficult for such people to live independently.

THE SOCIAL FUND

The 1986 Act solved the problem of regular weekly payments by abolishing individual payments and putting premiums in their place. This left one remaining problem: how to tackle the issue of so-called 'lumpy' needs – those occasional larger expenses which claimants face. A solution was offered in the form of the social fund. The social fund has two parts: one regulatory and one discretionary. It is the latter which has attracted particular criticism.

The regulatory social fund began operating in April 1987. It provides payments for maternity and funeral expenses and grants for periods of severe cold weather. Entitlement to these three payments is governed by regulations and, therefore, has attracted less criticism than the discretionary part of the fund. Maternity payments are paid to anyone on income support or family credit; funeral payments are paid to people on income support, family credit or housing benefit; and cold weather payments to people on income support only. This part of the social fund is not subject to a cash limit and anyone dissatisfied with a decision has the right to an independent appeal.

It was the discretionary social fund which attracted almost universal criticism. It did nothing to attempt to solve many of the problems that had been identified with previous systems of lump sum payments, such as unequal treatment between claimants, failure to claim, and the mismatch between needs and grants available. The social fund was set up to address only government concerns with cost and administration. The new legislation abolished single payments and urgent needs payments and in their place put community care grants, budgeting loans and crisis loans.

Community care grants are available to people on income support and to those who will be, for example, on discharge from an institution. The law states that these social fund payments must promote community care. Payments are made (i) to help people re-establish themselves in the community following a stay in institutional or residential care; (ii) to help a person or a family member remain in the community rather than entering institutional or residential care; (iii) to ease pressures on a person *and* their family; and (iv) to help a person with travel expenses to visit someone who is ill, to attend a funeral, etc. Though the law sets out these four areas, there is nothing in the *legislation* to stop grants being made for many other expenses which might enable the recipient to live in the community (Lakhani *et al.* 1989, p. 309).

Certain categories of applicants are treated as priority for community care grants. The priority groups are: older people, people with learning difficulties, with physical disabilities or mental health problems, chronically sick people, especially the terminally ill, people who have misused alcohol or drugs, ex-offenders requiring resettlement, 'families under stress', people without a settled way of life and young people leaving care. Although grants can, in law, be made to other people, in practice a payment is more likely if one of the above labels can be attached to an applicant. Thus, in a research project on the social fund conducted by the Social Security Research Consortium (SSRC), a social worker working with people with learning difficulties reported that if parents of an adult with learning difficulties applied for help with, for example, a washing machine to cope with the extra washing caused by their son or daughter's incontinence, they were unlikely to be successful. However, if the application was made in the name of the adult child, then it stood a much greater chance of success. The need and the circumstances were the same, but the label attached to the applicant was crucial.

Probably the most contentious aspect of the social fund was the establishment of a loans system. There are two types of loans: budgeting loans which are intended to cover large items of expenditure for which it is difficult to budget on income support, and crisis loans which cover living expenses for a short period in an emergency or for another urgent need. Budgeting loans are paid for a wide variety of expenses which are accorded high, medium or low priority. High priority needs include essential items of furniture, bedding, fuel meter installation and reconnection charges; medium priority includes non-essential items of furniture and household equipment, redecoration costs, and clothing; and low priority includes rent in advance and leisure items. As these examples show, in theory, loans can be made for anything – a television or a table tennis table! In practice only high priority items are met because limited local office budgets cannot cope with more.

Anyone who receives a loan has no difficulty repaying it, as repayments are deducted direct from benefit; deductions can be made from a wide range of benefits including national insurance benefits. There are three repayment rates depending on the applicants' other commitments: 5, 10 or 15 per cent of the income support applicable amount, less housing costs. The maximum repayment time is 72 weeks, or 104 weeks in exceptional circumstances. This means that repayments can be extremely high. For example, in 1991/92 a couple with two small children whose head is out of work and who have no other income, could pay over £12.21 out of their £81.40 benefit in loan repayments. The maximum loan(s) which a claimant may have is £1,000. For some it might be lower. If an applicant has other commitments and is judged only to be able to afford to pay 5 per cent of the applicable amount in repayments, then the maximum loan is 5 per cent of applicable amount multiplied by 72. Applicants who have very considerable other commitments, most commonly other debts, can be refused a loan on the grounds that they cannot afford to repay it. For them, there is no help whatsoever provided by the social fund.

In the early years of the social fund, there were a number of research and monitoring projects set up to examine the operation and impact of the social fund (see, for example, SSRC 1991; Evason *et al.* 1989; ACOP 1990; Barnardo's 1990; Becker and Silburn 1990; NACAB 1990a; Stewart, Stewart and Walker 1989). The DSS later commissioned its own research on the social fund. This was undertaken by the Social Policy Research Unit

(SPRU) at the University of York (Huby and Dix 1992; Walker *et al*. 1992). All, including the SPRU research, were critical of the fund and found it to be severely wanting as a mechanism for helping with the needs of the poorest people (SSRC 1991). In its Seventh Report, the Social Security Advisory Committee (SSAC) commented that 'on the evidence available to date, there is no reason to withdraw our fundamental objections (to the social fund)' (SSAC 1990, para. 3.2). The consensus of opposition before the introduction of the social fund centred on four issues. First, the fund is cash limited – the first time that any part of the British social security system has not been demand led. Second, most of the fund's budget is allocated in the form of loans; only a third is paid out in grants. Third, all decisions relating to the fund are discretionary and, fourth, there is no independent right of appeal. In the light of these early reservations, the additional criticism, which has been a feature of analysis of the social fund since its introduction – the unpredictability of the decision-making process – was almost inevitable.

The establishment of a cash limit on the amount of help that could be given to the poorest was opposed on principle. The problem of single payments had been that many people could not or did not get the help they needed. The establishment of a cash limit could only mean that still more people would not get help, regardless of the level of need, because there was no money in the budget. When the budget was announced it came under further fire because it was set so low. In the first year the budget was set at £203 million, virtually the same as the cost of single payments in their last year but considerably less than the £360 million spent on single payments before the savage cuts of 1986.[1]

The budget for both loans and grants was underspent in the first year. This was due to a number of factors which only applied at that time. First, the scheme was new so it took time for demand to build up. Second and probably more significantly were the numerous single payments take-up campaigns which had been organized in 1987/88 and which had led to a huge increase in applications, many of which were still being processed after April 1988. Third, the low level of expenditure led Ministers to acknowledge that social fund officers were interpreting the Guidance in the Social Fund Manual too strictly and a circular was sent out to encourage them to use their discretionary powers more generously. To avoid an embarrassing underspend in the first year, towards the end of the financial year there was a 'closing-down sale' to try to spend up to budget (SSRC 1991, p.4). One welfare rights worker reported to the writer that applicants were rung up by social fund officers (SFOs) during the weekend to expedite applications. Such stories may be apocryphal. They certainly illustrate the unusual mood of the time. However, a subsequent increase in demand on the system means that such generosity is unlikely to be seen again.

The government attempted to freeze the budget in the second and third years. However, from December 1989 it became clear that many offices were likely to exceed their budgets. The government's desire to hold the budget fast received a further blow in January 1990 when High Court Rulings on three cases considered under judicial review challenged the priority given to the local office budget. The Court argued that officers' ability to use their discretion was effectively negated by the budget constraints. In September 1990 the Secretary of State responded by issuing new Directions and Guidance to social fund officers on the control and management of local budgets. The new Directions sought to restore the primacy of the budget and introduced new sanctions against SFOs who overspent. By the end of 1989/90, the social fund's second year in operation, the government had been forced to make three extra allocations of money totalling £4.7 million and a total of 200 out of the 450 local offices received part of this extra allocation. Not all of this was new money. Some came from viring money between offices and the rest came from shifting money received from loans repayments into the grants budget. (Money received in loans repayments does not go back into the local office budget. The loans budget is spent only once in any financial year.)

For the third year, 1990/91, the budget was raised to £215 million which represented an increase over two years of approximately 7 per cent per year, less than the rate of inflation. This meant that at the beginning of the third year, some offices were paying out (net) barely one-eighth of the money they had spent on lump sum payments five years earlier (SSRC 1991, p. 9). Not surprisingly, problems soon began to emerge. In August 1991, some London offices reported that they would be making no further grants or loans that month. Within the week, and only one-third into the financial year, the Social Security Minister announced a further £40 million would be put into the social fund, the largest injection of extra cash since its creation. The reason given for this extra money was the 'current temporary trend of rising unemployment' (*Guardian*, 9 August 1991).

Although the budget was underspent in the first year, demand still exceeded supply. Even in that year, when the fund had been under least pressure and eventually only 89 per cent of the budget had been spent, over one-third of applications were refused and this rose to nearly two-fifths in 1989/90. If crisis loans, which have enjoyed a higher success rate of about 90 per cent throughout, are excluded, the refusal rate for all other applications rose from 43 per cent in 1988/89 to 47 per cent in 1989/90. The Social Security Research Consortium (1991, chapter 1) reported that this average concealed even higher figures:

(there were) 'record' refusal rates of between 80 per cent and 90 per cent

... at a number of local offices in November and December 1989 during the period of – to date – greatest budgetary pressure.

(SSRC 1991, chap. 1)

The success rate for crisis loans stands above that for the other two types of payment. The high success rate has been attributed to the suspicion that a large number of applications are turned away informally, without being recorded as a formal application and rejection (Berthoud 1991). It is also due to the type of applications that have been made. For example, in 1989/90 over half the crisis loans awarded were for ordinary daily living expenses. Since 1988 claimants under 60 receive their benefit two weeks in arrears. Many are forced to take out a crisis loan to tide themselves over this period and are consequently in debt to the social fund even before their weekly benefit comes through. When it does, they have to live below the poverty line in order to repay a loan which replaced what previously would have been paid as benefit as of right. As a result of this minor administrative change, crisis loans take up a far larger part of the total loans budget than anticipated (over one-quarter), leaving less money to be paid out in budgeting loans.

The Secretary of State for Social Security's *Annual Report on the Social Fund* (1991) showed that in 1990/91 the refusal rates for grants had increased to 60 per cent and to 44 per cent for budgeting loans. In total 895,000 applications for grants or loans were rejected in 1990/91. In August 1991 the *Guardian* (9 August 1991) reported that leaked guidance to social fund officers in the South Tees social security district showed that grants were being refused to *all* battered wives, drug or alcohol abusers, homeless people, families under 'exceptional' stress and young people leaving care, regardless of individual circumstances.

The main reasons for refusals in the first two years were that the applicant was not on income support (11 per cent in 1988/89; 9 per cent in 1989/90), had not met the qualifying condition of being on income support for six months (31 per cent in 1988/89; 27 per cent in 1989/90), or their application was of 'insufficient priority' (26 per cent in 1988/89 to 32 per cent in 1989/90). This phrase is a euphemism for there being insufficient money in the budget. Thus, one-third of applications were refused – not because the need did not exist – but because there were insufficient funds. Still more disconcerting are the 37,000 applicants (4 per cent of all refusals) who were unable to get help from the social fund because they were deemed to be unable to afford the repayments – they were too poor to get any help from even the safety net of the state safety net. Even this high level of refusals is probably an underestimate of the true rate. The SSRC research found that many people were dissuaded from making an application to the social fund by income support staff. Others withdrew their applications 'not because their needs had suddenly vanished, but because they had made a quite realistic judgement that they could not repay loans on top of other existing commitments' (SSRC 1991, p. 38).

Defending the social fund at a conference organized by *Community Care* and the Social Security Research Consortium in November 1989, Bill Taylor, Head of the DSS Policy Division responsible for the social fund, argued that the system was working because it was keeping within its budget. This statement proved to be dubious on two counts. First, it was only in the first year that the budget held firm. Extra money had to be put in *during* the financial year in both the second and third years of operation. The budget was only contained in the first year because demand was uncharacteristically low and in the second and third years by injections of money in the course of the financial year when it seemed an overspend was likely. Secondly, expenditure was only kept as low as it was because over two million refusals were made (SSRC 1991, p. 9).

The second objection to the social fund was the introduction of the loans principle. The major part of social fund expenditure – 70 per cent each year – is earmarked for loans. The predominant use of loans to help people with urgent needs or to make occasional lump sum expenditures means that before long the loans budget will be virtually self-financed by repayments and will have saved the state £1/4 billion annually, when compared to the cost of the pre-1986 single payments system. This saving by the state has been made possible at the cost of growing indebtedness among the poorest people. By the end of 1990, approximately £100 million was owed to the state by nearly half a million income support claimants – nearly one in six of the total caseload; nearly one in five of those under 60 years of age (SSRC 1991, p. 37).

This increasing indebtedness to the state has occurred at a time when debt is increasingly common among income support claimants (see Chapter 5). A consistent finding of many research projects on the social fund has been the high level of debt held by those people who approached another agency, such as social services departments or advice centres, for financial help. In its study conducted in early 1989, the SSRC (1991) found that in its sample of 1200 cases identified by 23 social services and social work departments in England and Scotland more than half overall, and two-thirds of families with children, were in debt; a similar proportion of people identified in the SSRC's advice centres' monitoring were also in debt. The SPRU research revealed that two-thirds of their survey respondents were making payments from their cash income to cover credit and borrowing (Huby and Dix 1992, p. 28). The average repayment rates for those in receipt of social fund loans were 13.2 per cent of weekly income (before social fund repayments). The unsuitability of loans for poor people was highlighted in the social fund monitoring conducted by the Nottingham Benefits Research Unit:

> This case concerned a couple with children ... recently been turned down for a Crisis Loan from the Social Fund. The Social Worker observed: 'Client already has maximum loan from Social Fund. The amount of repayments have reduced the weekly budget to such an extent that more debts are occurring. Staff are helpful, but regulations stifling'.
>
> (Becker and Silburn 1990, p. 66)

One-third of the social services staff interviewed by the SSRC said they would never advise service users to apply to the social fund for a loan. Their main reservation was that loans were not an appropriate solution to the person's problem but would only serve to increase indebtedness: a perfectly logical conclusion given the prevailing level of debt. Becker and Silburn (1990, p. 67) found similar examples:

> Application was made for a bunk bed so children could sleep in own room, not with parents. Children probably at risk. We were told initially (that) children with problems would get help ... they were offered a loan instead. They were very angry. I then had to telephone and I was told to rewrite a letter in the wording to get a grant, I did so and they were given a grant. Ethically I feel I can *never* recommend a family for a loan when benefit is paid for needs. Any loan in this case would have affected money spent on food. In any case the family were sensible enough to realize they could *not* afford a loan.

The respondents in the SPRU research pointed up some of the advantages of the system, such as the fact that loans were interest-free and the administrative simplicity of repayments, but most only applied for a loan because, usually correctly, they did not think they could get a grant. The inability to repay a loan was the main deterrent from applying. The SPRU research also showed vividly how the social fund was encouraging indebtedness. Sixty per cent of social fund applicants had a previous social fund loan; one-third had more than one previous loan. Seventy per cent of people with social fund loans said they did not have enough money to live on (Huby and Dix 1992, p. 125).

The third objection to the social fund stemmed from the shift from a rights-based to a discretionary system. In its 1979 White Paper on the *Reform of the Supplementary Benefits Scheme* (Cmnd 7773 1979) the Conservative government had been keen to promote claimants' rights, even at the expense of reductions in benefit for some. By 1985, the government was arguing that while the regulatory framework introduced in 1980 had worked well for weekly additions, it had proved too complicated for occasional lump sum expenses. The arguments put forward in favour of discretion were presented positively but with no apparent recognition of the problems which had led to the abolition of many discretionary powers and decisions in 1980.

(The social fund) will be better able to respond to individual needs as they arise. This does not mean there will be no guidelines or that decisions will be capricious. But it does mean that decisions will not be constrained by a very detailed framework of rules and precedents .... decisions will be made locally by specialist officers with the minimum of formality.

(Cmnd 9517 1985)

The SPRU research found that in practice the degree to which social fund officers could exercise their discretion was severely curtailed by local office practice and especially the budget. 'The presumed and actual impact of local budgets is critical in helping shape the interpretation of definitional categories such as "exceptional stress" or "risk of entering care" ' (Huby and Dix 1992, p. 127). In addition, the discretionary social fund has given rise to the same kind of iniquities which were a feature of the discretionary systems operated by the SBC and the NAB, plus some new ones. First, social fund spending varies between different regions and offices. Therefore, success can still depend on *where* the applicant lives. For example, in the first three months of the scheme, some offices in the same region had spent eight times more of their grants budgets than others (SSRC 1991, chapter 1). Craig reported for the SSRC that by the end of the second year, one office in Sheffield had overspent its loans budget by £1,121, while the neighbouring office still had £41,000 in hand (16 per cent of its loans budget). Similarly, in Barnsley, one office spent all but £32 of its grants budget, whereas its neighbour was left with £35,000 (24 per cent) of its grants allocation. Craig (SSRC 1991, p. 12) has shown similar disparity between regions, not all of which could be explained by differing levels of need:

expenditure between regions reflected many of the patterns familiar from the old ENP... and single payments ... regimes. Thus the NE and Scottish regions tended to 'overspend' (that is, demand exceeded supply of cash)... The SE of England, covered by the two London regions, were persistent 'underspenders', a fact which enabled the overall expenditure to be held more or less in balance as budgetary pressures developed.

As well as varying according to area, spending also varies during the course of a financial year. In order to manage its annual allocation, each office draws up a monthly profile of expenditure for both loans and grants. These monthly allocations are not recognized in law or by the Social Fund Inspectorate (SFI) and offices vary in how strictly they adhere to them. Some operate them quite stringently, others have been prepared to overspend some months in anticipation of making savings in later months. Analysis for the SSRC found that 'Clearly, it did matter *when* an applicant sought cash help from the social fund' (1991, p.3). If an applicant gets the timing wrong, then it is not possible to make another application for the same item for six months.

The profile of recipients of social fund payments very much resembles that of people getting lump sum payments before and after 1980 and does not necessarily correlate to different levels of need. Lone parents are considerably over-represented relative to their proportion of the income support caseload, receiving 32 per cent of loans and 37 per cent of grants in 1989/90. Pensioners are considerably under-represented, receiving in 1989/90 26 per cent of grants and just 3 per cent of loans. The SSRC monitoring revealed that the greatest reluctance to take out a loan was among people over retirement age. The social fund offers very little help, therefore, to this group of people who have always been reluctant to claim the extra help which social assistance has offered in the past. As under national assistance and supplementary benefit, unemployed people are under-represented in the social fund payments received, despite the accepted evidence that they include many of the poorest claimants. The SPRU research found that grants were more likely to be paid to owner-occupiers, people with an advocate and those on higher incomes. By contrast, loans were likely to be given to younger applicants, to those without severe health problems, those living in overcrowded accommodation and, most ironically of all, to those on lower equivalent incomes (Huby and Dix 1992, p. 125).

One of the criticisms that was made of the discretionary SB scheme was that success was as much dependent on the arguments put forward to support the claim as on the level of need. This argument is even sharper in relation to the discretionary social fund, as the cash limit means that one person's success inevitably means someone else's failure. Thus, as happened with supplementary benefit, an applicant who is able to understand the official criteria governing payments and to muster good arguments in writing and verbally, or an applicant who has an advocate who can do this on his or her behalf, will have a much greater prospect of success. The SSRC monitoring found that the success rate for the applicants supported by social workers in the study was higher than the national success rate (SSRC 1991).

Applicants who have little or no English are particularly disadvantaged when applying to the social fund. First, they are confronted with a 14-page application form. Secondly, they would have more difficulty in mustering the appropriate arguments necessary to get a discretionary decision in their favour either in writing or at the interview with the SFO which constitutes the first step in the review process. The National Association of Citizen's Advice Bureaux (NACAB 1990b, para. 7.14) has reported some examples where the lack of knowledge of English clearly worked to applicants' disadvantage:

> A CAB in North London reports the case of a refugee applicant whose husband was in prison in Somalia and who spoke no English. She was refused a community care grant for a pushchair for her disabled child because the applicant could not present a case as to the health and safety of the family being affected.

> A CAB in Derbyshire reports that an Asian family who did not speak English were referred to the bureau by the DSS after an interview about a social fund application. This meant their application was delayed while they obtained help about what information was relevant in their application for starting up a new home.

Such disadvantage is unlikely to be put right at the review stage as local offices are not under an obligation to provide an interpreter and in most cases it is up to the applicant to make provision.

> If the claimant gets as far in the review procedure as the interview at the local office, the onus will be on the client to bring an interpreter. If the person attends alone, CABx report that a cross is marked against the applicable box on Form SF600 for the claimant to sign, no other details are recorded and the review interview is over. A client of a CAB in North London did not even know she had attended a review interview.
>
> (NACAB 1991)

In their study of Social Services Departments, Becker and Silburn (1990, p. 58) found that 'there was little evidence to suggest that the refusal rate for those who had made an application to the Social Fund was differentiated by ethnic origin': 56 per cent of black applicants were unsuccessful compared to 51 per cent of white applicants. NACAB suggests that they might have reached a different conclusion had they looked at the results in relation to whether or not the applicant spoke or wrote English and also if they had looked at the situation of asylum seekers/refugees who in the NACAB survey had suffered worse treatment than others (NACAB 1991, p. 62). It is also important to note when considering the Becker and Silburn finding that this does not show the number of people who did not make a claim. As discussed earlier, many people are discouraged by the DSS from making an application to the social fund, others are unwilling to make an application and others do not claim because they are unaware that any help is available. It is likely that black people will be over-represented in all of these categories. Black claimants are subject both to formal discrimination when claiming benefits, for example by being asked to show passports (NACAB 1991; Gordon and

Newnham 1985), and to informal discrimination by DSS staff (Cooper 1985), which may result in either their not being told of the help available or being told that it is not appropriate in their circumstances. The danger that discretion could be used to disguise discrimination has been raised by Gordon and Newnham (1985):

> The extensive discretion afforded to staff can mean that staff who are so minded can demand from black claimants documentation in support of a claim which would not be asked from a white claimant. Those who have encountered such behaviour, whether they are claimants or advisers, know only too well that there is little that can be done by way of redress and certainly little that can be done to ensure that a payment is made speedily.

There is even greater risk of abuse with discretion in the social fund because there is no independent right of appeal. Even if there is no discrimination, which given the evidence is unlikely, if black applicants *believe* they receive unfair treatment, then it will deter them from applying.

'The positive side of discretion is *flexibility*... The negative is *inconsistency*' (Berthoud 1991, p. 9). While in the same article Berthoud reported a senior official as saying that 'consistency is not one of the objectives of the social fund', any system which is based on the principle of prioritizing need should, all things being equal, offer similar help in similar circumstances. This does not happen. The unpredictability of the discretionary social fund was one of the main criticisms made by social services staff interviewed for the SSRC research (1991, p. 30). The discretionary decision-making process, together with the cash limit, means that it is impossible to advise applicants on the likelihood of success.

> In the past I knew what I could achieve, now I am just relying on pot luck which is rather sad.

> I am confused by the system. There doesn't seem to be any correlation between what one is supposed to be able to apply for and what one is actually able to get when a client applies.

This unpredictability and the high failure rate led many social workers and others in the SSRC study to look for alternative sources of help (1991, p. 30). Over one-third of those interviewed said that they were using statutory powers more frequently to provide financial help to people. One-half were using charities more often and one in five were encouraging people to explore informal sources of help from family or friends. When asked what action they would take after the refusal of a social fund application, nearly one-fifth said they would approach a charity, only slightly lower than the number who would take the 'correct' route of applying for a review. It was felt in many cases that they would stand a better chance of getting help or at least of getting it more quickly through unofficial channels.

> Access to charities much easier, speedier response and more likely to be successful.

> Section 1 money is quicker and a local charity sometimes helps with debts.

> The state doesn't give much assistance any more; it's quicker and easier to use other sources.

> (SSRC 1991, p. 30)

The fourth major criticism of the social fund concerned the removal of the right to an independent appeal. The abolition of appeal rights was crucial to the successful operation of a cash limited system. When the discretionary supplementary benefits system was in place, the SBC found that their attempts to standardize the circumstances in which discretionary payments could be made were continually sent off track by the individual decisions of appeal tribunals. An independent appeals system would have posed an even greater threat to a cash limited system and probably made it unworkable. However, the absence of an independent appeals system means that an important check on the possible inappropriate use or misuse of discretion by officers is lost.

Instead of an independent appeal, applicants may seek a review of a decision. The review process is very cumbersome. First, the application is re-examined by the SFO who made the decision and the applicant is invited to an interview. If the decision is unchanged then the case is looked at by a senior member of staff in the local office. Only after these two stages have been completed is the case referred outside the local office for independent review by the Social Fund Inspectorate (SFI). The Social Fund Commissioner has gone to great lengths to establish her and the Inspectorate's independence from the DSS and has made attempts to bring in some non-DSS staff to the Inspectorate. The SFI receives all the papers relating to the case and sends copies to the applicant. This welcome innovation, which caused not inconsiderable consternation in local offices, offers applicants the first opportunity to see the full reasoning behind a decision. The SFI investigation is purely a paper exercise and therefore it presents difficulties for people who are less able to make a case in writing.

In the first year, few cases were sent to the SFI for review and the SFI generally sent back decisions to the office for further consideration. Since then pressure has begun to build up, and the SFIs have shown a greater willingness to substitute their own decisions for those of the local SFO. In doing so they have been more inclined to exercise discretion in applicants' favour. As the system develops under increasing pressure it will be interesting to see the outcome of this for, although the SFI is aware of budget constraints, its officers are not subject to the day-to-day pressure of having responsibility for remaining within a local office budget. Some local offices have already reported that a sizeable proportion of their monthly budget is being committed by the SFI.

As the discussion so far shows the social fund has led to a number of new problems for social assistance claimants. It is particularly unfortunate, therefore, that it did not solve any of the old problems faced by claimants before 1988. The income support rates did not provide for the loss of extra help provided by single payments so the continued low level of weekly benefit means that the need and demand for additional help remains. The SPRU research found that 87 per cent of their sample who had applied to the social fund in the summer of 1990 had felt really anxious at some time during that year because they did not have the money to meet an essential expense. Needs most frequently mentioned were clothing, household goods and furniture, fuel costs, food and community charge payments (Huby and Dix 1992, p. 125). The SSRC (1991) found that in one-fifth of the cases included in their sample people were seeking help with basic living costs, such as food and fuel. In most cases, help was sought with items, such as furniture and household equipment, which would previously have been met under the single payments regulations. They were, therefore, seeking discretionary help, which, if paid at all, would probably be paid as a loan, help which previously would have been available as of right. Many people get no help either because there is insufficient money in the budget or because they cannot afford the repayments. Consequently, the various monitoring exercises on the social fund have found that people have very great difficulty in meeting any additional expenses which occur.

> There are a tremendous number of people for whom, when a large item wears out, they have no recourse – no way of replacing things at all.
>
> (SSRC 1991, p. 23)

The social fund has further exacerbated the major problem of unmet need. First, even where a payment is made, it may not be sufficient to meet the need. Over half the awards made to people interviewed in the SPRU research were lower than the amounts requested. Seventeen per cent of recipients had had to supplement their awards with money from other sources (Huby and Dix 1992, p. 125). Second, the Directions, which have the force of law, exclude help with a wider range of items than had been in force under the single payment regulations. In addition to the exclusion of help for most services which a local authority is empowered to provide (regardless of whether they are actually provided) and help with any education or training expenses, help can no longer be given for work-related expenses, such as travelling expenses to attend work interviews. In addition, community care grants cannot be made for the cost of any fuel or standing charges or any housing costs. Budgeting loans cannot be made for the cost of mains fuel or standing charges, or most housing costs, including deposits to secure accommodation. In general, help cannot be provided with any of the main debts which claimants have: housing costs or fuel charges and, increasingly since the 1988 changes, the poll tax and water charges. It is hardly surprising that eight out of ten agency workers interviewed for the SSRC study felt that the introduction of the social fund had made it more difficult for them to help people with their financial problems compared with only 6 per cent who thought it had made it easier.

CONCLUSION

In the 1990s the social assistance scheme will, after many delays and false starts, be fully computerized. This has been achieved because the reforms in the Social Security Act 1986 were designed to create a structure which would conform to the inflexibility of a machine. This could only be done by disregarding the diversity of needs of social assistance recipients. The advantage to claimants is a weekly benefits system which is easy to understand. Claimants should be more likely to get their full entitlement, though the income support error rate is still a cause for concern. The disadvantage is that income support is inflexible to individual need. People may be more likely to receive all they are entitled to, but many people are entitled to less than they would have been under supplementary benefit. The structure of the personal allowances and the premiums are neither adequately honed to meet the needs of even those groups picked out for help, nor are they sufficient to offer claimants a decent standard of living (see Chapter 5).

The low level of income support means that there are still demands from claimants for more help. The pressure thus created will not jeopardize the running of the main income support system, as it is administered quite separately, but only three years after the introduction of the discretionary social fund it was bending under immense pressure. A cash limit can control output, it cannot control the number of applications which are made and have to be processed. The DSS had to make available the equivalent of 1,615 extra social fund staff (4 per cent per office) to cope with the anticipated demand in 1990/91 (SSRC 1991, p. 12) Approximately one-third of social fund expenditure goes on administration. The discretionary social fund is failing claimants (people on income support), it is also failing applicants (those who apply to the fund). It does not provide any real solution to the financial difficulties of income support claimants. Grants are hard to get, restricted, because of the budget, to high priority needs and groups and complicated to claim. Loans offer no solution to people on poverty line incomes, many of whom are already in debt.

The government's own research on the social fund, like independent work published earlier which the government chose to ignore pending the result of its own investigation, showed serious shortcomings in the working of the social fund. The authors found that:

> ... we cannot show that those who got awards were in greater need than those who did not; nor can we conclude that the social fund is meeting its objective 'to concentrate attention and help on those applicants facing greatest difficulties in managing their income'.
>
> (Cm 1580 1991) (Huby and Dix 1992, p. 127)

The social fund is also failing the government. The introduction of the cash limit has, as planned, drastically reduced expenditure on urgent or 'lumpy' needs. In this respect it has proved to be an effective tool of financial management as SFOs are forced to reject many claims in order to meet their financial targets. However, neither the cash limit nor the inherent disincentive of loans has prevented the new system from being put under intense pressure. After only three years, leaks have appeared in the dam. On several occasions the government has had to inject further money into the social fund to prevent local office budgets running out. Not even a government which, in theory, was prepared to close the doors on some of the most vulnerable people in society has, yet, been able to bring itself to let it happen too obviously in practice. Individual refusals to help people who cannot afford repayments can be hidden; a decision by a local office to cease all payments cannot.

Only three years after the introduction of the discretionary social fund, it is showing the same signs of failure which beset the supplementary benefits discretionary payments scheme. More and more staff will be needed to process a growing number of applications. Though no more people will be helped, it is just as time-consuming, probably more so, to process a negative decision as to process a positive one. This will no doubt lead to demands to simplify administration and cut back on social fund provision. *Déjà vu*! Should this happen yet again, it will be because once more a government refused to tackle the real problem of British social assistance. As long as weekly benefits are too low, any system of extra help cannot work.

NOTE

1   The subsequent discussion is based on an analysis of the national summary sheets

and local office data published monthly by the DSS, from parliamentary answers and from other Government published material, including the first two Annual Reports of the Secretary of State for Social Security (1988/89 and 1989/90), conducted by Gary Craig and published in SSRC 1991.

8 Retaining dignity in adversity
Being a claimant

The adequacy of the standard of living of claimants is obviously primarily dependent upon them receiving financial support at a level which is sufficient to meet their needs. In the previous chapters it has been argued that British social assistance schemes have failed to do this for the majority of recipients either in the weekly benefit rates or in the provision for 'lumpy' needs. This chapter examines another, less tangible, aspect of claimants' well-being, their status within society. This is a function of how users are treated by the social security system, how they are perceived by those administering the system, and by the general public, and how they view themselves.

There has always been a conflict at the heart of the state's attitude towards the alleviation of poverty: put simply the conflict is between the state's caring role and its control function. Consequently, at the same time as the administration of social security has responsibility for meeting need, it also operates controls and sanctions designed to deter and root out the dishonest and the 'undeserving'. Each government determines which of these two roles should take precedence and what the *main* objective of the social security system should be: to pay benefits to those who are entitled to them, or *not* to pay benefits to those who are not entitled, and, more contentiously, to those who do not deserve them. The answer to this question is central to the development and structure of any social security system. Which function is paramount at any particular point in time will determine both how much is paid in benefits and the character of the benefits' administration. Over-zealousness in one sphere will have ramifications in the other. This chapter considers how, in the means-tested sector, the emphasis on controlling claimants' behaviour inevitably has affected the ability of social assistance to achieve its goal of meeting basic need. It also considers why the control function has become pre-eminent and the impact this has had on both users and potential users of the service.

IRRECONCILABLE GOALS

Welfare state services have rightly been criticized by those on the right and the left of the political spectrum, though for different reasons, for failing to put the needs and demands of users to the fore. That criticism is particularly true of the two main 'pro-poor' services (Le Grand 1982) of social security and the personal social services. In many respects changes in social security and social assistance in particular have been implemented *despite* their impact on users (Walker 1987). Moves to redress this imbalance in the late 1980s and 1990s have tended to concentrate on user participation in universal services such as education and health, though social security has been included briefly within the Conservative government's proposals for a Citizen's Charter (DSS 1991). Participation can only be possible if providers and users of services have a degree of respect for each other. The terms on which social security has been debated and administered in the post-war period have engendered a degree of scepticism, and even hostility, on each side of the counter that is particularly difficult to break down.

The debate on social security throughout its modern history has shown distinct signs of schizophrenia. On the one hand, governments wish to show their compassionate, caring side by persistently maintaining that benefits are adequate; on the other hand they wish to show that they are 'responsible' and financially prudent by making frequent pronouncements against those who, because of alleged fecklessness, laziness or dishonesty, should not receive state support. While few would argue with the principle that social security payments should go only to those who are legally eligible, many find the justification (made by Labour and Conservative governments alike) that crackdowns on fraud and abuse create 'an atmosphere ... in which "honest" people will feel more able to claim' unconvincing (see Smith 1985, p. 113). More realistic is the assumption that 'myths about widespread fraud deter people from applying for benefits, because all claimants are tarred with the same brush and the stigma of claiming is intensified' (Smith 1985, p. 113). The stigma, which the concentration on the dishonesty of claimants creates and reinforces, affects both those already in receipt of benefit and potential claimants.

Because of the dual functions they perform, British social assistance schemes have always had an 'image' problem. With the exception of income support in 1988, the major changes in British social assistance have resulted at least in part from a desire to improve the image of the state safety net. The obvious failure of what were mainly cosmetic changes stemmed from the inherent flaw in any means-tested system, stigma, and the policy of putting the need to control claimants' behaviour over the duty to meet need. The introduction of national assistance in 1948 was hailed as 'a major break-

through: the end of a whole period of social history' (Fulbrook 1978, p. 177).
Bessie Braddock echoed the sentiments of many, when, in the debate on the
National Assistance Bill, she said 'I think of what we are repealing more than
of what we are proposing' (quoted in Titmuss 1969, p. 155). However, the
new system deliberately incorporated many elements which guaranteed that
social assistance should be perceived as inferior to social insurance. In his
report, Beveridge (1942, para. 369) had argued the importance of this
inequality:

> Assistance ... must be felt to be something less desirable than insurance
> benefit; otherwise the insured persons get nothing for their contributions.
> Assistance therefore will be given always subject to proof of needs
> and examination of means; it will be subject also to any conditions as
> to behaviour which may seem likely to hasten restoration of earning
> capacity.

It is not surprising, as Hall and her colleagues subsequently pointed out, that
national assistance, like its predecessor, was also tarred with the brush of
stigma:

> In just four years the note had changed from one of self congratulation to
> one of concern with the image of national assistance ... it reflects the
> beginning of a gradual increase in the degree and specificity of the
> disenchantment with which members of the Labour party viewed national
> assistance.
>
> (Hall *et al.* 1975, p. 142)

As a result, history repeated itself and, in 1966, the Labour government
introduced a new social assistance scheme with a new name and, it hoped, a
new image. The new scheme was a poor substitute for more ambitious plans
drawn up in Opposition to reduce dependence on means-tested social
assistance. In government the aim was merely to make the means test more
attractive. Like national assistance, the new system, supplementary benefit,
was presented as a fresh start, distinct from the problems of its predecessor.
As with national assistance, the attempt failed.

The reforms introduced in the Social Security Act 1980 continued the
move that had begun with the introduction of supplementary benefit in 1966
towards a more rights-based approach. It was presented by government as a
way of enabling claimants better to understand and claim their rights; a gain
that the Conservative government argued justified the cash losses suffered
by many thousands of people (Cmnd 7773 1979). However, when claimants
took up those rights and increased demand, especially on the single payments
system, it proved to be a Pyrrhic victory. The government attributed the
increase to claimants' misuse of the system, although they had no firm

evidence to substantiate this beyond the increase in claims (see Chapter 7). The response to what might have been regarded as a policy 'success' was to make extensive cutbacks in single payments in 1986 before finally abolishing additional payments in 1988 (see Chapter 7). A further justification for the switch from discretion to rights was that the establishment of clear rules of eligibility would remove much of the conflict in the scheme, which had long been attributed to a discretionary system (SBC 1977). Beltram (1984) concluded from his study of the post-1980 scheme that staff generally welcomed being able to put the regulations between themselves and the claimants. The introduction of income support in 1988 differed from previous social assistance reincarnations. This reform was not trying to address the image problem of the existing scheme or indeed trying to make the scheme more acceptable to claimants. The driving forces were purely administrative and financial.

Ultimately, none of the attempts to give social assistance a face-lift were successful; the old negative image kept re-emerging because, as the National Consumer Council warned over 15 years ago (1976, p. 7):

> Improved publicity, however excellent, cannot over any length of time sell a poor product, and so it is with means-tested benefits.

The link between means-testing and stigma is unbreakable. The consequences are devastating both for the service and for service users, a point which Miller (in Titmuss 1987, p. 1) selects as being one of Titmuss's key messages from the 1960s onwards.

> Stigma threatens the person stigmatized, the programme, and the society which condones stigmatization. The stigmatized person experiences the fact of being separated from the rest of society, of being treated as someone different, marginalized, as less than others, as not worthy of the everyday exchanges and transactions that make up the community... 'If people are treated as burdens', Titmuss declared, 'they will behave as burdens'. He could have added that if they are treated as untrustworthy, subject to harsh checks of their eligibility, they will often fulfil that prediction.

In addition to the deterrent presented by the application of a means test itself, controls have been used to deter both claimants and claims. Most time and energy has been expended against the unemployed from the wage stop in the 1970s to the availability of work tests and restart interviews introduced in the 1980s (see Chapter 2). Periodically lone parents have also been subjected to various pressures, either by the fierce application of the cohabitation rule or, first by exhortation and later by law, to name the father of their children (Cm 1264 1990).

BLAMING THE POOR

The history of social security has been chequered with outbursts of hostility towards benefit recipients. These have shown themselves in sensational headlines in the popular press and administrative campaigns to clamp down on alleged abuse. In the 1920s over three million claimants were refused benefit on the grounds that they were not genuinely seeking work, though there was little evidence to show that such work existed (Deacon 1976). The late 1960s and early 1970s saw the issue of fraud and abuse within the social security system coming on to the public agenda more frequently. Each time such a campaign gained momentum, the government of the day showed its concern by introducing measures to crack down on possible abuse or misuse of the system, regardless of the actual evidence which existed. The introduction of the four-week rule and the cohabitation rule in 1968 followed a welfare backlash. Newspapers and politicians painted emotive pictures of '... genuine old-age pensioners reduced to tears by pushful young men elbowing them to one side, some with bulging wallets' (Gresham Cooke MP, *Hansard*, vol. 586, col. 914, 20.10.69).

The next wave of concern, which arrived in the early 1970s, led Sir Keith Joseph, the Secretary of State for Social Services, to set up a Committee on *Abuse of Social Security Benefits* (1973). Under its Chairman, Sir Henry Fisher, the Committee was asked to 'review the measures taken by the DHSS and the Department of Employment to prevent and detect abuse through wrongful claims to social security benefits' and 'to recommend any necessary changes'. This Committee, whose approach was not on the whole sympathetic to claimants, concluded that the amount of abuse was very small as a percentage of total expenditure on benefits but still serious because 'substantial sums of money are misappropriated each year' (Cmnd 5228 1973, p. 5).

One of the most virulent outbreaks of 'scroungerphobia' (Deacon 1978) occurred in 1976. Newspaper headline writers were attracted by the claims of Ian Sproat, Conservative MP, that 20 per cent of supplementary benefits claims were fraudulent and that 50 per cent of those registered as unemployed could find jobs if they wanted. Though these claims were later to be discredited, they undoubtedly contributed to the general hostile environment in which the Labour government set up a Departmental Co-ordinating Committee on Abuse in 1976.

Much of the criticism made of the social security scheme in the press in 1976 was concerned not only with fraud and abuse but also with the level of benefits and their administration. Golding and Middleton (1982) found that the most explicit theme in the media during this period was the generosity and inefficiency of the welfare apparatus. In the month that the review of the supplementary benefits scheme was announced the *Daily Express* (30 September 1976) carried the headline 'Social Security ... the giant that's gone out of control' and the *Daily Mirror* (17 September 1976) declared that welfare is 'so complicated that the system can no longer be policed'.

In 1976 the Labour government imposed a third year of pay restraint, tax thresholds were falling and, in return for help from the International Monetary Fund, significant cuts were made in public expenditure. However, while those in work were subject to a strict wages policy, social security payments increased in line with inflation. For some claimants this amounted to more than the £6 per week pay limit. The fall in the standard of living felt by many workers provided fertile ground for the popular press to wage its anti-claimant campaigns. This backlash against welfare recipients was one of the reasons put forward by the Labour government for the establishment of the first SB review.

Most post-war governments have highlighted the issue of fraud and abuse in response to criticism, which has usually come from the press. However, in 1980 the government itself took the lead in creating anti-claimant sentiment. When strikes took place in local offices in protest at the lack of staff to undertake everyday benefit administration, the DHSS was allowed to recruit over 1,000 additional staff to intensify the crackdown on fraud. That year also saw the introduction of Specialist Claims Control teams in some regional offices and in 1983 came the establishment of Regional Benefit Investigation Teams (RBITs). Both these initiatives were in addition to existing local office fraud staff. They were, however, much more proactive in seeking out abuse by, for example, trawling the case papers of so-called 'risky groups' such as unemployed people and lone parents. In addition to the introduction of increased and proactive policing methods, the public standing of claimants was undermined by other strategies in the 1980s. First there was the assertion that the poor were not really poor and second that some claimants should be supported not by the state but by their families (young people) or their absent parents (children in lone parent families). There were also a number of changes in the administration of benefit, particularly to the unemployed, to tighten up control procedures.

The attack against social security claimants, and social assistance claimants in particular, in the 1980s went beyond endorsing and talking up old familar accusations of fraud and abuse. New forms of criticism emerged and a new vocabulary grew up, including: 'the why-work syndrome', the 'dependency culture', the 'benefits culture' and the rehabilitation of the term 'underclass' (Murray 1990; Moore 1987; Moore 1989). Very little empirical evidence has been put forward to substantiate these many criticisms. On the contrary a considerable body of evidence which refutes one of the major criticisms – the disincentive effect of benefits – has done little to silence the critics (e.g. Moylan *et al.* 1984). Little research has been done to obtain the views of claimants on their experience of 'being a claimant'. Instead, as discussed in Chapter 2, critics including politicians and academics have made assumptions about why claimants behave the way they do and the impact that receipt of benefits has on their behaviour. This chapter draws together what empirical evidence is available to help inform the debate.

The frequent sniping at the easy claimant target inevitably has an impact on how claimants perceive themselves and how they are perceived by others. It leads to a sense of inferiority among claimants and a sense of suspicion both by staff who administer the scheme and by the general public. Given the poor public image of the social security system and claimants it is not surprising that, in his study of public attitudes to the welfare state, Taylor-Gooby (1985) found that social security was the least popular service. Among benefit claimants, there was a clear hierarchy from 'deserving' to 'undeserving'; pensioners and people with disabilities were placed at the top of the list and unemployed people at the bottom.

MIXED MESSAGES: THE PROBLEM OF TAKE-UP

Efforts to prevent the 'undeserving' from receiving benefits have not been matched by measures to ensure that benefits reach all those who should receive them. As a consequence, one of the main problems of British social assistance schemes, though all too often ignored by governments and certainly ignored by the two supplementary benefit reviews, has been their failure to reach all those who are eligible.

The introduction of supplementary benefit was a watered down attempt to tackle the take-up problem that had emerged in studies published in the early 1960s (Cole with Utting 1962; HMSO 1966). Initially it appeared that the change had been successful. Douglas Houghton (1967), Chancellor of the Duchy of Lancaster in the Labour government, claimed that 'the abolition of the National Assistance Board, and the deletion of the word "assistance" from the dictionary of Social Security, has had remarkable success. Some half a million more people applied within a few weeks'. However, this initial optimism was soon seen to be unfounded. Atkinson (1970, p. 61) estimated that, although the total receiving benefit had increased by 20 per cent between September and December 1966, in fact between one-half and two-thirds of the increase in the number of retirement pensioners in receipt of a supplementary pension between December 1965 and November 1968 was due to the more generous scale rates and not to the greater acceptability or knowledge of the new scheme.

A study carried out for the SBC found that take-up of benefit did not exceed 76 per cent in the first ten years of operation. Subsequently, the overall take-up level fell to 70 per cent in 1979, and for pensioners (the group targeted by the 1966 change) to 65 per cent. In the same year expenditure-based take-up was 85 per cent. Expenditure-based take-up tends to be higher than the take-up figure based on caseload because people are more likely to claim higher amounts of benefit. It is the expenditure-based figure that the Conservative government has preferred to use in recent years. In 1985 (the latest available) the comparable figures were 84 per cent and 91 per cent, a significant improvement. This might be the result of the higher profile given to supplementary benefit in the 1980s because of the numerous reforms and take-up campaigns, or a change in the Family Expenditure Survey (FES) figures on which they were based. Roughly a year after its introduction, the take-up rate for family credit increased from one-third to one-half as a result of a recalculation of the figures, not as a result of a higher proportion of people claiming. Even on the basis of the 1985 supplementary benefit take-up figures, which were significantly higher than the estimate for previous years, there were 840,000 people not getting the benefit to which they were entitled. Though government ministers have often tried to minimize the take-up problem by arguing that non-claimants tend only to qualify for small amounts of benefit, the average unclaimed weekly amount in 1985 was £12.60 per week. According to official estimates £550 million was not paid out in 1985 in social assistance alone (DSS 1990, table H5).

Take-up of benefits is a complex issue which is affected by a number of factors including lack of knowledge and the complexity of the benefits system. However, the stigma attached to the means test is probably the most enduring. The SBC recognized the significance of this back in 1977:

> Attitudes to means-tests vary widely both among those subjected to them and among those who administer them, but it is extremely difficult to avoid altogether their stigmatizing effects. To claim supplementary benefit is to admit that one is poor, and this in itself is a major barrier to overcome in a society which tends to equate poverty with failure if not with moral defects.
>
> (DHSS/SBC 1977, p. 29)

Not only does the stigma associated with claiming deter people from taking up their rights but it subtly discourages potential claimants from thinking that they might be entitled; after all they do not wish to think of themselves as having anything in common with the kind of social security recipients they read about in the newspapers. Consequently, whatever name has been in use at the time, no British social assistance scheme has managed to shake off its stigmatizing public image and all have failed to reach everyone who is eligible for help.

ATTITUDES TO SOCIAL ASSISTANCE AND BEING A CLAIMANT

On the surface, those in receipt of benefit appear to have overcome the problems associated with take-up of benefit since they have already made a claim. However, many people claim *despite* their reluctance to do so. Many in receipt of benefit are embarrassed or even ashamed of being a claimant.

In the Leeds study of supplementary benefit claimants (Walker with Dant 1984), one-third of the pensioner group, half the lone parents and sick and disabled groups and as many as three-fifths of the unemployed respondents reported that they were unhappy about having to claim state benefits. Roughly half of those receiving supplementary allowance said that claiming SB 'bothered them' in some way. This is not surprising given that in 1985 the British Social Attitudes Survey (Jowell *et al.* 1986) found that half the people interviewed felt that social security made people feel like second class citizens. This rose to 60 per cent of those within social classes IV and V, from which benefit recipients are most likely to be drawn. Though these answers referred to all social security benefits, for reasons discussed earlier the problems of stigma are even greater for recipients of social assistance.

Some people go to considerable lengths to conceal the fact that they are receiving social assistance. One pensioner interviewed in the Leeds survey used to keep her book hidden in the post office until 'the last minute'; another asked for her orders to be payable at a post office some distance from her home so that neighbours would not know she was drawing social assistance. Both these women were receiving their benefit on the same order book as their state pension, but even so they were still embarrassed. Many did not tell anyone that they were receiving supplementary benefit:

I don't talk to anyone about it except my daughter. It's a private affair.

I have to laugh when I'm with friends – they say 'they're alright (those people) on SB'. I don't say a word.

The majority of claimants interviewed thought that some people would not claim social assistance even though they were entitled to it. Pride was thought to be the main reason which would stop people claiming. Claimants below pension age also thought that ignorance of the benefits system was an important factor but few over retirement age gave this as a reason. The reasons respondents gave for other people not claiming reflected their own present attitude towards claiming, or the way they had felt at the beginning. In some cases, the objection to claiming was that the level of benefit was too low and had led to a drop in the standard of living:

Don't really feel good about it, I'd rather be working... Yes (it bothers me) when you see your friends working and can afford to go out. There's a youth club. It only costs 20p but I can't afford it. I've got some nice clothes, but can't afford to go anywhere in them.

(unemployed man)

More often, however, the reason was that claimants felt guilty or ashamed at not being able to support themselves and their families. Comments were frequently prefaced by the remark 'I'd rather be working'. This guilt was felt even by those who said that they were no longer bothered about claiming, even if they had been in the past:

I don't like it but somehow it's something that you have to do. You've got to feed your kids... It doesn't (bother me) now, it did at first. We'd been in the army, all over the world and we had a car and a phone and a colour TV and I had to get rid of all of them.

(lone parent)

I don't like it. I would much rather be working. I try very hard to get a job. I'm always at the Job Centre but it is impossible... I don't like it but I have no choice. If we didn't claim how could we live and take care of our children?

(unemployed man)

Takes your pride away a bit but if that's what you have to do, you do it. Didn't like it one little bit at first, bit embarrassing when you first do it, like charity ... then someone said you couldn't get it if you didn't deserve it. Now I look at it like that ... I always worked before and never relied on anybody, that's the embarrassing part.

(lone parent)

Respondents in the Leeds survey often legitimized claiming to themselves on the grounds that they had previously worked and paid contributions. One pensioner said she felt 'entitled to what I'm claiming... We've worked all our lives' and the following lone parent said:

When I first went on, I was very grateful for the money that we got. Still am. I were reluctant to ask at the beginning 'cos never had to ask before, I felt ashamed. Before, I'd been able to go out to work and it's frustrating to know that you can't go out and earn money. You feel useless, but then when you've been at it a long time you have to get over it, find an excuse for being on it. Some say ... husband's paid contributions... I think I'm beginning to feel like that.

Respondents who had sufficient confidence in their role to overcome any loss of dignity associated with claiming were exceptions to the general rule:

I'd rather claim it than her go away, but I'd rather I had the money to look after her. I call it my wage.

> (mother looking after daughter with disability)

(It bothers me) Yes I'd rather not. Prefer to be financially independent... I have to do it... Women do anything to make sure children are fed and clothed. In one parent families we're doing a very valuable job for the country looking after children... Given the choice between claiming benefit and going out to work, would rather do (former)... it will be repaid later.

> (lone parent)

The foregoing discussion and quotations show that many claimants feel demeaned by having to turn to the state for support. This is quite different to the impression painted by many critics, including members of the Conservative government and their supporters, that claimants often claim benefit unnecessarily and too easily fall into the 'sullen apathy of dependence' (Moore 1987). There are few people who easily adapt to a life on social assistance without a sense of loss of pride or dignity. Unfortunately the administration of the system and the unthinking protestations of relatively affluent politicians only serve to make them feel even more insecure.

In the pilot survey for the Leeds research of supplementary benefits claimants, respondents were asked whether they regarded receiving benefit as a right or a charity, a standard question used in some previous studies. This question was dropped in the main questionnaire because all respondents said that benefit was a right. However, in all the *comments* which were made it was clear that it *felt* like charity. Such sentiments reveal how difficult it is for means-tested benefits to be regarded as rights. Unfortunately, the demise of the national insurance system discussed in Chapter 2 means that more and more people are being subjected to means tests. Furthermore, the adminis-tration of national insurance benefits, particularly to the unemployed, has been so altered that many of the stigmatizing conditions previously attached only to means tests are now also applied to national insurance benefits. Not only have the contributions conditions been made tougher but claimants have to show that they are taking positive steps to find work and that they are immediately available for work. The availability for work test requires unemployment benefit applicants to state, for example, how far they are prepared to travel to work, how much (or how little) they are prepared to work for, and to show they have suitable child-care arrangements. Beveridge's requirement that claiming social assistance should *feel* worse than claiming national insurance was changed in the 1980s. Social assistance payments to the unemployed and unemployment benefit are jointly admin-istered by the Department of Employment. Payment of unemployment benefit now depends not only on an adequate contributions record but on passing the numerous tests of behaviour described above. These changes to unemployment benefit administration mean that people claiming it are expected to feel *as bad* as those getting social assistance. The stigma, therefore, arises not so much from which benefit is being claimed but the benefits administration and the status of being unemployed.

IT'S NOT JUST THE MONEY THAT MATTERS

As is clear from the discussion so far, being a claimant involves more than financial hardship. A government sponsored survey of the living standards of unemployed people (Heady and Smyth 1989) found that, despite 'pervasive financial anxiety' among respondents, 'material and financial deprivation are not always seen by the unemployed people themselves as the worst aspect of their situation. Over half named non-material reasons'. Thirty-eight per cent said that the worst thing about being unemployed was the lack of money, compared to over half who identified a range of broadly 'psychological' factors. Twenty-seven per cent said the worst thing was boredom, 10 per cent depression, 8 per cent a sense of inferiority. Only 5 per cent said they were not bothered about claiming and most of those were older people without dependent children who were approaching retirement age. The authors of this report concluded that psychological well-being was related to 'the family's financial situation and to their level of consumption' (p. 66) and for that reason unemployment had as much impact on the psychological well-being of the partner as on the claimant.

There is other evidence to suggest that wives feel their own status is undermined when their partners become unemployed. Being the wife of an unemployed man does not feel the same or share the same public acceptance as being the wife of an employed person. In addition, there are the well-known difficulties that face couples when the man becomes unemployed. Unemployed men, already suffering from a loss of status, are less likely to help their wives with domestic tasks. The wives of unemployed men are less likely to work than the wives of working men partly because of the financial disincentive created by the earnings rules of the benefits system but also because a wife's employment can cause difficulty in the traditional bread-winner/wife relationship. Heady and Smyth (1989) found that once the man was back at work the sense of psychological well-being of *both* husband and wife improved. Lone parents and some people with disabilities are also subject to social pressure. Doubts are often expressed about the authenticity of some claimants' situation and how far it really is necessary for them to be supported by the state. Thus many claimants, and particularly those under retirement age, face problems of identity and self-esteem as well as the practical difficulties of supporting themselves on low fixed incomes.

It is worth emphasizing again that both lone mothers and wives of unemployed men face difficult decisions. Their families are vulnerable, often coping not only with economic difficulties, but with problems of family relationships to adjust to changed circumstances and new family patterns.

(Brown 1989, p. 97)

ATTITUDES ACROSS THE COUNTER

Titmuss loved to tell of how on his visits to local Supplementary Benefits offices around the United Kingdom he would first use the toilet. He believed that the quality of the toilet facility – its cleanliness, its paint and lights – revealed the staff's concern about the claimants. For that concern is basic to the claimant's well-being.

(Miller 1987, p.15)

Social assistance offices have been notorious for their inhospitable appearance and lack of facilities. The contrast between offices or sections of the same office which administer social assistance and those dealing with national insurance benefits is often considerable. The difference between them and tax offices, let alone banks, can be dramatic. The poor state of office facilities was recognized by the SBC nearly twenty years ago (SBC 1976) but there have been few improvements since then. DSS local office staff have often been reluctant to see improvements in facilities for claimants because of the belief that they would be misused. Instead staff have sought greater security precautions to protect themselves from aggressive claimants. As a result, in the last 15 years social assistance offices have taken on the forbidding appearance of fortresses designed to keep out the people they are supposed to serve. Chairs are screwed to the ground and counter screens between staff and claimants have gradually been raised to the ceiling. Such an environment is not conducive to high morale on either side of the counter and it adds to the loss of dignity felt by those on the public side.

Within this inhospitable atmosphere, claimants are faced with a service which is far from perfect. An automatic ticket machine often controls the queue, but can do little to limit delays. The receptionists deal with all queries from a request for a leaflet to a complicated benefits query. Interviews in which claimants are expected to reveal personal information about themselves are held within earshot of everyone waiting; private facilities are available but many claimants are too reticent to request them. The receptionist has no direct access to claimants' files so has to leave the counter to consult colleagues who may or may not be available. Before computerization, the 'lost file', which could be in any one of forty places in a supplementary benefits office, was part of benefits folklore. If the claimant does not speak English then there is no requirement that the DSS should provide an interpreter. After all this, the receptionist may be unable to give an answer then and there, or may not give the answer that the claimant is so desperate for.

The Benefits Agency, which took over responsibility for the administration of social security, including social assistance, from the DSS in 1990, has said that it is concerned to run its services to the advantage of what it calls in its literature its 'customers'. It is too early to see what impact the new organizational structure will have. In the short term, the most noticeable change since the Benefits Agency was set up has been that ministers refuse to answer many parliamentary questions on social security on the grounds that its administration is the responsibility of the Benefits Agency. Computerization should prevent some of the most simple errors but cannot make good human error. However, these innovations will have only a limited impact if there is not enough staff to provide a prompt and efficient service nor enough money to put an end to the 'two nations' (Lister 1989a) of benefit offices by improving the physical environment. Even more important, the quality of service can only improve if government ministers and others cease to cast doubt on the integrity of claimants, and staff are encouraged to treat all 'customers' on their merits and not, as now, as potential shoplifters.

In such an unattractive environment it is easy for the frustration which claimants feel against the *system* and the *service* to manifest itself in frustration and aggression against staff. From the staff's side of the counter the alienating user conditions and the hostility they sense from users, taken together with a prevailing ethos which undermines the integrity of claimants and puts a premium on saving money, all combine to alienate staff from the people who are seeking help.

FROM THE INSIDE LOOKING OUT

One of the intentions and effects of the changes to social assistance in 1980 and in 1986 was to improve the relationship between staff administering the scheme and claimants by depersonalizing benefit administration. This had been a major consideration, for example, when the SBC argued for the end of discretion (see Chapter 6). There is very little reason for new or existing social assistance claimants to go to their local office unless something goes wrong. Postal claiming has been introduced for all claimants. Applications for extra weekly or lump sum payments under the post-1980 supplementary benefits scheme were increasingly dealt with on a postal basis. Applications for income support and the social fund can also be handled without any face-to-face contact between claimants or applicants and staff. Home visits were gradually cut back until they were virtually eliminated. In the 1990s the computerization of the scheme will be completed, accompanied, it is proposed, by the gradual change from local benefit offices to regional centres supported by 'shop front' style offices with computer link-ups. This will further distance claimants from the administration of the system, with the advantages and disadvantages that will involve.

The switch to a more rigid structure in supplementary benefit and then income support, together with less personal contact between claimants and staff, reduces the scope for discrimination on the grounds of race or any other personal prejudice, such as the claimant being 'undeserving' or just too demanding. But there is still room for unfair or inconsistent treatment. Within any administrative system, officers are often required to use judgement, for example on whether to tell people that they might be able to get help from the social fund or whether to expedite a request or not; social fund officers still have to exercise discretion to decide whether someone should get help. In these areas there is scope for discriminatory practice and there are indications that it exists. A study in local supplementary benefit offices in 1983 found a prevalence of racist attitudes among DHSS staff (Cooper 1985). The official response to this was to delay publication of the report and criticize the findings. Since then, there have been several local studies, as well as a plethora of anecdotal evidence, to suggest that black people are discriminated against by local office staff (NACAB 1991). In the case of the social fund, officers can hide discriminatory actions behind the cash limit and internal criteria on priorities to justify their decisions.

Some claimants may welcome the depersonalization of administration because they prefer to have no contact with the benefits system beyond cashing their weekly giro or order. However, the loss of contact between staff and claimants not only removes a source of anxiety or even tension, it also removes the opportunity for advice to be sought and given. Many claimants are reluctant to seek help. Through routine contact, NAB and SBC officials often picked up underlying problems and claimants' worries, or misunderstandings could surface. The new computerized income support structure and administration marks the final abandonment of the welfare role which was a feature of both national assistance and supplementary benefit, though it is important not to exaggerate the limited popularity of even these schemes with users (Ritchie and Wilson 1979; Briggs and Rees 1980).

During the 1980s, the Conservative government created a 'do-it-yourself' social assistance scheme (Walker 1987). The onus was put on claimants to identify their own needs, to find out about help which might be available, to obtain any appropriate forms and to fill them in correctly. Although very considerable effort has gone into their design, the long application forms for both income support and the social fund demand a good command of English and a high level of literacy. Anyone without these skills is disadvantaged. The forms are designed to collect the full range of information needed to assess the eligibility and ineligibility of a wide range of people claiming in a wide range of circumstances. They are not an effective way of enabling claimants to express their needs. The social fund application form has a space of 8cm by 4cm in which claimants should provide 'all the relevant facts' that will determine 'why you need help' (Berthoud 1991, p. 8). There have been some individual local office initiatives to provide information and advice on benefits to members of ethnic minority groups but overall a NACAB report (1991) on the treatment of black claimants gave little reason for complacency. The government has abdicated its responsibility for ensuring that social assistance reaches everyone who is eligible. There would be an outcry if fraud investigations were conducted by post. Should expectations be lower and investigations less thorough when the DSS is pursuing what should be its primary role, of getting benefits to those who are entitled to them? (Walker 1987, p. 108).

Staff's loss of contact with ordinary claimants, the ones who have no specific problem or who do not wish to ask for help, is important. A study for the DHSS found that nine out of ten social assistance claimants had not been to their local office in the previous twelve months (Cmnd 9519 1985). Those who do go are the ones with problems: the people whose giro has not arrived, the person who cannot pay the electricity bill, the person who wants more. Unfortunately, all too often the Olivers who ask for more are held in less regard than 'those people who just stay at home getting on with things'. Unfortunately, this point of view, expressed by one member of staff in a local office, is shared by many others. If staff deal personally with only those people who are in difficulty, they form a one-sided view of claimants. That somewhat jaundiced view is reinforced by the negative public images of social security claimants seen in the press and exhortations from departmental management to be vigilant against fraud and abuse, as one account of working within a supplementary benefit office reported:

> Concern to prevent abuse was probably the single most significant influence on staff's attitudes to and dealings with claimants. The prevalent view was that abuse, whether trivial or serious, was rife throughout the scheme... It was ... the more outrageous cases of fraud or abuse that had become the common gossip of the office, and so further infected the general attitude... Questioning a claimant with one eye on his welfare needs and the other on the possibility of fraud, was an impossible

schizophrenic role. And with some staff, the suspicious eye became much the sharper of the two.

(Moore 1980, quoted in Golding and Middleton 1982)

Over ten years later, Cook (1989, p. 97) found similar attitudes which set staff apart from the feelings and motivations of claimants:

> For departmental staff the agenda for dealing with claimants is set in adversarial terms, dominated by the concern to prevent abuse. By contrast, the fraudsters' self-justifications emphasize the issues of poverty, inequality, powerlessness and degradation.

An analysis of the responses to the report of the first supplementary benefits review team showed that staff working in local supplementary benefit offices held markedly different views to the many other groups and people who responded.

> The two staff groups ... were both significantly more likely than any other group to agree to a cost-saving proposal and less likely to agree to proposals necessitating an increase in resources. The individual staff responses were considerably more sympathetic to the review than the official response from the Staffside unions.

(Walker 1983, p. 116)

A leaked internal DHSS report was highly critical of some staff who were 'abrupt, even discourteous' (Moore 1981). Cook (1989) found that 'mucking around' was as prevalent a style of administrative practice in supplementary benefits offices in the 1980s as it had been in NAB offices in the 1960s (Hill 1969). Too often, benefit administration seems to ignore the reality of the lives of users. A delayed giro is routine for a busy office; it is a crisis for the family which finds itself with no money on Saturday morning. Similarly, noting the changed status of the unemployed person who reports sick may be necessary for record purposes, but there is no reason why it should lead to delays in payments, as was found in the Leeds study, when the amount of money due is unchanged. Such administrative insensitivity and inefficiency is likely to be counterproductive. For example, it deterred some people in the Leeds survey from declaring occasional part-time earnings, not because they were trying to be dishonest, but because doing so could lead to an interruption in the payment of benefit. In an effort to minimize the possibility of abuse, respondents who reported a possible change of circumstances to the local office were often told to send in their book immediately, the problem would *then* be sorted out. Claimants find it very difficult to cope, emotionally or financially, with that kind of insecurity.

When people first make a claim for social assistance, they are often not only in financial difficulty but also facing a domestic or emotional crisis: the loss of a job, the loss of a partner or the onset of illness or disability. Unfortunately, in their efforts to ensure that a claim is genuine, staff fail to see and are unable to respond to the personal tragedy that lies behind the claim. Though apparently only cosmetic, staff treatment of service users is important. Good manners cost nothing and, although they have no impact on the amount of money claimants have to live on, they do have a crucial impact on how claimants perceive the service, and that in turn affects their own sense of self-esteem.

FROM THE OUTSIDE LOOKING IN

In the Leeds survey, claimants' views on staff reflected their position in the claimant hierarchy. Satisfaction was clearly related to the way benefit was administered to each group. Lone parents and unemployed people – the 'undeserving' – had and still have more checks and controls on their entitlement to benefit. It is not surprising then that they feel more dissatisfied with their treatment. Neither would it be surprising if the culture of mistrust which sceptical administrative procedures can engender leads to staff treating some less favourably than others. In the Leeds survey, people over pension age were far more likely (47 per cent) to report that staff were helpful. The group of sick and disabled respondents showed considerably less satisfaction (30 per cent) than those over pension age, but considerably more than either those in the unemployed (11 per cent) or lone parent (14 per cent) groups. Dissatisfaction with staff was most frequently expressed by the unemployed and lone parents: almost three-quarters of the former and two-thirds of the latter were unhappy with the treatment they received. A substantial minority of these thought that the unsatisfactory service was due to pressures on staff, who did not have sufficient time to deal with each claimant. However, substantially more thought that staff 'did not try' to provide full information. The suspicion seemed to be that a policy of minimum information was being pursued. Thus, respondents might get a reply to a specific query, but staff did not go beyond this to see if there were any other ways in which the claimant might be helped. Getting full entitlement depended upon being able to ask the right questions.

Although the Leeds survey showed older people to be the least dissatisfied of the groups of social assistance claimants, a more recent survey (British Gas 1991) has shown that less than two-fifths of the older people interviewed thought that social security treated them very well or fairly well. Though social assistance was not specified, this is the part of the benefits system which is most likely to cause problems. A leaflet produced by the Benefits

Agency suggests that their approach will be different. It is to be hoped that these good intentions find their way into good practice.

In the Leeds survey, claimants' attitudes to staff also correlated with how well each group managed on benefit and the frequency of and reasons for contact with staff. Thus, the unemployed and one-parent groups, who had greatest difficulty in managing, found their dealings with staff most unsatisfactory. Attitudes are, of course, affected by whether the claimants concerned receive the answer or help they want. Those who asked for help most often (unemployed people and lone parents) were most likely to have experienced disappointment and blame was often laid at the door of the staff member making the decision – not the rules of the system. One respondent commented about staff 'they're a load of rubbish', but even she made a point of excluding one visiting officer who had pointed out that she was entitled to a single payment.

It is extremely difficult to separate out claimants' attitudes towards staff and their attitudes towards the system. Many, though by no means all, complaints voiced by respondents in the Leeds survey arose from the scheme staff were operating, and were not directed against the staff as individuals.

(They) try to help you but they're working from instructions. Deep down they can't help you because they have to work to higher up.

(lone parent)

It's hard work because everyone goes down shouting about benefits. Just frustrating because they haven't got enough money.

(unemployed claimant)

Chaos. That many things they have to do – forms, sorting out ... not all as organized as they should be. Got referred to one then another on the phone.

(pensioner)

They try to tell you but they don't always know themselves. They always say 'it's in the post'.

(disabled claimant)

It is inevitable in any system employing thousands of low-paid staff that some, on some days, will not act with the degree of sympathy and efficiency which might be desirable. However, appropriate training and a sympathetic rather than a suspicious office ethos could minimize such behaviour. Complaints made by respondents in the Leeds survey went beyond staff merely having a bad day. The first complaint was that staff looked down on them:

> Makes you feel as though you're begging, as though I can't provide for me family ... makes you feel as though they're better than you.
>
> > (unemployed)

> I don't like it because they treat you as a second class citizen. Yes (it bothers me) very much, I would rather be working. I would prefer to stand on my own two feet and get on with it.
>
> > (unemployed)

> Terrible. I feel as if I am begging. There is nothing like being independent. I hate to have to claim for my son, but (I) have little choice.
>
> > (mother with son with disability)

> You feel as if you're beholden to government and to people, taxpayers. The majority of people look down on you.
>
> > (disabled respondent)

A second complaint was that staff failed to judge each claimant on his or her own merits; it was felt that all claims for extra help seemed to be treated with suspicion:

> The attitude of the people who work there is terrible. It is all wrong. They treat everybody the same like they are layabouts.
>
> > (unemployed respondent)

> I know they have their hardships but they treat everyone the same – they haven't got much time for anyone.
>
> > (unemployed respondent)

> Some of them are very high-handed. They make you feel as if it's your fault that you're there.
>
> > (lone parent)

Cook (1989) found that claimants experienced feelings of degradation and worthlessness which were created through the process of claiming and receiving supplementary benefit. She argues that such feelings encourage people to behave fraudulently not least because, as one of her respondents remarked (in a similar vein to Titmuss two decades before): 'They think I'm fiddling so I may as well be'. She argues that claimants' behaviour is affected by the way they are perceived and treated by staff and others:

> Fraud can be seen partly as a product of a staff–claimant nexus of distrust on the one side and ... a feeling of degradation claimants feel as a result of being perceived as 'undeserving' scroungers.
>
> > (Cook 1989, p. 93)

Despite dissatisfaction with the treatment they received from some staff, many respondents in the Leeds survey recognized that staff did not have an easy job. The majority of respondents (three-quarters of the pensioner and sick and disabled groups, and two-thirds of the unemployed and lone parent groups) thought that working in a local office was not pleasant. It was widely recognized that staff were under considerable pressure and were often subjected to unpleasant or abusive behaviour. Some respondents' impressions of what it is like working in an office are given below:

> Dreadful. Because people who come in are unpleasant; (they're) over-worked, under stress, trying to keep out the people that are scrounging.
>
> (lone parent)

> Can't be very nice. People asking you for money all the time and shouting at you if they don't get what they want.
>
> (pensioner)

> Terrible, some of the people they have to deal with but at least they have a job.
>
> (unemployed man)

DIVIDE AND RULE

Like staff, claimants are also members of the general public. They share the likes and dislikes and prejudices of wider society. Most read a popular press which, when it does tackle issues concerned with social security, generally does so in a sensational, oversimplified and derogatory way. Claimants, who are themselves often struggling to manage on a low fixed income, are exposed to stories of others who abuse the system and hearsay about other claimants who have received large sums of money from the benefits system. Golding and Middleton (1982, p. 178) noted this in their study, which remains the major attempt to explore this issue in some depth:

> ... perhaps the most striking finding is the overall virulence and nature of hostility to welfare claimants. It is strongest among the low paid and unskilled – those most threatened by economic gloom and looming unemployment. But it is also voiced by claimants themselves. Indeed, claimants and the low paid are frequently the most bitter and hostile commentators on welfare recipients.

Most claimants only meet other claimants in the local office, an atmosphere in which concern and frustration often give rise to anger and, then, abusive behaviour. In the Leeds study, one of the most frequently mentioned objections to going to the local office was 'the other kinds of people there' (see, also, Ritchie and Wilson 1977). Respondents did not want to be associated with 'people like them'. Such feelings are encouraged by the divisive nature of benefit administration and government pronouncements on benefit recipients. Thus, statements which claim that the unemployed are not really unemployed, or that lone parents are to blame for their situation or that pensioners, along with other claimants, are not really poor, set one group of claimants against another.

One of the longstanding criticisms of all British social assistance schemes by governments, officials (see Chapter 6), and also by claimants, has been that some people do better than others, and the assumption has been that those who do best are not necessarily those in greatest need. One of the perceived advantages in 1980 of basing decisions on rules not discretion was that all claimants would be, and would be seen to be, treated uniformly. Research conducted after the introduction of the 1980 reforms (Walker with Dant 1984) showed that the view that some people were, unjustifiably, getting more than others was still widespread. Although many respondents thought that some claimants needed more money than others, they did not feel that those were the people getting the most.

The most frequent explanation for the perceived disparity in treatment was not related to specific needs or groups of claimants but to recipients' willingness to seek help, and the differing degrees of knowledge held by claimants. Thus, a distinction was drawn between 'those who know' and 'those who don't', and 'those who ask, and them like me that won't'. Below are some of the comments on those that respondents thought did best from the scheme:

The ones who know what to ask for.

(disabled respondent)

Don't know how they do it, maybe they know all the ins and outs.

(pensioner)

I'm sure these young families do better than elderly people – when you see people drawing all those (grants).

(pensioner)

Oh, the people who demand it, leave kids on the counter and say 'right you have "em" '.

(lone parent)

And those who did worst:

Those that are contented and can manage.

(pensioner)

Those ones who don't know enough.

(disabled respondent)

The people with lack of knowledge about their entitlement.

(lone parent)

The ones that use their money as it should be used.

(lone parent)

Poor sods that don't go in for it, who can't lower themselves to go, which I wouldn't.

(pensioner)

The sense of grievance expressed by respondents arose because they felt that they struggled to manage and that others should also. They felt they were being penalized for their thrift, while others were being rewarded for their profligacy. A survey of attitudes towards social security generally conducted for the 1983 social security reviews (Cmnd 9519 1985, paper 4), found that the 'best thing' about social security was that it helped the needy, but that one of the 'worst' aspects was that it helped those who did not need it.

There is little evidence available to show whether the more rigid structure provided by income support has eliminated such divisiveness. The premium structure merely formalizes the claimant hierarchy, the order of which not all claimants agree with. For example, several childless couples in the Leeds survey felt that they were disadvantaged relative to families with children, and that was *before* the government began to target the latter group. The very nature of the social fund with the establishment of priority groups is liable to foster divisiveness, especially given the very high refusal rate. The policy of targeting resources can give rise to dissatisfaction among those who feel equally hard up but are not identified as being in need of extra help, and may even have their benefit cut. As long as one group of poor people feels that another (albeit also poor) group is getting more attention and possibly more help, there is scope for rivalry and divisiveness within the benefits system.

The second reason for antagonism between claimants is, not surprisingly, the issue of fraud and abuse. In a national survey of claimants and non-claimants, the British Social Attitudes Survey (Jowell *et al.* 1986, p. 131) found in both 1983 and 1985 that two-thirds agreed with the statement that 'large numbers of people falsely claim benefits'. The Leeds survey of supplementary benefit claimants also found that two-thirds of respondents thought that some people abused the system; approximately one-half of these thought it happened 'in a lot of cases'. The majority of respondents (over half the unemployed and lone parent respondents and two-thirds of the sick and disabled and pensioner respondents) were extremely critical of those who tried to cheat the system: first, because they objected to the greed and dishonesty of such people; secondly, and more commonly, because they thought that such people made things worse for other, honest, claimants:

> That's not fair. If these things get played on, they spoil it for others.
>
> (pensioner)

> Unfair to other people. Someone probably needs it more than someone getting it unfairly. They're the people that are never satisfied.
>
> (lone parent)

> It's not fair. It's put there for a proper reason and it has to be spun out and they're taking it from people who need it.
>
> (man with a disability)

> It's not right, (they) should get what they are entitled not what they fiddle. It makes it bad for genuine cases. On reception at social security they can't tell which are the genuine cases and which aren't.
>
> (unemployed man)

However, a significant proportion of respondents thought that fraud or abuse was understandable given the low level of benefit and the meanness of some of the rules. For example, many argued that the low earnings disregard (which for many people is even less generous at the time of writing) encouraged claimants to behave dishonestly. More recent research conducted into tax and benefit fraud, and the differences in attitudes to and treatment of the two, has confirmed the link between poverty and fraud. In this study, Cook (1989, p. 71) concluded that benefit fraud is 'understandable only in terms of the material conditions of disadvantage, poverty and degradation in which (claimants) live out their lives'. She argues that most benefit fraud, including working while claiming benefit which accounts for 49 per cent of offences, is 'unsophisticated' and 'risky', revealing that it stems from desperation rather than criminality.

> Almost all the (benefit) fraudsters I interviewed invoked vocabularies of poverty, need, stigma and despair in justifying their actions. It was, for most of them, impossible to separate the *means* of benefit fraud from the allegedly legitimate *ends* which they felt it served.
>
> (Cook 1989, p. 86)

CONCLUSION

The circumstances which lead people to claim social assistance generally involve a loss of social status. Whether they have had to resort to means-tested support because of unemployment, sickness, disability, caring responsibilities or retirement, the circumstances which have brought it about can be personally traumatic. The benefits system, and especially the prevalence of the means-tested system, compounds that sense of inferiority. The low level of benefits ensures that social assistance recipients are excluded from full participation in the society in which they live. In addition to that social exclusion brought about by poverty, they are confronted by a system which is both intentionally and unintentionally stigmatizing. Attempts to improve the image of social assistance, for example by changing the name, have been purely cosmetic and totally inadequate to overcome the stigma ingrained in means-tested provision.

Successive governments have been too willing to accept the premiss that the fecklessness and dishonesty of many claimants is a major problem. The active promotion of such negative stereotypes of claimants by those in authority, as well as the press, creates a climate in which claimants are fully justified in feeling ashamed about being claimants. It also creates an administration which itself holds very negative views about its users, as the claiming process is more concerned to weed out the undeserving than to help those in need. In such a system, it is the honest who lose most; those intending to deceive are more likely to ignore such hostility. This loss of self-confidence among claimants is all the more damaging as the responsibility for ensuring entitlement has shifted from the service provider to the service user. The depersonalization of the administration of social assistance means that many people without a sufficient level of confidence, knowledge and skill will not see a claim through to the end. For government, this is revenue saved; for potential claimants it means a life of greater poverty.

9   Conclusion
Claimants first

Since the second world war, the means test has played a role of growing importance in British social security provision. Beveridge's vision of a society protected by a national system of social insurance, set out in *Social Insurance and Allied Services* (1942), was never realized. Instead social assistance, which was designed as a residual and diminishing means of support, gradually expanded to make up for the inadequacies of a national insurance system which was at first neglected and then attacked by governments. This important shift in the founding principles of the income maintenance programme occurred without any public or parliamentary debate on the merits of such a transition and without public acknowledgement by government that it was indeed happening. As a result British social assistance provision has continually been stretched beyond reasonable limits.

Social assistance is now only one of three major national means-tested benefits, alongside family credit and housing benefit, but it is the most important and the most influential. It has been taken as the focus of this book because it has a crucial significance to wider social security policy and to recipients of all state benefits. Despite the rejection by governments of the adoption of the social assistance rates as a 'poverty line', the levels of benefit which are set each year do represent a state definition of minimum income. It is, therefore, appropriate to ask whether that definition is adequate and whether the standard of living which that income affords is appropriate to British society in the 1990s. Examination of the structure and delivery of social assistance also tells us much about how people who have to turn to the state for support at certain periods of their life are to be regarded by wider society. Both the level of benefits and the treatment of claimants have an important bearing on individuals' personal standing within the community and their ability to be full members of the society in which they live.

WRONG AGENDAS

Social assistance has been one of the most closely examined and most frequently reformed parts of British social security policy since the war. Each reform has reinforced its significance in income maintenance provision. The need for a plethora of changes arose because the structure of the system was not appropriate to the size at which it was required to operate. The first national system of social assistance – national assistance – had been designed as a flexible, individualized scheme catering for small and diminishing numbers of people but in practice had to operate on a much larger scale. From the beginning, the number of claimants was greater than anticipated and grew throughout the post-war period.

The attempt to operate on a mass scale a scheme which had been designed to cover relatively few claimants put huge pressure on the administrative machine and led to increasing frustration for claimants. Many attempts were made by those administering the schemes and by governments to make social assistance administratively manageable, often with only a token or no regard to the impact on claimants. The numerous reforms made prior to the Social Security Act 1986 failed to reduce pressure on the scheme permanently because they sought internal, administrative solutions to much broader problems. In particular, the two major problems which beset each social assistance programme and which were the real cause of the administrative difficulties were not addressed. The numbers of people claiming benefit and the inadequate level of benefit were ignored.

TOO MANY PEOPLE ...

It was not until 1976 (DHSS 1978) that it was officially acknowledged that social assistance was not performing the residual role intended for it by Beveridge (1942), but that it was having to operate on a mass scale (DHSS 1976) and that it would clearly continue to do so. Prior to this first public admission, both Labour and Conservative governments had pledged their commitment to reducing the number of people receiving social assistance, but their actions conveyed a different message. Various benefit upratings which increased assistance more than, or instead of, insurance and the introduction of new non-contributory benefits, paid below even the short-term contributory national insurance rates, led to more people claiming means-tested assistance.

The first significant moves to remove people from social assistance were made by the Thatcher governments in the 1980s. However, these reductions were not achieved by the introduction of positive measures to lift people above social assistance level; they were made by removing the right to benefit from some groups, most notably young people. The introduction of housing benefit in 1982/83 also meant that some did not have to claim social assistance but the alternative was also means-tested and, especially in the beginning, complex and chaotic (Hill 1984)). These reductions in the number of claimants were more than compensated for by increases brought about by cuts in national insurance provision, for example the abolition of children's allowances for short-term benefits and the abolition of the earnings-related supplement. The cuts in the State Earnings Related Pensions Scheme (SERPS) made in the 1986 Social Security Act will mean that in the future fewer pensioners will receive an income from the state which is sufficient to keep them above social assistance level.

Having eventually taken the major step of breaking the previous official conspiracy of silence on the role social assistance was having to play in practice rather than the one attributed to it in theory, the Labour government's supplementary benefits review team went on to recommend that the scheme should be restructured to enable it to operate effectively on a mass scale. Although it was clear that the Labour government agreed with their review team's proposal to do this (Walker 1983), it fell to the 1979 Conservative government to implement the necessary changes. The main thrust of the ensuing legislation, the Social Security Act 1980, was to change social assistance from a scheme which was flexible to the needs of the individual to a mass scheme covering 'the common and predictable needs of the broad categories of claimants' (DHSS 1978, p. 5).

In their second and third terms, the Thatcher governments went on actively to proselytize the principle of selectivity and, following its own review of various aspects of social security including social assistance, put forward a package of reforms which emphasized the importance of means-tested benefits. This espousal of the means test as a mechanism for paying benefits did not extend to any affection for the name itself. The familiar, but much criticized, label of 'means test' was dropped in favour of new euphemisms, among the most favoured of which was first 'targeting on those in greatest need' (Cmnd 9517 1985) and later 'income-related benefits'.

Instead of trying to reduce the numbers of claimants, a search has been conducted over the past thirty years to find a means-tested scheme which could cope on a mass scale. In so doing, administration had to be simplified by reducing the flexibility of provision, and the structure of social assistance gradually changed from a system seeking creative justice to one based on proportional justice (Donnison 1982). In any such scheme the needs of the individual have to take second place to the needs of the group; and the needs of claimants have to be subordinated to the needs of the bureaucracy.

... WITH TOO LITTLE MONEY

The second underlying problem that governments preferred to ignore, which had a knock-on effect both for claimants and for the administration of social assistance, was the inadequate level of benefits. Here again, policy changes dealt with symptoms: the pressure put on the subsidiary system of help with regular or occasional needs. They did not address the question of why so many people needed help or heed the well-known answer of the Supplementary Benefits Commission (DHSS/SBC 1977) that help was required because weekly benefit rates were insufficient to meet even basic needs, let alone any extras.

For obvious reasons, governments have been reluctant to acknowledge the poverty of those who depend on the state for support. No government has been prepared to replicate Beveridge's attempt to justify empirically the levels of benefit which it sets. In 1990 an independent research project began work which is designed to establish budget standards for different family types (FBU 1991). This might go some way to making good governments' reluctance to substantiate the benefit levels which they set. The reason governments have refused to undertake this task is clear: the benefit rates do not stand up to close scrutiny. Numerous studies from the 1960s onwards, many of which are discussed in Chapters 4 and 5, have shown that people living on social assistance suffer considerable hardship and deprivation. Far from lifting people out of poverty, social assistance over the years has ensured that its recipients remain poor. The rates have been set too low to allow claimants to have a standard of living comparable to that of the rest of the community in which they live. The means test provides claimants with few ways of increasing their disposable income. Unless claimants earn more than they receive in benefit, they cannot improve their standard of living above the meagre income disregards. The means test thus ensures that the benefit rates represent not only a minimum income but a maximum also, and locks people into poverty.

WHERE IS THE JUSTICE IN ROUGH JUSTICE?

Attempts to find a permanent solution to the problems facing the various British social assistance schemes have been inhibited by the more pressing government aims of controlling and then cutting public expenditure. Since the mid-1970s social security has been given no special protection and has been expected to offer up its sacrificial lambs. Consequently the reforms to social assistance made in the late 1970s and early 1980s were drawn up within the context of standstill resources. Later they were expected to yield savings. With such an overriding constraint, it is not surprising that they could not find permanent solutions to their own administrative agendas, let alone to the needs of claimants.

It was the first supplementary benefit review team set up by the Labour government in 1976 who were first confronted with the difficult task of finding effective solutions to the problems of social assistance without spending any more money. The solution they found was the redistribution of resources *within* the scheme, with inevitable consequences.

> This course is bound to involve some element of rough justice and some losers as well as gainers, as it would seem impracticable to expect that extra money would always be found for the process of always levelling up to ensure that nobody would ever be worse off than now. The real question is how much loss, and for how many, would be acceptable. Rough justice must not be too abrasive.
>
> (DHSS 1978, p. 5)

Both the major sets of changes introduced since publication of that review team's report, in the Social Security Act 1980 and the Social Security Act 1986, applied rough justice. Both sets of reforms involved losers as well as gainers. In 1980, two-thirds of claimants lost. Estimates of the impact of the 1986 legislation vary. However, at the time of the changeover from supplementary benefit to income support, one-third of claimants received transitional protection to maintain the level of benefit at pre-1988 levels in cash terms (Social Services Committee 1989, p. iv). (Transitional protection is paid until the claimant's entitlement under the new system overtakes the amount which was payable under the old. No increases in benefit are paid for inflation or changes in circumstances until the two figures balance.) In order to direct extra resources to the group which had been identified as being in greatest need – families with children – other 'less poor' groups received less. In 1980, claimants over retirement age were the main losers. They lost again in 1988 but were joined by other childless couples and, especially, young people.

Applying the principle of rough justice to the distribution of incomes of the poor is bound to increase hardship among the losers, and it ignores the hardship that many people who find themselves classed as the 'less poor' already face. Although the evidence discussed in Chapters 4 and 5 showed that not all groups of claimants were equally badly off and that some groups of claimants do face more difficulties than others, the overriding conclusion was that many claimants in *all* groups face difficulty in managing on benefit. People's ability to manage depends on a number of factors, the first and most important of which is the amount of money they receive each week. The reason hardship is found to be less common among older social assistance claimants than among younger claimants is that they usually receive higher levels of benefit (see Chapter 4). Income from social assistance varies according to family size *and* claimant status. Under national assistance, pensioners were the group most likely to have their weekly benefit enhanced by regular weekly additions for special needs. Supplementary benefit paid higher weekly rates to pensioners, and some other long-term claimants, as well as paying weekly additions which favoured these groups. Income support includes a system of premiums which means, in effect, that different groups of claimants get different rates of weekly benefit. There is no longer one weekly rate for all claimants. The variations in the premiums owe as much to judgements about the 'deserving' and 'undeserving' as to the actual needs of benefit recipients. Thus, despite the fact that even the Conservative government acknowledged that families with children were the group facing greatest hardship, it set the family premium at approximately half the rate of the pensioner premium.

In the Green Paper, *The Reform of Social Security* (Cmnd 9517, 1985), the Conservative government prioritized families with children because they formed the largest group in the bottom quintile of income distribution. It has been argued elsewhere that this statistic reveals nothing about whether older people are in poverty or not (Walker 1990), but it was used as the main justification for the priorities which were set. Numerous studies (see Chapter 4) on the standard of living of claimants have also shown that a larger proportion of people below retirement age (and particularly of families with children) than people above retirement age, cannot meet their basic needs on social assistance. One way of responding to the disparity in the rate of hardship between groups would have been to acknowledge the disparity in income and recognize that it is the higher rates of benefit paid to older people that reduce the incidence of poverty. The most obvious solution to the problems of the poorest, therefore, would have been to increase *their* incomes. As the government was not prepared to commit any extra resources the only way of paying some claimants more was to pay others less. The policy of redistributing resources *among* the poor merely redistributes poverty and can only lead to more poverty not less. The official statistics (DSS 1990) on income distribution for 1988 show that the proportion of pensioners in the bottom quintile has increased. Thus, according to the criteria used in the Green Paper, the not-so-poor had become the poor once again. The same figures showed that young single people, who were also victims of the policy of rough justice, formed a growing proportion of those living below social assistance levels (Oppenheim 1990).

MANAGING THE UNMANAGEABLE

The standard of living of claimants is, of course, most crucially influenced by the amount of money they have to spend. However, there are various factors which influence how well people can manage their money (see Chapter 5). Some people might spend less because they have lower expectations. Older people who experienced severe hardship before and during the second world war may be more accustomed to going without or having little, although this is no justification for expecting them to do so. Indeed the incidence of hypothermia among older people during the winter is testimony to the dangers of their putting the worry of the fuel bill before their concern for their own health and welfare. A more important factor is the degree to which people are able to control and predict their spending. People who live alone are much more likely than claimants with children to be able to keep a tight rein on what they spend and how they spend it.

The only conclusion that can be drawn from the evidence on the living standards of social assistance recipients which has been presented is that the majority of claimants cannot manage on their benefit. They are in good company. Various people who tried it for a week or so, including a Conservative MP and a member of the SBC, failed to make their money last. Nevertheless, the poverty of claimants is often put down to their own bad management (e.g. Moore 1987; Murray 1990). This book has sought to dispel such aspersions and put forward the alternative explanation that claimants have too little money and few strategies available to them to make ends meet. As discussed earlier, the means test prevents people from boosting their income to any meaningful extent. The earnings disregards are far too low to make it financially worthwhile to take part-time work. The full value of maintenance payments is deducted from benefit. Benefit is reduced for anyone with savings over the capital limit (£3,000 in 1991) and savings of as little as £500 (in 1991) disqualify a claimant from receiving help from the social fund. With a lack of opportunities to increase their weekly income, claimants have to look for other ways to make ends meet. The strategy most frequently adopted by people to manage their poverty is to reduce expenditure, either by cutting down or by going without. So-called luxuries like social activities and new clothes are the first expenses to go but they are soon followed by lower expenditure on essentials such as food and heating.

Despite such sacrifices, many people fail to make both sides of the domestic balance sheet tally. Many fall into debt. It is the increasing numbers of people faced with debt who are often assumed to be the 'bad' managers. However, this book has shown that debt is seldom the result of profligacy or mismanagement, it is the inevitable result of having too little money to live on. Social assistance claimants are constantly having to make hard choices: whether to meet today's need or put aside for tomorrow; to replace the worn-out pair of children's shoes or to save for the electricity bill. It is impossible to judge from the outside whether a family is managing on benefit or not. When living on a low fixed income, whether one falls into debt or not is the difference between turning off the heating in a cold spell or keeping warm and running up a bill. Many people who show the outward signs of managing by keeping up to date with their bills may only do so because they do not heat their homes adequately or have a nutritious diet.

A SAFETY NET, A SOP OR AN EXCUSE?

Beveridge built into social assistance a system of subsidiary support to meet extra or special needs, which could not be covered by a subsistence level benefit. Though governments soon abandoned the subsistence principle in practice, the theory remained an important influence in the determination of benefit levels, and the various schemes for providing extra financial help with regular weekly needs or occasional *ad hoc* expenses became an integral part of social assistance provision (see Chapter 2). One of the main outcomes of the failure of successive governments to reduce the numbers of people living on social assistance, or to set the main scale rates at a high enough level to meet basic needs, was to increase the demand for this extra help. Consequently, one of the main goals of many of the reforms to social assistance was to bring this system under control. Such attempts were doomed to failure because they ignored the questions of why the demand was there and why it persisted. Early attempts at reform, with the introduction of supplementary benefit in 1966 and the long-term addition in 1973, did try to reduce the need for extra help. The 1980 reforms were noted most for the introduction of the simpler administrative arrangements discussed earlier which led to many losers. However, they were equally significant for the reduction in the availability of extra help. In 1986, lone parents and unemployed claimants lost their right to the most frequently made grants, and in 1988 the single payments scheme was abolished entirely.

The time and effort devoted to administering and reforming the various systems of supplementary support which have existed in the post-war period were totally out of proportion to the cost of such schemes. When the SBC launched its campaign against discretionary payments in 1976 (SBC 1977), it estimated that together extra weekly and occasional lump sum payments accounted for less than 5 per cent of total supplementary benefit expenditure. After the introduction of the regulatory scheme in 1980, the problem of administering weekly additional payments was largely solved, though there were still many unresolved problems for claimants (see Chapter 6). However, lump sum payments remained an administrative headache. In 1986, the cost of single payments reached its peak of expenditure, £360 million, much more than ten years earlier but still less than 5 per cent of SB expenditure. The 1986 cuts, which the government made because they felt that the single payments system was again getting out of hand, halved that share (DSS 1990a) and in 1989 the social fund, which was the most criticized of the 1986 reforms, was only 2 per cent of the cost of income support.

These systems of extra help maintained their high profile, despite their relative insignificance in terms of overall social security expenditure, for two reasons. First the supplementary systems of support were the symbol of social assistance provision which could be flexible to the needs of the individual. Increasingly, as the numbers of people on benefit and the numbers seeking extra help grew, governments and administrators of the system found such flexibility unwieldy and anachronistic. A scheme which could adapt to the needs of the individual was not a viable option in a scheme supporting millions of people.

The systems of extra help were important also because, in the short term, they provided a convenient escape chute for both government and claimants. Despite the many complaints of unfairness and inequity inherent in both the discretionary and regulatory schemes, the system of extra payments provided some relief for claimants struggling to survive on social assistance (see Chapter 6). Under both the national assistance and the discretionary supplementary benefit schemes, governments found it convenient for these extra payments to be made more available. They provided a cheap way of responding to emerging needs while deflecting criticism of the low basic scale rates. However, in the longer term, the widespread use of additional payments became an administrative nightmare and a political embarrassment. The persistently high level of demand for extra help was a constant reminder that the main benefits structure was not providing an adequate minimum income. Consequently, what had been a convenient device until the 1980s to assist governments obfuscate on the issue of the adequacy of the main scale rates became more of a burden than an asset.

None of the attempts to control the systems of supplementary support in the various British social assistance schemes has succeeded, either for the government or for claimants. They failed governments because the level of demand stretched administration to breaking point. They failed claimants because they did not provide sufficient help to meet all their outstanding needs. All such schemes have been and are still doomed to failure as long as governments are unwilling to grapple with the underlying problem of inadequate weekly benefit. The tail has wagged the dog. The problems presented to the main benefits system by an inexorable demand for extra help have been dealt with by changing the basis on which additional help is available and the level at which it is given, when what was needed was a total rethink about whether the main benefit rates were capable of providing the majority of beneficiaries with sufficient money to meet all their basic needs.

BACK BEYOND BEVERIDGE

In the Social Security Act 1986 the Conservative government, unlike its Labour and Conservative predecessors, came clean about its aims and intentions for British social assistance. This legislation espoused the principle of selectivity and accepted the extension of the role for means-tested social assistance, a trend which previous governments had been reluctant to admit to publicly. The government argued that selective benefits were a more efficient use of resources; by concentrating help on fewer people, each individual could receive more and overall costs could be reduced. The arguments against selectivity, which were so well rehearsed in the 1960s and 1970s, remain equally valid in the 1990s. Experience has shown that an increasingly means-tested system has failed claimants. British social assistance has never reached all those eligible. The means test locks people into their poverty as it is impossible for them to make any significant improvement in their income. It creates dependency within the family and makes unsound assumptions about the distribution of resources within a household. And, as Lister (1989, p. 220) has pointed out, it leads to social exclusion:

> Means-tested benefits, confined to the poor, isolate them so that the rest of society no longer has a real stake in defending and improving what is becoming an increasingly stigmatized system associated with failure.

Such alienation is intensified by the increasing emphasis on controls against 'suspect' groups, such as unemployed people (who have to prove they are 'genuinely' unemployed), people from ethnic minorities (especially black people who have to prove their residence status by showing a passport) and women (who as lone parents have to prove they do not have a partner, and to assist the DSS secure maintenance from the fathers of their children). In the light of these criticisms, together with an overstretched insensitive benefits administration and inhospitable benefit offices, it is little wonder that many people, especially from ethnic minority communities, do not claim and that those who do continue to feel stigmatized (see Chapter 8).

With the implementation of the Social Security Act 1986, the link with Beveridge's vision of residual means-tested provision and with the idea of a scheme responsive to individual need was finally officially broken. It is even possible that this attempt to find a means-tested system which can be operated on a mass scale might be successful in administrative and political terms. If it is, then it will be because it is unconcerned with the needs of claimants. The introduction of income support was not accompanied by any increase in the real levels of benefit, as had happened when supplementary benefit replaced national insurance (Oppenheim 1990a). And yet it drastically cut back the system of supplementary help, even for those expenses which a subsistence benefit was never expected to cover.

On introducing income support, the then Secretary of State for Social Services, Norman Fowler, said that his first priority was to establish a suitable structure. In income support he established a simple classical structure which was administratively convenient but which cannot meet all the needs of a diverse range of claimants who require an edifice of rather more gothic proportions (Chapter 7). Having failed to find a technology which could adequately tackle a flexible system of social assistance sensitive to the diverse needs of claimants, the government founded a benefits system which was sensitive to the needs of the computer. The new computerized system and simplified structure should improve the service to claimants. However, could that important gain only be made at the cost of a less generous benefits system? The ultimate test of a social assistance scheme should be whether it provides claimants with an adequate standard of living. Income support does not do that. Consequently, three years after its introduction, it is clear that claimants living on income support suffer similar hardships to those faced by recipients of supplementary benefit and, before them, the recipients of national assistance.

The continued inadequacy of the main benefits rates in the 1990s is shown by the rising pressure on the social fund (see Chapter 7), the sop which the Conservative government created to diffuse criticism of the abolition of single payments. Within three years of its creation, the social fund was under enormous pressure, with some offices having refusal rates as high as 80 per cent (SSRC 1991). For the vast majority of claimants, the social fund offers no help at all; the bulk of the help given is in the form of loans, which are entirely inappropriate for a group of people for whom debt is already a major problem. For the government the social fund is only a qualified success. It has achieved the main goal of cutting back expenditure. However, the government has found it impossible to stick rigidly to the cash limit because of the volume of applications and the speed with which some offices used up their budgets. Furthermore, the social fund is an administrative nightmare, much worse than either the discretionary or regulated single payments system, costing one-third of social fund expenditure.

The problems for the social fund are only just beginning. The demand for help can only increase and the long-term effects of a Social Fund Inspectorate, which is showing greater inclination to overturn local office decisions, and the prospect of further challenges in the High Court are going to ensure that the social fund will remain a running sore as long as it survives. The Conservative government deflected the growing criticism of the social fund made by independent researchers, SSAC and the National Audit Office pending publication of its own research conducted by SPRU. This 'official' evidence confirmed serious weaknesses in the working of the social fund (see Chapter 7). Despite this extremely critical report, Nicholas Scott, Minister for Social Security and Disabled People, maintained in television interviews that the principles on which the social fund was based were sound. The authors of the SPRU report concluded with this statement:

> The challenge for the future is to continue the search for a realistic, manageable and fundable policy which will meet the needs of vulnerable people in a timely, efficient and just manner.
>
> (Huby and Dix 1992, p. 127)

Whether the government will rise to that challenge is as yet uncertain.

DOWN WITH THE POOR

A claim for a social security income maintenance benefit is normally made after the occurrence of a major life change. Most of these changes are unexpected: the loss of a job, the onset of illness or disability, or the break-up of a relationship. Some, like retirement, are predictable. Whether unexpected or anticipated, the transition from a situation of supporting oneself in work, or being supported, financially or domestically, by a partner, to reliance on the state for support is traumatic even if it happens several times in a lifetime. This leads to a sense of lost status by the majority of claimants. The problem is compounded for those who have to turn to social assistance, either to supplement a national insurance benefit or as their primary source of income, because of the way eligibility is assessed. The process of assessing entitlement can easily reinforce the feelings of stigma. Claimants have to provide information of 'a searching and detailed kind... Questions about the claimant's private affairs – not only his income but what savings he has, who else lives in the house and on what terms – are necessary and in most cases inoffensive; but such questioning is not involved in a claim for a national insurance benefit' (DHSS/SBC 1977, p. 29).

There have been several attempts to shed the negative image of the various British social assistance schemes. The name has been changed twice since 1948 and an emphasis put on rights-based entitlement rather than discretionary help (with the important recent exception of the social fund). The failure of these attempts was inevitable. First, and most important, the introduction of both supplementary benefit and income support represented important, but only superficial, changes. The least attractive aspect of social assistance, the means test and the stigma which 'inevitably' (DHSS/SBC 1977, p. 32) accompanies it, survived.

While superficial attempts have been made to improve the image of the scheme, governments have done little to improve, and much to harm, the public image of claimants. Successive governments have concurred with press criticisms of claimants being undeserving or dishonest. In the 1980s the Conservative government actually took the lead in casting aspersions of one kind or another on nearly all the main groups of claimants.

Over the years, governments have been so concerned that the benefits system should not lay itself open to fraud or abuse that benefit administration has been geared more to catching the dishonest than helping the needy. The desire to curb the excesses of the minority has affected the way benefits are administered to all, mostly honest, claimants. This conflict between the control and helping functions of social assistance is reflected in staff attitudes towards claimants, and the way claimants see themselves (see Chapter 8). As Titmuss said, people will respond in the terms in which they are treated: if they are treated as burdens, they will behave as burdens (see Miller 1987); and as Cook found twenty years later, if claimants are assumed to be dishonest, some will be (Cook 1989).

The active promotion of stigma in the social assistance scheme, through both the means test and a sceptical and distrustful administration, affects both current claimants and potential claimants. Non-claimants are discouraged from claiming. Those who have made a successful claim have had to override any sensitivities in order to survive, but it does not mean that they relish the status of being a claimant. For many, receiving social assistance feels quite different to receiving a national insurance benefit. The latter is a right which has been earned; the other is help reserved for the poor.

The steps to depersonalize and regulate social assistance allows people to have the distance from the scheme that some want. More regulations and a more rigid structure require less intrusion once entitlement to benefit has been established. However, this is not true at the point of the initial claim. The income support claim form is considerably longer than the old supplementary benefit application form. The cost to claimants of this change is that there is less help available. Claimants have less need to meet staff on a routine basis which means that staff see mainly those with complaints of problems and, therefore, form a very one-sided view. Claimants never get the opportunity to seek verification or clarification of the scheme. Thus, there is little opportunity for the common anxiety, that they might be breaking the rules without realizing it, to be alleviated. The DSS now provides a free telephone line for social security enquiries. This is a welcome innovation but it would be better if it supplemented rather than substituted for personal contact.

It is unlikely that any means-tested social assistance scheme can be non-stigmatizing. However, modest steps forward could be made, if governments promoted the positive role of social security rather than the negative attributes of a minority of claimants. Benefits administration needs to be much more proactive in providing information. Most importantly, the ethos of administration needs to change dramatically. Supermarkets do not make every customer feel like a shoplifter, even though they do take stringent steps to prevent thieving. Similarly, there is no reason why a social security system cannot guard against the dishonesty of some people while still respecting all its beneficiaries. Social assistance claimants are punished twice: first, by having to live on means-tested benefits and secondly by being villified or denigrated for receiving that financial support.

THE REAL PROBLEM IS POVERTY – NOT POOR PEOPLE

Social assistance is the second most expensive social security benefit after the retirement pension, accounting in 1990/91 (HM Treasury 1988) for nearly one-fifth of benefits expenditure (excluding administration). It supports one in seven of the British population. It is thus a major component of social security policy. It is also the area which has received more attention, generally adverse, than any other aspect of benefit provision. Despite the amount of time and effort, and money, spent on social assistance, it has failed to provide claimants with a high enough standard of living or a decent and sensitive service.

The failure of social assistance is first and foremost the result of failures outside the scheme. The adverse ramifications of an inadequate social insurance scheme have been compounded by application of the means test, which has been proved to be totally inadequate to the task of either preventing or alleviating poverty. The means test has been applied too harshly and administered in such a way as to deter large numbers of people from claiming. The many reforms to social assistance which have been introduced in the post-war period have been the social security equivalent of shifting the deckchairs on the *Titanic*, when what was needed was a thorough evaluation and improvement of the substructure.

Social assistance does not exist in a vacuum. Its immediate environment is a social security system which is failing to provide for all the needs of its recipients. That is then set within a wider economic climate which determines the extent to which people will, or will not, be able to provide for themselves through the labour market. Changes need to be made in both these spheres if social assistance is to be made redundant, or at least rehabilitated. If the problem of poverty caused by social assistance is to be prevented, then the problem of poverty elsewhere needs to be tackled. That will require radical but not impossible change.

The most effective way of reducing the number of people living on any benefits system is to provide them with jobs. An effective employment and training policy is therefore vital. The poverty of those in work must be tackled not only in the interests of social justice but also to enable benefit rates to rise alongside wages. This involves measures to secure decent wages, such as a minimum wages policy, a fairer tax and national insurance system, and child benefit, so that incomes in work reflect family responsibilities. A proper framework of social services provision is needed. It is time Beveridge's five giants stopped stalking the land. Homelessness is one of the major scandals of our time; poor people still suffer more ill health, they die younger and more of their children die in infancy. Children from poor families are still less likely to stay on at school or go on to higher or further education, and the financial support that enabled some to do so has been reduced in recent years.

Numerous alternative strategies for the reform of social security have been put forward in the last decade. These fall broadly into three types, all of which have been discussed more fully elsewhere (Lister 1989a; Alcock 1987). The first two of these strategies would involve scrapping existing structures and starting again. Proposals to combine tax and benefits into one system, negative income tax (NIT), were mooted by the 1970–72 Heath government and still retain support on the Right. The main criticisms of them are that they are not sufficiently flexible to the economic circumstances of the poor. They have also been criticized because they are merely the 'logical conclusion' (Lister 1989a) of the means test and so incorporate many of the disadvantages which are associated with it, such as the poverty trap and the aggregation of incomes within the family. They also provide 'a more blatant subsidy of low pay' (Lister 1989a, p. 224).

The second model is that of a basic income. In its ideal form, this would provide an unconditional tax-free cash payment to each individual, and as such would not isolate the poor to a separate and, therefore, stigmatized system. Advocates of the basic income (e.g. Parker 1982) have recognized that its main weakness is its cost. In its pure form the cost is seen to be too great to attract either the political or public support necessary for its implementation (Atkinson 1989). However, the cost could only be reduced by making important concessions which could undermine its effectiveness; either benefits would have to be too low to provide genuine security; or conditions would have to be imposed, which, as experience of the current social security scheme has shown, could be misused for both economic and ideological ends. None the less, after examining the costs of practical implementation, Atkinson concluded that it did present a 'practicable' option with the advantage (or, according to one's point of view, disadvantage) of having no major redistributional consequences:

> In a rational world, the partial basic income may have a lot to recommend it, but political decisions are not made in this way. Less transparent forms of redistribution may be more successful.
>
> (Atkinson 1989, p. 334)

A third way of gradual (and therefore less transparent), but planned and fundamental, reform has been put forward by Lister (1989a) and the Child Poverty Action Group (Lister 1987; Becker and Bennett 1991). Briefly, the kind of changes suggested to provide a social security system which can prevent and alleviate poverty include: increases in child benefit; an increase in national insurance benefits to unemployed people to the level of long-term benefits such as invalidity benefit, and its extension for as long as unemployment lasts; the development of a disability income scheme which covers disability costs as well as providing an income for those unable to work; provision for carers, including lone parents; a phased increase in all NI benefits to a level which allows 'social participation'; the gradual phasing out of contributions tests; a system of housing support which helps tenants and owner-occupiers equally; and allowances for young people who stay on in education beyond the minimum school-leaving age (Lister 1987). Additional changes included in CPAG's contribution to the 1992 election (Becker and Bennett 1991) included payment of benefits at a level which allows full participation in society; further moves towards rights-based benefits and away from discretion (as used in the social fund and the payment of benefits for 16 and 17 year olds); benefits paid on the basis of need or contingency rather than means tests; benefits which promote the autonomy of individuals by using the individual, not the family unit, as the basis of assessment; and benefits which ensure equal access to, and equal treatment from, the social security system, thus ending the inequitable treatment given to black and ethnic minority claimants.

The culmination of these many proposals, which could be implemented gradually, would preclude entirely the need for social assistance, as well as the other major means-tested benefits, and, given the proven difficulties of producing means-tested benefits which reach all potential recipients in a non-stigmatizing way, their elimination should be the ultimate goal. However, in the real world it has to be recognized that, even if a government embarked on such an adventurous voyage, it would be some time before it reached its destination, and there would be many a storm to be survived on the way. In the mean time social assistance should be and could be improved. Income support is a mass scheme. As the computerization programme settles down, there is no administrative reason why it could not deal with even more people. Thus, an increase in the level of social assistance, without a commensurate increase in national insurance, which would lead to more eligible claimants, could be managed administratively. Such an increase would improve the standards of living of those receiving benefit. It would not, of course, do anything for those people who are deterred from claiming by the means test.

It is only by increasing the basic scale rates that the provision for extra and special expenses can be contained to a level which is workable and manageable. It has been argued that, 'human nature being what it is', the demand for extra help will persist as long as there is help available. However, that cynical assumption has never been put to the test. The great majority of needs with which people have consistently sought additional help have been basic subsistence needs such as clothing and footwear, and necessary but expensive household items, such as furniture, for which they have not been able to save from subsistence incomes. Contrary to the comments of some authorities (Berthoud 1991) it is possible to begin to establish an order of magnitude of the increases necessary (see, for example, Piachaud 1979; Mack and Lansley 1985). The findings of the Family Budget Unit (1991) will assist in this endeavour. Only when benefit rates are increased to an adequate level will it be possible for claimants to meet basic expenses from their weekly benefit and for social assistance to provide extra help only in a limited and clearly defined set of circumstances.

Considerable effort has been put into looking for ways of improving the social fund. The most comprehensive discussion of an alternative to the present structure of the social fund has been provided by Craig (SPRU 1992; see also Berthoud 1991 for an alternative option). Craig proposes a system of (a) regular and regulated grants for all income support claimants (and possibily other low-income people) to cover lump sum expenses which people inevitably meet; (b) regulated grants paid for specific life events such as births, deaths, setting up home, etc.; (c) discretionary grants for unpredictable crises. Craig costs this scheme in 1992 at £675 million, compared to gross expenditure on the discretionary social fund in the same year of £345 million and £1 billion had single payments been continued. Craig is adamant that his new scheme has no place for loans but suggests that the government could explore, separately, the establishment of a low- or no-interest social lending scheme. In its current form, the social fund can never be a success from the claimants' perspective. Any cash limit imposed on a system designed for the very poorest is bound to mean that many needs will not be met. The removal of the cash limit on loans, which though not cost-free to the government are relatively cheap, would reduce the refusal rate, but would only compound the problem of rising debt among recipients.

In recent years 'realism' has dominated the debate on social security reform. In this vein, proposals for change have been mainly confined within each part of the system. We would not wish to underestimate the importance of small-scale incremental change – even small improvements (and deteriorations) can have a considerable impact on people living on very low fixed incomes. However, there is the danger that a piecemeal approach to change can reinforce the divisions that are already entrenched in social assistance. At least one major pressure group has been arguing for improvements in the income support premiums rather than in the basic scale rates. But such a strategy will inevitably lead to greater differentials between different groups of claimants, which do not necessarily closely reflect need. Most importantly, such a 'realistic' strategy needs to take on board 'the real world' in which such a change might be made. In the world of no-cost reform, improvements in the premiums paid to some would lead to reductions in payments to others. All pressure groups can make a genuine case for improvements in benefit for the users they represent – people with disabilities, older people, young people, lone parents and others. The sheer number of pressure groups arguing for improvements for the users they represent is evidence of a social security system that is failing many people in many different circumstances.

The proposals described above are second-best because they accept a sustained and even increased role for means-tested provision. Those arguing for more radical, and therefore expensive, change will be accused of being utopian or at least 'unrealistic'. However, the money can be found to make significant improvements in social security and the reduction of poverty (Lister 1989a; Walker 1990) if there is political will to do it. Opinion polls have shown considerable and growing support for increased spending on welfare services, even at the cost of higher taxes, though that commitment has not yet been strong enough to prove salient at the ballot box. Considerable improvements could be made in social security provision, even without any overall increase in public expenditure. The abolition of the married man's tax allowance could pay for a substantial improvement in child benefit; withdrawing subsidies to the private pensions industry would fund an increase in the retirement pension. However, such a policy would involve losers as well as gainers. And though rough justice has been deemed to be good enough justice for the poor, it is not a concept which governments have been willing to apply to the more affluent.

At the heart of any strategy to improve social security is the need to promote positive attitudes towards the recipients of benefits, and that must start at the top. For too long it has suited governments to support and join in the disparagement of benefit recipients because it has enabled them to justify containing and cutting expenditure. It is easier to justify not helping the 'undeserving'. It is easier to cut back on benefits if it can be established, or just intimated, that the beneficiaries are not really poor. Much is spoken of rights and entitlement but they mean nothing if claimants are vilified for needing state support and then for claiming it. Social assistance has been designed to ensure that those who are not eligible for help do not get it; it has been less concerned to ensure that those who are eligible take up and receive their entitlement. Consequently, many people who, as the result of some traumatic life event, have to turn to the state for support, find themselves guilty by association. Social assistance claimants deserve to be treated with the same dignity and respect as the rest of the community. They are no more or less dishonest, feckless or undeserving than any other group in society. But they are more vulnerable. The least that a civilized society owes to those people who face adverse times, for reasons which are usually outside their control, is mutual respect which allows them to maintain their self-esteem and personal dignity; this begins with decent and fair treatment by policy-makers and administrators and is maintained by a reasonable income which allows them full membership of the society in which they live.

Bibliography

Abbott E and Bombas K (1943), *The Woman Citizen and Social Security*, London, K Bombas.

Abel-Smith B and Townsend P (1965), *The Poor and the Poorest*, London, Bell.

ACOP (1990), *Surviving Poverty: Probation Work and Benefits Policy*, London, Association of Chief Officers of Probation.

Alcock P (1987), *Poverty and State Support*, Harlow, Longman.

Allbeson J and Smith R (1984), *We Don't Give Clothing Grants Any More*, London, CPAG.

Andrews K and Jacobs J (1990), *Punishing the Poor: Poverty under Thatcher*, London, Macmillan.

Arnott H (1987), 'Second-class Citizens', in Walker A and Walker C (eds), *The Growing Divide: A Social Audit 1979–1987*, London, CPAG.

Ashley P (1983), *The Money Problems of the Poor: a Literature Review*, London, Heinemann.

Atkinson A B (1970), *Poverty in Britain and the Reform of Social Security*, Cambridge, Cambridge University Press.

Atkinson A B (1989), *Poverty and Social Security*, London, Harvester Wheatsheaf.

Atkinson A B (1991), 'A National Minimum? A History of Ambiguity in the Determination of Benefit Scales in Britain', in Wilson T and Wilson D (1991), *The State and Social Welfare: The Objectives of Policy*, Harlow, Longman.

Atkinson A B and Micklewright J (1985), *Unemployment Benefits and Unemployment Duration*, London, STICERD.

Barnardo's (1990), *Missing the Target*, Barkingside.

Becker S (1991), *Windows of Opportunity: Public Policy and the Poor*, London, CPAG.

Becker S and Bennett F (1991), 'Conclusion: A New Agenda', in Becker S (ed), *Windows of Opportunity: Public Policy and the Poor*, London, CPAG.

Becker S and MacPherson S (1988), *Public Issues, Private Pain*, London, Social Service Insight Books.

Becker S and Silburn R (1990), *The New Poor Clients: Social Work, Poverty and the Social Fund*, Wallington, Community Care/Benefits Research Unit.

Bell K (1975), *Research Study on Supplementary Benefits Appeals Tribunals: Summary of Main Findings: Conclusions: Recommendations*, London, HMSO.

Beltram G (1984), *Testing the Safety Net*, London, NCVO/Bedford Square Press.

Ben-Tovim G, Gabriel J, Law I and Stredder K (1986), *The Local Politics of Race*, London, Macmillan.

Bennett F (1991) 'A Window of Opportunity?', in Becker S (ed), *Windows of Opportunity*, London, CPAG.

Berthoud R (1984), *The Reform of Social Security*, London, PSI.

Berthoud R (1986), *Selective Social Security: an analysis of the Government's plans*, London, PSI.

Berthoud R (1991), 'The Social Fund – Is It Working?', *Policy and Politics*, Vol 12.1.

Berthoud R and Kempson E (1990), *Credit and Debt in Britain: First Findings*, London, PSI.

Beveridge Report (1942), *Social Insurance and Allied Services*, Cmd 6404, London, HMSO.

Bosanquet N (1987), 'Interim Report: Public Spending and the Welfare State', in Jowell R, Witherspoon S and Brook L, *British Social Attitudes: The 1986 Report*, Aldershot, Gower/SCPR.

Bradshaw J (1982), 'Public Expenditure on Social Security', in Walker A. (ed), *Public Expenditure and Social Policy*, London, Heinemann.

Bradshaw J and Holmes H (1989), *Living on the Edge: a study of the living standards of families on benefit in Tyne and Wear*, York, Tyneside CPAG.

Bradshaw J, Mitchell D and Morgan J (1987), 'Evaluating Adequacy', *Journal of Social Policy*, 16.2, pp 165–182.

Bradshaw J and Morgan J (1987), *Budgeting on Benefit*, London, Family Policy Studies Centre.

Briggs E and Rees A (1980), *Supplementary Benefits and the Consumer*, London, Bedford Square Press.

British Gas (1991), *The British Gas Report on Attitudes to Ageing 1991*, British Gas.

Brown J (1989), *Why Don't They go to Work? Mothers on Benefit*, SSAC Research Paper No 2, London, HMSO.

Bull D (1983), '"Free" Education: shirking and shifting responsibilities', in Bull D and Wilding P (1987), *Thatcherism and the Poor*, London, CPAG.

Bull D and Wilding P (1983), *Thatcherism and the Poor*, London, CPAG.

Burghes L (1980), *Living from Hand to Mouth*, London, FSU/CPAG.

Byrne D (1987), 'Rich and Poor: The Growing Divide', in Walker A and Walker C, *The Growing Divide*, London, CPAG.

Caplovitz D (1963), *The Poor Pay More*, New York, The Free Press.

Carlen P (1988), *Women, Crime and Poverty*, Milton Keynes, Open University Press.

Clark A (1989), *After the Social Fund*, Edinburgh, Citizens Advice Scotland.

Cm 1264 (1990), *Children Come First: The Government's proposals on the maintenance of children*, London, HMSO.

Cm 1580 (1991), *Annual Report by the Secretary of State for Social Security on the Social Fund*, London, HMSO.

Cmd 6404 (The Beveridge Report) (1942), *Social Insurance and Allied Services*, London, HMSO.

Cmnd 5228 (Fisher Committee) (1973), *Report of the Committee on Abuse of Social Security Benefits*, London, HMSO.

Cmnd 5629 (The Finer Report) (1974), *Report of the Committee on One Parent Families*, London, HMSO.

Cmnd 7773 (1979), *Reform of the Supplementary Benefit Scheme* (White Paper), London, HMSO.

Cmnd 9296 (1984), *The Supplementary Benefit (Requirements and Resources) Amendment Regulations 1984, SI No 1102, SI No 938. Report of the Social Security Advisory Committee.*

Cmnd 9517 (1985), *Reform of Social Security*, Volume 1, London, HMSO.
Cmnd 9518 (1985), *Reform of Social Security: Programme for Change*, Volume 2, London, HMSO.
Cmnd 9519 (1985), *Reform of Social Security: Background Papers*, Volume 3, London, HMSO.
Cmnd 9691 (1985), *Reform of Social Security: Programme for Action* (White Paper), London, HMSO.
Cmnd 9791 (1985), *The Supplementary Benefit (Requirements and Resources) Miscellaneous Provisions (No 2) Regulations 1985, SI No 600. Report of the Social Security Advisory Committee.*
Cole D with Utting J (1962), *The Economic Circumstances of Old People*, Welwyn, Codicote Press.
Cole-Hamilton I and Lang T (1986), *Tightening Belts*, London, London Food Commission.
Cook D (1989), *Rich Law, Poor Law: different responses to tax and supplementary benefit fraud*, Milton Keynes, Open University Press.
Cooke K and Baldwin S (1984), *How Much is Enough? A review of supplementary benefits scale rates*, London, Family Policy Studies Centre.
Cooper S (1985), *Observations in Supplementary Benefit Offices*, London, PSI.
CPAG (1983), 'Price Index for Poor Families', *Poverty*, 55, pp 37–40.
CSO (1990), *Family Spending: a report on the 1990 Family Expenditure Survey*, London, HMSO.
CSO (1991), *Social Trends 21*, London, HMSO.
Deacon A (1976), *In Search of the Scrounger*, London, Bell.
Deacon A (1982), 'An End to the Means-test: social security and the Attlee Government', *Journal of Social Policy*, vol. 11, pt 3.
Deacon A and Bradshaw J (1983), *Reserved for the Poor*, Oxford, Basil Blackwell and Martin Robertson.
Dean H (1991), *Social Security and Social Control*, London, Harvester Wheatsheaf.
Dean H and Taylor-Gooby P (1992), *Dependency Culture: the explosion of a myth*, Hemel Hempstead, Harvester Wheatsheaf.
DHSS (1972), *Families Receiving Supplementary Benefit: a study comparing the circumstances of some fatherless families and families of the long-term sick and unemployed*, London, HMSO.
DHSS (1978), *Social Assistance: A Review of the Supplementary Benefits Scheme in Great Britain*, London, DHSS.
DHSS (1979), *Review of the Supplementary Benefits Scheme: Analysis of Views and Comments*, London, DHSS.
DHSS (1979a), *Report of a Survey of Claimants' Attitudes to Central Issues of the Supplementary Benefits Review*, London, DHSS.
DHSS (1988), *Low Income Statistics: Report of a Technical Review*, London, DHSS.
DHSS (1988a), *Low Income Families*, London, DHSS.
DHSS/SBC (1975), *Exceptional Needs Payments*, London, HMSO.
DHSS/SBC (1977), *Low Incomes: Evidence to the Royal Commission on the Distribution of Incomes and Wealth*, London, HMSO.
DHSS/SBC (1977a), *Supplementary Benefits Handbook: A Guide to Claimants' Rights*, London, HMSO.
DHSS/SBC (1979), *Response of the Supplementary Benefits Commission to 'Social Assistance: A Review of the Supplementary Benefits Scheme in Great Britain'*, SBA Papers No 9, London, HMSO.

Dilnot A W and Kell M (1987), 'Male Unemployment and Women's Work', *Fiscal Studies*, vol. 8.3, pp 1–16, August.

Dilnot A and Walker I (eds) (1989), *The Economics of Social Security*, Oxford, Oxford University Press.

Donnison D (1976), 'Supplementary Benefit: Dilemmas and Priorities', *Journal of Social Policy*, vol. 5.4.

Donnison D (1982), *The Politics of Poverty*, Oxford, Martin Robertson.

DSS (1989), *Social Security Statistics 1989*, London, HMSO.

DSS (1990), *Households Below Average Income 1981–87: A Statistical Analysis*, London Government Statistical Service, HMSO.

DSS (1990a), *Social Security Statistics 1990*, London, HSMO.

DSS (1992), *Households Below Average Income: a statistical analysis 1979–1988/89*, London, Government Statistical Service, HMSO.

Evason E, Allamby L and Woods R (1989), *The Deserving and the Undeserving Poor*, Derry, CPAG (NI).

Expenditure Committee (General Sub-Committee) (July 1977), *The Civil Service*, vols I–II, 1976–77, London, HMSO.

Family Budget Unit (1991), *Summary Budget Standards for Three Families*, University of York, FBU.

Ford J (1991), *Consuming Credit: debt and poverty in the UK*, London, CPAG.

Franey R (1983)), *Poor Law: the mass arrest of homeless claimants in Oxford*, London, CHAR/CPAG.

Fulbrook J (1978), *Administrative Justice and the Unemployed*, London, Mansell.

Glendinning C and Millar J (eds) (1992), *Women and Poverty in Britain: the 1990s*, London, Harvester Wheatsheaf.

Golding P and Middleton S (1982), *Images of Welfare*, Oxford, Martin Robertson.

Gordon P and Newnham A (1985), *Passport to Benefits: Racism in Social Security*, London, CPAG/The Runnymede Trust.

Graham H (1976), 'Smoking in Pregnancy: the attitudes of expectant mothers', *Social Science and Medicine*, 10, pp. 399–405.

Graham H (1984), *Women, Health and the Family*, Brighton, Harvester Wheatsheaf.

Greenwood W (1933), *Love on the Dole*, London, Jonathan Cape.

Hall P, Land H, Parker R and Webb A (1975), *Change, Choice and Conflict in Social Policy*, London, Heinemann.

Harris J (1977), *William Beveridge: a biography*, Oxford, Clarendon Press.

Heady P and Smyth M (1989), *Living Standards During Unemployment: Volume 1, The Results*, OPCS, London, HMSO.

Hill M (1969), 'The Exercise of Discretion in the National Assistance Board', *Public Administration*, 47.

Hill M (1984), 'The Importance of Housing Benefit', *Journal of Social Policy*, Vol 13.3, pp 297–420.

Hill M (1990), *Social Security Policy in Britain*, Aldershot, Edward Elgar.

Hills J (1987), 'What Happened to Spending on the Welfare State?', in Walker A and Walker C, *The Growing Divide*, London, CPAG.

Hills J (1990), *Changing Tax: How the Tax System Works and How to Change It*, London, CPAG.

HM Treasury (1988), *The Government's Expenditure Plans, 1988–89 to 1990–91*, Cm 288–I, London, HMSO.

HMSO (1966), *Financial and Other Circumstances of Retirement Pensioners*, London, HMSO.

HMSO (1991), *Citizen's Charter*, London, HMSO.

Huby M and Dix G (1992), *Evaluating the Social Fund*, Department of Social Security Research Report No 8, London, HMSO.

Jacobson B (1981), *Beating the Ladykillers: women and smoking*, London, Pluto Press.

Johnson P and Webb S (1990), *IFS Commentary, Poverty in Official Statistics*, London, IFS.

Jones K, Brown J and Bradshaw J (1978), *Issues in Social Policy*, London, Routledge Kegan Paul.

Jowell R and Airey C (eds) (1984), *British Social Attitudes: the 1984 Report*, Aldershot, Gower/SCPR.

Jowell R and Witherspoon S (eds) (1986), *British Social Attitudes: The 1985 Report*, Aldershot, Gower/SCPR.

Jowell R, Witherspoon S and Brook L (eds) (1987), *British Social Attitudes: The 1986 Report*, Aldershot, Gower/SCPR.

Judge K (1980), 'Beveridge: past, present and future', in Sandford C, Pond C and Walker R (eds), *Taxation and Social Policy*, London, Heinemann Educational.

Kerr S (1983), *Making Ends Meet: An Investigation into the Non-claiming of Supplementary Pensions*, London, Bedford Square Press/NCVO.

Kirk D, Nelson S, Sinfield A and Sinfield D (1991), *Excluding Youth: Poverty Among Young People Living Away from Home*, Edinburgh, Bridges Project/Edinburgh CSWR.

Lakhani B *et al.* (1989), *National Welfare Benefits Handbook 1989/90*, London, CPAG.

Le Grand J (1982), *The Strategy of Equality: redistribution and the social services*, London, George Allen and Unwin.

Leicester City Council (1988), *Language and Benefits: a study of DHSS service delivery to ethnic minority communities*, Leicester, Leicester City Countil.

Lister R (1975), *Social Security: The Case for Reform*, Poverty Pamphlet No 22, London, CPAG.

Lister R (1976), *National Welfare Benefits Handbook, 6th Edition*, London, CPAG.

Lister R (1978), *Social Assistance: the Real Challenge*, Poverty Pamphlet No 38, London, CPAG.

Lister R (1979), *The No-Cost No-Benefit Review*, Poverty Pamphlet No 39, London, CPAG.

Lister R (1987), '*Conclusion II: there is an alternative*', in Walker A and Walker C (eds), *The Growing Divide: a social audit 1979–87*, London, CPAG.

Lister R (1989), 'Assessment of the Fowler Review', in Dilnot A and Walker I (eds), *The Economics of Social Security*, Oxford, Oxford University Press.

Lister R (1989a), 'Social Benefits – Priorities for Redistribution', in The Sheffield Group (eds), *The Social Economy and the Democratic State*, London, Lawrence and Wishart.

Lister R (1989b), *The Female Citizen*, Eleanor Rathbone Memorial Lecture, Liverpool, Liverpool University Press.

Lister R (1990), *The Exclusive Society: Citizenship and the Poor*, London, CPAG.

Lunn T (1990), 'This Customer Business', *Community Care*, 16 August.

Lynes T (1981), *The Penguin Guide to Supplementary Benefits*, 4th edition, Harmondsworth, Penguin.

McCarthy M (1986), *Campaigning for the Poor: CPAG and the Politics of Welfare*, Beckenham, Croom Helm.

Mack J and Lansley S (1985), *Poor Britain*, London, George Allen and Unwin.
McKee L and Bell C (1985), 'His Unemployment, Her Problems', in Allen S *et al.* (eds), *The Experience of Unemployment*, London, Macmillan.
McLaughlin E, Millar J and Cooke K (1989), *Work and Welfare Benefits*, Aldershot, Avebury.
Marsden D (1969), *Mothers Alone: Poverty and the Fatherless Family*, Harmondsworth, Penguin.
Martin J and White A (1988), *The Financial Circumstances of Disabled Adults Living in Private Households*, OPCS surveys of disability in Great Britain, Report 2, London, HMSO.
Millar J (1989), 'Social Security, Equality and Women in the UK', *Policy and Politics*, 17.4, pp 311–319.
Moore J (1987), *The Future of the Welfare State*, mimeo, 26 September.
Moore J, (1989), *The End of the Line for Poverty*, Speech to the Greater London Area CPC, 11 May.
Moore P (1981), 'Scroungermania again at the DHSS', *New Society*, 22 January.
Moylan S, Millar J and Davies R (1984), *For Richer, for Poorer*, DHSS Cohort Study of Unemployed Men, DHSS, Research Report No 11, London, HMSO.
Murray C (1990), *The Emerging British Underclass*, London, IEA Health and Welfare Unit.
NACAB (1990a), *Hard Times for Social Fund Applicants*, E/1/90, London, NACAB.
NACAB (1990b), *Barriers to Benefit*, London, NACAB.
National Audit Office (1991), *The Social Fund*, London, HMSO.
National Consumer Council (1976), *Means-Tested Benefits: Discussion Paper*, London, NCC.
Noble M *et al.* (1989), *The Other Oxford: Low Income Households in Oxford*, University of Oxford, Department of Social and Administrative Studies.
Oppenheim C (1990), *Poverty: The Facts*, London, CPAG.
Oppenheim C (1990a), *Holes in the Safety Net*, London, CPAG.
Oppenheim C and McEvaddy S (1989), *Christmas on the Breadline*, London, CPAG.
Pahl J (1983), 'The Allocation of Money and the Structuring of Inequality within Marriage', *Sociological Review*, 31, pp 237–62.
Pahl J (1989), *Money and Marriage*, Basingstoke, Macmillan.
Parker G (1990), *Getting and Spending: Credit and Debt in Britain*, Avebury, Gower.
Parker H (1982), *The Moral Hazards of Social Benefits*, Research Monograph no 37, London, IEA.
Pascall G (1986), *Social Policy: a feminist analysis*, London, Tavistock.
Piachaud D (1979), *The Cost of a Child*, Poverty Pamphlet No 43, London, CPAG.
Piachaud D (1987), 'The Growth of Poverty', in Walker A and Walker C (eds), *The Growing Divide: A Social Audit 1979–87*, London, CPAG.
Ritchie J (1990), *Thirty Families: Their Living Standards in Unemployment*, DSS Research Report No 1, London, HMSO.
Ritchie J and Wilson P (1979), *Social Security Claimants*, London, OPCS.
Rowntree B S (1901), *Poverty: a Study of Town Life*, London, Longman.
Rowntree B S (1941), *Poverty and Progress*, London, Longman.
Runciman W G (1972), *Relative Deprivation and Social Justice*, Harmondsworth, Penguin.
SBC (1976), *SBC Annual Report 1975*, Cmnd 6615, London, HMSO.
SBC (1977), *SBC Annual Report 1976*, Cmnd 6910, London, HMSO.

The Sheffield Group (eds), *The Social Economy and the Democratic State*, London, Lawrence and Wishart.

Smith R (1985), 'Who's fiddling? Fraud and Abuse', in Ward S (ed), *DHSS in Crisis*, London, CPAG.

Social Policy Research Unit (1992), *The Social Fund: reform or replacement*, York, University of York.

Social Security Advisory Committee (1982), *First Report of the Social Security Advisory Committee 1981*, London, HMSO.

Social Security Advisory Committee (1983), *Second Report 1982/83*, London, HMSO.

Social Security Advisory Committee (1985), *Fourth Report 1985*, London, HMSO.

Social Security Advisory Committee (1987), *Fifth Report of the Social Security Advisory Committee 1986/7*, London, HMSO.

Social Security Advisory Committee (1989), *Sixth Report of the Social Security Advisory Committee 1988*, London, HMSO.

Social Security Advisory Committee (1990), *Seventh Report of the Social Security Advisory Committee 1989*, London, HMSO.

Social Security Consortium (1987), *Of Little Benefit: An Update: A Critical Guide to the Social Security Act 1986*, London, AMA.

Social Security Research Consortium (SSRC) (1991), *Cash Limited, Limited Cash*, London, AMA/ACC.

Social Services Select Committee (1988), *Fourth Report: Families on Low Incomes: Low Income Statistics*, Session 1987–88, London, HMSO.

Social Services Select Committee (1989), *Ninth Report: Social Security: Changes implemented in April 1988*, vol. 1, London, HMSO.

Stewart G, Stewart J and Walker C (1989), *The Social Fund: a critical analysis of its introduction and first year in operation*, London, Association of County Councils.

Tarpey M (1984), *English Speakers Only*, Islington, Islington People's Rights.

Taylor-Gooby P (1985), *Public Opinion, Ideology and State Welfare*, London, Routledge & Kegan Paul.

Thatcher M (1990), Inaugural National Children's Home George Thomas Society Lecture, mimeo.

Titmuss R (1971), 'Welfare "Rights" Law and Discretion', *Political Quarterly*, vol. 42, no 2, April.

Titmuss R (1987), *The Philosophy of Welfare*, London, Allen and Unwin.

Townsend P (1979), *Poverty in the UK: A Survey of Household Resources and Standards of Living*, Berkeley, University of California Press.

Townsend P and Davidson N (1982) (eds), *The Black Report*, Harmondsworth, Penguin.

Townsend P and Gordon D (1989), *Unfinished Statistical Business on Low Incomes?: A review of new proposals by the Department of Social Security for the production of public information on poverty*, Bristol, Statistical Monitoring Unit, University of Bristol.

Unemployment Unit/Youthaid (1991), *Working Brief*, London, Unemployment Unit/Youthaid, October.

Veit-Wilson J (1989), 'The Concept of Minimum Income and the Basis of Social Security Scales', mimeo.

Walker A (1986), 'Pensions and the Production of Poverty in Old Age', in Phillipson C and Walker A, *Ageing and Social Policy: a Critical Assessment*, Aldershot, Gower.

Walker A (1990), 'The Strategy of Inequality: Poverty and Income Distribution in Britain 1979–89', in Taylor I (ed), *The Social Effects of Free Market Policies*, Hemel Hempstead, Harvester/Wheatsheaf.

Walker A (1990a), 'The Economic "Burden" of Ageing and the Prospect of Intergenerational Conflict', *Ageing and Society*, vol. 10, pp 377–396.

Walker A (1991), 'The Persistence of Poverty under Welfare States and the Prospects for its Abolition', *International Journal of Health Services*, vol. 2, no. 1, pp. 1–17.

Walker A and Walker C (eds) (1987), *The Growing Divide: A Social Audit 1979–1987*, London, CPAG.

Walker C (1982), 'Social Assistance: the reality of open government', *Policy and Politics*, vol. 10, no 1.

Walker C (1983), *Changing Social Policy: the case of the supplementary benefits review*, London, Bedford Square Press.

Walker C (1983a), 'The Reform of the Supplementary Benefits Scheme – for whose benefit?', in Jones C and Stevenson J (eds), *The Yearbook of Social Policy in Britain in 1982*, London, Routledge & Kegan Paul.

Walker C (1986), 'The Impact of the Reformed Supplementary Benefits Scheme', *Social Policy and Administration*, Summer.

Walker C (1987), 'Reforming Social Security – Despite the Claimant', in Walker A and Walker C (eds), *The Growing Divide: A Social Audit 1979–1987*, London, CPAG.

Walker C with Dant T (1984), *The Reform of the Supplementary Benefits Scheme*, University of Leeds.

Walker R, Dix G and Huby M (1992), *Working the Social Fund*, Department of Social Security Research Report no 8, London, HMSO.

Walley Sir J (1972), *Social Security: Another British Failure*, London, Charles Knight.

Weale A, Bradshaw J, Maynard A and Piachaud D (1984), *Lone Mothers, Paid Work and Social Security*, London, Bedford Square Press/NCVO.

Whitehead M (1988), *The Health Divide*, London, Health Education Council.

Whiteley P and Winyard S (1983), 'Influencing Social Policy: the effectiveness of the poverty lobby', *Journal of Social Policy*, Vol 12.1.

Williams F (1977), *Why the Poor Pay More*, London, Macmillan.

Williams F (1989), *Social Policy: A Critical Introduction*, Oxford, Polity Press.

Wilson T and Wilson D (1991), *The State and Social Welfare: the objectives of policy*, Harlow, Longman.

Name index

Subject index